CONTEMPORARY ETHNOGRAPHY

Kirin Narayan and Alma Gottlieb, Series Editors

A complete list of books in the series is available from the publisher.

IN CHOCOLATE WE TRUST

THE HERSHEY COMPANY TOWN UNWRAPPED

PETER KURIE

PENN

UNIVERSITY OF PENNSYLVANIA PRESS

PHILADELPHIA

Published by
University of Pennsylvania Press
Philadelphia, Pennsylvania 19104-4112
www.upenn.edu/pennpress

Printed in the United States of America
on acid-free paper

2 4 6 8 10 9 7 5 3 1

Library of Congress Cataloging-in-Publication Data

Names: Kurie, Peter, author.
Title: In chocolate we trust : the Hershey company town unwrapped / Peter Kurie.
Other titles: Contemporary ethnography.
Description: 1st edition. | Philadelphia : University of Pennsylvania Press, [2018] | Series:
Contemporary ethnography
Identifiers: LCCN 2017036446 | ISBN 978-0-8122-4987-3 (hardcover : alk. paper)
Subjects: LCSH: Hershey (Pa.)—Economic conditions. | Hershey (Pa.)—Social conditions. |
Milton Hershey School Trust. | Hershey Trust Company. | Milton Hershey School (Hershey, Pa.)
| Company towns—Pennsylvania—Hershey. | Trusts and trustees—Pennsylvania—Hershey. |
Hershey, Milton Snavely, 1857–1945—Estate.
Classification: LCC HC108.H47 K87 2018 | DDC 371.9309748/18—dc23
LC record available at https://lccn.loc.gov/2017036446

CONTENTS

≋ INTRODUCTION ≋

Hershey's is the currency of affection.
It's the childhood symbol of love.

—Ad man Don Draper,
pitching to Hershey Company executives
in *Mad Men* (2013)

THE HERSHEY'S MILK CHOCOLATE BAR is an iconic American consumer good. The product—210 calories per serving, made mostly from sugar and milk—satisfies the common craving for low-cost, ready-to-eat, sweet foodstuff. But the brand name Hershey's goes beyond the product itself and appeals to consumers through symbols, values, and cultural heritage. After more than one hundred years in the marketplace, Hershey's is deeply embedded in the memories and imaginations of generations of modern consumers in the United States and across borders.

The brand was founded by Milton Snavely Hershey (1857–1945), the Gilded Age entrepreneur who built a chocolate company and model industrial community in the farmlands of central Pennsylvania and who, for want of an heir, entrusted his multimillion-dollar candy fortune to American orphans. Since his death, the Hershey Company has expanded the brand and repackaged the founder's life story and legacy for markets in North America and beyond. I have been closely following the "afterlife" of Milton Hershey since 2010 when I began a year of research in Hershey,

Pennsylvania—headquarters of the Hershey Company, home of the Milton Hershey School (formerly the Hershey Industrial School for orphans), and site of the popular amusement park Hersheypark, among other regional attractions.

Inside the chocolate company, the story of the founder is carefully managed and curated to sell merchandise. But the story assumes a life of its own on the bucolic streets outside, where town residents, chocolate company employees, students and alumni of Milton Hershey School, and leisure-seeking tourists live and circulate among each other. In present-day Hershey—a predominantly white, working-class, rural-suburban community of 25,000, one hundred miles west of Philadelphia[1]—the story of the founder and the significance of his legacy is more than a commercial concern: it is an existential matter, implicating livelihoods and lifeways.

The Hershey story has been written numerous times by biographers and historians.[2] But something about the narrative—its moral qualities— eludes conventions of history, biography, or for that matter, marketing and advertising. Its subject is a poor, unschooled, Mennonite farm boy who, after failing in multiple business ventures, "succeeds" through a combination of genius and grit, and then "pays forward" his fortune to children in need. Though it intersects with the Horatio Alger rags-to-riches legend, this is not a story about striking it rich. It is, rather, about the making of the entrepreneur-philanthropist—a hero figure of our time.

The interpretation of the story lends itself to ideologies on both left and right, yet the tale as popularly told is not ideological. Milton Hershey was a dyed-in-the-wool capitalist, to be sure, but he was also a communitarian. Whether he made money in order to serve community, or served community in order to make money, is impossible to resolve. For those who know the narrative well, it is beside the point. Hershey's was an impure, offbeat capitalism. The contrary impulses and blended motivations of the man and his various enterprises make the story credible, entertaining, and, perhaps, enlightening.

Until the Hershey chocolate company came along in 1894, edible chocolate was a specialty item off-limits to working classes because of its price. Through a processing innovation that allowed for mass production and distribution, the company made this luxury accessible to anyone who could afford five cents. Most manufacturing took place inside the model industrial town of Hershey, established in 1906, which offered relatively high standards of living and generous benefits to workers and their families. American consumers embraced the harmony of a good product made in a good way.

With a long shelf life and a tangy, sour taste, the Hershey bar became an American staple. When G.I.s went to battle in World War II, they took the bar with them to give away to children in war zones. The bar democratized the pleasure and enjoyment of chocolate and, in the process, helped export the culture of American consumerism to the world. It also ushered in a global market for cocoa beans.

Milton Hershey's major philanthropic endeavor—an orphanage established in Hershey in 1909—is the least well-known chapter in the story. The founder and his wife, Catherine Sweeney Hershey (1872–1915), evidently could not conceive children of their own. As a substitute, they deeded most of their local land holdings to a trust fund that supported the housing and education of orphans "in perpetuity"—that is, forever. In 1918, following Catherine's early death (perhaps because of complications from syphilis [D'Antonio 2007]), Milton Hershey donated to the trust fund his full stake in the Hershey chocolate company, valued at $60 million. In 1945, one year after retiring as chairman of the board of trustees, he died. That is the start of the story.

At present, the Milton Hershey School educates and houses, year-round and free of cost, upward of two thousand children who lack adequate support from parents or caregivers. Thanks to its enduring stake in the successful Hershey Company, the Milton Hershey School Trust has grown in value to an estimated $12 billion—a remarkable sum for a former orphanage in an unassuming part of the country and, it turns out, a persistent source of local and national intrigue.

TRUST MATTERS

Hershey's entrepreneurial and philanthropic enterprises are contemporary with the great Gilded Age corporations and foundations established by Rockefeller, Ford, Carnegie, and others; and they may be regarded as antecedents to present-day endeavors by the likes of Gates, Buffett, and Zuckerberg. The legacy of these enterprises takes on new significance in our Second Gilded Age, in which inequality reaches degrees not gauged since the turn of the twentieth century, in which business corporations are popularly regarded as a primary engine of that inequality, and in which successful entrepreneurs increasingly devote themselves to philanthropic pursuits.

The Hershey story speaks to the role of business and the business entrepreneur in modern society. It offers one answer to the question of what business is good for other than turning a profit. Can business take care of people? Can it build and sustain communities? Can it save lives? Milton Hershey demonstrated it could; or at least he believed it could, and he acted on his belief. This makes all the difference to those who hold the story sacred.

How does the Hershey story continue to capture imaginations and sell merchandise when other First Gilded Age American entrepreneur-philanthropists arguably have made a larger economic and political footprint? Ford gave us automobiles and, through his son Edsel, the Ford Foundation, dedicated to the advancement of human welfare. Carnegie gave us steel and an unprecedented plethora of educational, cultural, and arts institutions. Rockefeller gave us oil and the Rockefeller Foundation, dedicated to medical research and public health and welfare. Hershey gave us chocolate candy and a single residential school in south-central Pennsylvania that remains little known outside the region.

Undoubtedly the lasting reputation of Hershey has something to do with the happiness and pleasure that chocolate brings, especially to children. Oil, steel, and even automobiles cannot compete with the simple, widespread enjoyment of candy. But there is a more formal, structural reason for Hershey's enduring charisma: the legal arrangement by which the Hershey chocolate fortune is managed and spent.

The Rockefellers, Fords, and Carnegies each dispensed their massive fortunes by means of general purpose foundations. These foundations were the most significant innovation of turn-of-the-twentieth-century U.S. philanthropy, permitting "an unlimited agenda of works, in which participants redefined goals as circumstances changed," observes historian Olivier Zunz (2011: 3). Liberated from the "the legal obligation… to follow strictures only because they were the donor's wishes," as Zunz puts it, they underwrote experiments in medicine, science, higher education, and beyond. The Sixteenth Amendment to the U.S. Constitution, which instituted a national income tax beginning in 1913, exempted general foundations from taxes, giving rise to what is commonly called the "third sector." Across the country and internationally, countless research grants, building projects, cultural institutions, and schools and universities exist thanks to the American third sector.

By contrast, Milton Hershey dispensed with his fortune through a charitable trust fund that benefits specific, living individuals: the students of Milton Hershey School. Unlike the charter of a general purpose foundation, Hershey's deed of trust specifies precise and unchanging instructions for how and where to spend money: it is to provide for the housing, clothing, feeding, and educating of Hershey students (originally, white orphan boys, in accordance with the dominant social and legal logic of the time). Moreover, the deed provides that the school will remain located inside the boundaries of Derry Township, Pennsylvania, which encompasses the census-designed place of Hershey. Milton Hershey School trustees—the board members responsible for managing both the trust fund and the school itself—are obliged by law and custom to adhere as closely as possible to the intentions of the deed of trust document. Sitting members of the board elect their successors to carry out this "fiduciary duty" in perpetuity.[3]

A perpetual charitable trust that benefits specific individuals is not in itself novel or distinctive, yet there is another feature of Hershey's trust that makes it exceptional: the trust has an ownership stake in the Hershey Company. This means Milton Hershey School trustees enjoy a majority vote in significant actions involving the publicly traded chocolate company—from hiring and firing the chief executive officer to buying and selling subsidiary companies. This also means that, technically, trustees have authority to sell control of the company to a different entity—a decision with potentially profound implications for the community in and around Hershey, Pennsylvania. Imagine if today the directors of the Ford Foundation controlled the Dearborn, Michigan–based Ford Motor Company; this is the case with Hershey.

The Hershey Trust would be at home in Northern Europe among other "industrial foundations:" not-for-profit organizations that control publicly traded business corporations (Thomsen and Hansmann 2012). Common across Scandinavia, especially in Denmark, such foundations are rare in the contemporary United States. Importantly, the Hershey Trust's control of the chocolate company has prevented the company from being acquired by a larger conglomerate and possibly relocated or liquidated. It has ensured that the town of Hershey remains, more or less, a company town—not wholly dependent on a single industry, as it was for much of the twentieth century, but still deeply entwined with the company's interests. It has also permitted the school to benefit financially from a hundred years of relatively steady income from candy sales.

Nothing about the trust's control of the Hershey Company is written into the Milton Hershey School's founding deed of trust document. The arrangement is not legally required. Rather, it is a matter of convention—a long-standing custom carried over by successive generations of Hershey trustees. Today's board of trustees—made up mostly of Pennsylvania-based professionals with business and law backgrounds, including prominent alumni of the school—are essentially adhering to the precedent set out by the founder during his lifetime. Milton Hershey maintained control of his chocolate company after its initial public offering on the stock market in 1927 and never let go. He apparently considered selling the company on several occasions, but no deal was ever completed. After his death, the board held on to control and continues to do so seven decades later—much to the chagrin of speculators who would like to bid on Hershey's at auction.

Arguably, if the founder had died with a simple last will and testament, or no will at all, the story of Hershey would resonate much differently today. If Hershey and his wife had borne biological heirs, for example, Americans likely would be living with yet another dynastic family and all that typically entails, for better or worse. Instead, the Hersheys left behind a distinctive, quasi-dynastic ecosystem in and around Hershey, Pennsylvania: an ensemble of for-profit and not-for-profit enterprises, variously interlinked;

and a clan of "Hersheyites" (the term is a winking conceit that some may embrace), whose common interest and identity lies in the customs and practices of the Hershey Trust. I analyze this ecosystem in detail in the chapters that follow.

HERSHEY'S ECOSYSTEM

Hersheyites—town residents, company employees, Milton Hershey School alumni, and others—readily compare their founder to entrepreneur-philanthropists bygone and living. They compare the town he founded to prominent U.S. company towns (e.g., the railroad-car neighborhood of Pullman, Chicago, or the mill town of Lowell, Massachusetts). They compare Hershey Company to Nestlé and Mars (chief competitors in the candy industry) and the Milton Hershey School to Kamehameha Schools (a residential boarding school in Hawaii with a comparable endowment and parallel institutional history). But these comparisons are carried only so far and no further. Hersheyites generally insist on Hershey as being "one of a kind."

Unlike most company towns and model communities established at the turn of the twentieth century, Hershey today stands intact (cf. Crawford 1995; Green 2011). The local economy prospers in comparison to the wider rural-agricultural and deindustrialized region in which it lies, thanks in large part to the variety of enterprises bearing the Hershey name. The locally headquartered Hershey Company owns more than eighty brands around the world and has annual revenues of over $7 billion, with half a billion in profits, and twenty thousand employees worldwide; the Penn State Milton S. Hershey Medical Center, the teaching and research hospital of Penn State University, employs upward of ten thousand, annually enrolls eight hundred medical students, and serves around thirty thousand patients; the Milton Hershey School privately houses and educates two thousand students on more than 2,500 acres of land, expending an estimated $110,000 per student per year.

Advertised as "the Sweetest Place on Earth" in U.S. Mid-Atlantic media markets, the town boasts an entertainment industry that attracts international performing artists, making it a regional hub for the consumption of popular culture. Hersheypark, an award-winning amusement park with roller coasters and water rides, draws over three million tourists annually. Multiple golf courses, dating from the early 1930s and designed by nationally celebrated architects, make the town a top golf destination. The Hershey Hotel offers luxury accommodations, spa treatments, and gourmet restaurants. Other attractions include the Hershey Story Museum, Hershey Gardens, Zoo America, Hershey Theater, and Hershey Chocolate World, the flagship of seven national visitor centers for the Hershey Company.

These enterprises operate at multiple, shifting scales: local, regional, national, international. Each participates in "global flows" of money, goods, and people (Appadurai 1990). And yet, Hershey retains a distinct sense of boundedness, enclosure, and small scale. Visitors and locals alike comment on its "bubble"-like character; a "bubble town," some call it. In a "world in pieces"—anthropologist Clifford Geertz's name for our global present (2001)—Hershey appears as an "integral whole," a "totality," even a "society" (Durkheim 1995 [1912]: 442–43). Something about Hershey exhibits, moreover, an untimely, out-of-joint, anachronistic quality: "like something from the 1950s," some say; "like *Pleasantville*."[4]

Neither "frozen in time" nor "backward" in outlook, Hershey remains firmly rooted in a distinct cultural history. The spirit of the place—its *Geist*, its ethos—is, I suggest, a unique expression of the core values of early consumer capitalist culture. Those values remain central to contemporary American life.

Hershey's ecosystem—an ensemble of enterprises, activities, and social relationships—took shape just as consumer capitalist culture was becoming the dominant culture of the United States. Cultural historian William Leach offers trenchant remarks on that period:

> From the 1890s on, American corporate business, in league with
> key institutions, began the transformation of American society
> into a society preoccupied with consumption, with comfort
> and bodily well-being, with luxury, spending, and acquisition,
> with more goods this year than last, more next year than this.
> American consumer capitalism produced a culture almost

violently hostile to the past and to tradition, a future-oriented
culture of desire that confused the good life with goods. It was
a culture that first appeared as an alternative culture—or as one
moving largely against the grain of earlier traditions of republi-
canism and Christian virtue—and then unfolded to become the
reigning culture of the United States. It was the culture that many
people the world over soon came to see as *the* heart of American
life. (Leach 1993: xiii, italics in original)

Early consumer culture in America is distinguished by a "cult of the new"
drawn from prior national traditions, Leach observes. This is a culture that
celebrates, even worships, novelty. Its rise coincides with an expanded money
economy and a new emphasis on growing incomes and rising standards of
living. Ingeniously, consumer capitalist culture combines principles of democracy with privileges of consumption. It holds that everyone—regardless
of differences in creed, color, gender, preference, ability, or political affiliation—has an equal right to enjoy consumer goods: automobiles, Coca-Colas,
and, of course, chocolate bars.

Now more than a century and a half old, consumer culture has become
practically traditional in the United States.[5] Despite periodic challenges by
countercultural and anticonsumption movements, American mainstream
culture remains consumerist through and through. Hershey reflects its
time-honored appeal. Present-day Hershey embodies some of the most
picturesque qualities of consumerism's early years: an innocent, hokey
playfulness; a Norman Rockwellian wholesomeness; a good-natured pro-
gressiveness. One need look no further than the public street lamps lining
downtown's "Chocolate Avenue," the tops of which appear as Hershey's Kiss
candies, to appreciate that culture's enduring (and for many, endearing)
hold on quotidian life.

Hershey's founder is, likewise, memorialized for propagating the ideals
of consumer capitalism—democratization of fun and enjoyment, equality
among citizen-consumers, and so on—while mitigating its unsavory aspects: namely, spiritual and moral vacuousness. "Mr. Hershey"—as he is
known among Hersheyites past and present—is strongly associated with

personal and collective redemption. Alumni of the school celebrate him for giving children from destitute families "an opportunity to succeed in life." Without his generosity and inspiration from his wife, Catherine, these youngsters likely would have grown up to be "badass criminals," alumni say. Townspeople commemorate the founder as a man who, after building a community, "saved his town from the Great Depression because of his own ingenuity." Local Italian neoclassical architecture attests to his privately financed effort to keep dollars circulating, making Hershey "one community in the United States . . . unaware of the depression," per the founder's *New York Times* obituary ("M. S. Hershey Dead" 1945). In the view of insiders, as well as outsiders looking in, Hershey remains a community of exception: an isle of prosperity and security in a precarious sea, buoyed by the founder's entrepreneurial and philanthropic legacies.

Hershey's perpetual deed of trust effectively immortalizes the founder, or at least, immortalizes his benevolent intentions. Seventy years after the man's death, his "dead hand"—the legal term for control over property after death—continues to orchestrate the Hershey estate and fortune in and around south-central Pennsylvania. This untimely arrangement will persist, presumably, for as long as the law provides.

But how Hershey's deed of trust is executed in the future will depend on the judgment and actions of generations increasingly removed from its author. Hersheyites who regard themselves as stewards of the legacy find this a cause for anxiety. Among those who have body and soul invested in it, the worry that some bad actor will make a travesty of Hershey's ecosystem out of either ignorance or avarice is very real. This is the context in which I arrived in Hershey in fall of 2010—just as a public scandal over the trust began to unfold.

PRIVATE TRUSTS AND PUBLIC LIFE

Cultural anthropologists who have trained their eye on trusts, most notably George Marcus and Peter Dobkins Hall in *Lives in Trust* (1992), have homed in on their foremost practical and, indeed, existential dilemma: one way or another, trust funds must be spent. They exist to benefit another person or class of persons and cannot simply be hoarded. The problem of spending wealth is, of course, the other side of the coin to the problem of accruing wealth; it is the rarefied preoccupation of dynastic families and professional fiduciaries, such as those who manage private family trusts and foundation endowments. In the case of charitable trusts such as Hershey's, a minimum expenditure is required by law every fiscal year to enjoy the legal status and tax benefits accorded to U.S. charities.

With an endowment on par with top American universities such as the Massachusetts Institute of Technology and major foundations such as Ford, Hershey's trust is under persistent pressure to spend on behalf of beneficiaries. Much of its yearly expenditures go directly into the educating, housing, feeding and health care of Milton Hershey School students. But the trust also spends as an investor on behalf of future beneficiaries. Its investments travel far afield from Hershey's school and produce wide-ranging, often unanticipated, and occasionally contentious social effects.

Casual observers may be surprised to discover that the trust acts an entrepreneur in the economy of south-central Pennsylvania. Directly or indirectly, it is responsible for opening a market for health services and medical education in Hershey, and a market for entertainment and resorts. Its expenditures and acquisitions have precipitated or accelerated much of the demographic and economic change that has shaped the local community over the past half-century. At the same time, its closely held control of the Hershey Company and landholdings in the region has forestalled or retarded other kinds of local transformations. Thanks in no small part to the trust's actions, Hershey's early twentieth-century ecosystem has effectively transitioned into the twenty-first century—but not without controversy.

Given its eclectic range of investments and interests—from chocolate candy, to roller coasters, to real estate and university medicine—the Hershey Trust has gained a wide array of stakeholders over time, including residents of the town and surrounding township, workers and small-business owners in the region, and alumni and employees of the school, among others. These publics are "external" to the trust in that they are not named in the deed document. They are neither trustors, nor beneficiaries, nor trustees. Yet they are substantively affected by trust-led activities and are thus concerned with the outcomes of those activities. Some of these stakeholders recognize the "original intent" of Milton Hershey in the trust's recent transactions; others detect little or none of it. But few would deny the trust is acting like an entrepreneur-philanthropist. In this respect, the trust is a faithful heir to the founder.

In recent years, stakeholders in the town, company, and school, as well as onlookers from the worlds of philanthropy, finance, and journalism, have been publicly scrutinizing the trust for diverse reasons. They have expressed concerns about whether the trust will retain its customary control of the Hershey Company, and whether it should; about the quality of the relationship between the Hershey board of trustees and Milton Hershey students, the latter of whom are made up predominantly of poor children of color from homes of origin outside the region; and about the trust's accountability to "the public," broadly construed.

Participants in the professional world of philanthropy—the "philanthrosphere," in David Callahan's apt coinage (2017)—tend to balk at the very idea of perpetual charitable trusts. Constricted by the "original intent" of the donor, they are simply too inflexible and shortsighted, critics claim. All too often, these funds lend themselves to appropriation by powerful, unaccountable interests. Short of "busting" them—a specialty of certain lawyers and advocates—it is difficult if not impossible to adapt perpetual trusts to evolving circumstances and to ensure effective oversight.

For my part, I remain agnostic about whether perpetual trusts are a good or a bad idea. As a cultural anthropologist, my aim is to account for cultural meanings and social effects. My methods in Hershey are ethnographic: participation in and observation of local public rituals and ordinary social activities; informal and semi-structured interviews; reading in local history books, archives, and newspapers; and in general, being present and alert to whatever might transpire among "the natives" (an anthropological term of art so outdated it has become fashionable again).[6]

Although I remain agnostic about perpetual trusts, I am not a disinterested observer of Hershey: I was born and grew up there in the 1980s and 1990s. As a native son, I was well acquainted with the legends surrounding the founding father. Yet I knew very little about the function of Hershey's trust, other than the basic fact that it finances the Milton Hershey School. In my ignorance I was not alone.

Under routine circumstances, local people not directly involved in the trust's activities have taken as an article of faith that those in authority— whoever they may be—discharge their responsibility for ensuring that the trust does what it has been designed to do—whatever that is. People have simply "trusted the trust." Beginning in 2002, however, ordinary citizens started paying closer attention to its functions and dysfunctions. That was when the Hershey board of trustees shocked Hersheyites by voting to sell the trust's controlling stake in the Hershey Company.

The trust's decision in 2002 to sell the Hershey Company sparked loud objections from many residents, company employees, and Milton Hershey School alumni—all of whom anticipated the subsequent relocation or even liquidation of the chocolate company. Selling the company would unravel Hershey's unique ecosystem and threaten local jobs, property values, and community cohesion, they reasoned. Though they had no direct authority over trustees, their campaign to "Derail the Sale" gained the attention of the Pennsylvania attorney general's office, which took the trust to court and successfully delayed the sale, effectively canceling it. Ever since 2002, Hershey's private trust has been a prominent public concern, subjected to exposé journalism and numerous legal arguments and actions.

This book, grounded in an initial year of fieldwork in Hershey from 2010 through 2011, picks up where the campaign to "Derail the Sale" of the chocolate company ends. It follows the recent and often contentious career of Hershey's trust and accounts for efforts by diverse stakeholders to associate with, accommodate, contest, make claims on, or otherwise influence the trust. These chapters reveals the extent to which the trust is embedded in the everyday life of the modern Hershey community: not only as an engine of charity but also as an economic investor, a moral authority, and a custodian of collective identity. Hershey's trust is distinctive but not unique among charitable organizations in this regard. Taken a step further, the book sheds light on the complex ways by which philanthropic institutions are woven into the social fabric of the United States. Hershey's trust, viewed from an anthropological perspective, gives us a timely appreciation of the central place of philanthropy and business corporations in contemporary American life.

In Chocolate We Trust is organized as a tour across five chapters of the Hershey ecosystem.[7] The book moves from town, to company, to school, and back again on the trail of Hershey's entrepreneurial and philanthropic legacy. In each different setting and scene, we meet local people for whom that legacy is both a practical and ethical concern—both a mundane and moral matter. They offer us a glimpse into their everyday lives and share stories about Hershey's past and present, as well as hopes and fears for the community's future.

Generally, these "Hersheyites" endeavor to see the best of themselves and their compatriots reflected in Hershey's institutions. This is why, in autumn 2010, the gossip that turned into scandal was so disturbing and exciting: public allegations of "self-dealing" among Hershey Trust board members shook local people's faith in the order of things. It may even have shaken their faith in chocolate. *In Chocolate We Trust* begins here, in pursuit of Hershey's entrepreneurial-philanthropic legacy and amid publicity about trouble at the trust.

CHAPTER 1

≋ THE SCANDAL ≋

EARLY AUTUMN 2010. I live in a neighborhood of two-story, vinyl-sided suburban homes constructed in the mid-twentieth century, a few miles southwest of downtown Hershey. My bedroom window faces pale yellow cornfields and blue-green, tree-covered hills. At the center of the landscape, the steam stacks of Three Mile Island stand like four granite monoliths. Thirty years after the nuclear plant's partial meltdown, two of the stacks continue to pump out white clouds of steam hovering atop the Susquehanna River.

I frequently hear echoes of gunshots from a nearby public shooting range on state game lands. On some evenings, the gunshots give way to reverb-laden drums from Hersheypark's concert arena. The Penn State Hershey Medical Center's helicopter swoops above, attending to a medical emergency in rural parts not easily reached by road. Airplanes around Harrisburg International Airport, ten miles away, are a common feature of the soundscape. But the most consistent sound is a modulating combination of rustling wind, birdsong, and faint automobile traffic. This is the sound of the "suburban-rural mix" characteristic of south-central Pennsylvania.

The odor outside betrays the season: decaying leaves. In winter, there will be mineral notes; in spring and summer, fragrant flowers. On breezy days, a mild smell of chocolate makes its way into the neighborhood. The odor from downtown occasionally mixes with whiffs of manure from farmland, creating a distinctively sweet, sulfuric scent: the smell of home.

I grew up in this neighborhood, in this house. My parents arrived from the New York City metropolitan area as part of a new wave of residents in the 1970s; I graduated from the local public high school in 2001. After a decade away, I return as a doctoral student in cultural anthropology—a role I did not imagine as a young person. I do not know what my neighbors and longtime local acquaintances will make of my intentions in Hershey. Some might regard me as a "local boy made good" writing a tribute to his hometown; others, as a "liberal elite" from Princeton digging up dirt and looking for trouble. The latter perspective concerns me, as I realize my questions will address an emerging scandal. Given recent headlines about the Hershey Trust, some people inevitably will receive me as a muckraking journalist.

"Scandal," writes anthropologist Sally Engle Merry, "occurs when gossip is elevated into the public arena, when 'everyone knows that everyone knows'" (1984: 51).[1] Hershey residents, chocolate company employees, and alumni of the Milton Hershey School have been gossiping for decades about the unseemly financial activities of their homegrown, multibillion-dollar charitable trust, the Milton Hershey School Trust. There have been rumors of shady deals among members of the board of trustees, along with speculation that the board will try again, as it did in 2002, to put the chocolate company on the auction block. Nothing has been proven or made official. But now, unexpectedly, a proper scandal erupts.

"Hershey Trust Probe Confirmed," reads the headline of the state capital's *Harrisburg Patriot News* (Malawskey 2010). Pennsylvania Attorney General Tom Corbett—charged with oversight of charitable foundations and running as Republican candidate for governor—is leading an official inquiry into "self-dealing," in which one or more trustees is alleged to have profited personally from transactions of trust property. The attorney general's "probe" focuses on a land deal made in 2006, in which the trust purchased an economically insolvent golf course on the outskirts of town for the sum of $12 million—double or more its appraised value. One of the golf course's investors is a former chief executive officer of the Hershey Company who sat on the board of trustees and, presumably, voted on the deal. If the allegations are true, such "self-dealing" amounts to a gross violation of a trustee's basic fiduciary duty to beneficiaries.

The trust board responds to the probe by explaining that the golf course is intended as a "buffer" between expanding Milton Hershey School housing and the surrounding residential community. The land was purchased at a fairly negotiated price with Milton Hershey School students squarely in mind, the board insists. This "buffer" rationale might not have raised eyebrows in Hershey a couple of decades ago; it might have been called a prudent investment. But these are different times.

"People have lost trust in the trust," remarks Nancy,[2] a longtime Hershey resident. "It appears trustees bought the property to bail out the three guys who had owned the golf course, one of whom is CEO of the Hershey Company. It just looks bad." Nancy tells me the land deal epitomizes what the local public has increasingly perceived in recent decades: Hershey trustees have lost their focus on needy children and become "self-interested." "The grievance of locals is that the Hershey Trust has forgotten what the real meaning of the Milton Hershey School is," she says. "They're out of touch with what the students need. I'm not sure if [this grievance] is based on fact; it's more based on what people think is going on. But one thing that's factual is how the money is spent. A 'buffer' doesn't justify spending that much money on a golf course!"

The Starbucks Coffee where Nancy and I meet is in a strip of outlet stores, such as Banana Republic and Calvin Klein, adjacent to Hersheypark and not far from her home. The reputed origins of the outlet mall turn out to be relevant to our conversation: the mall was constructed on Hershey Trust–owned farmland that had been sold to a board member, a prominent developer in the region. The developer received a "sweetheart deal," locals say, paying a small sum up front with a promise to pay in full a decade after developing the land. Though not technically "self-dealing"—nothing in the deed of trust specifically forbids such a transaction—it gives the appearance of unscrupulousness on the part of the trust board. "For the last thirty years, there's been this appearance of conflict of interest around money, and trustees have done nothing to dispel it," Nancy observes. "I haven't talked to people in the community who feel proud of what's happening."

As we sip coffee and take bites from a sour lemon square, I inquire into Nancy's background. A baby boomer born in Pittsburgh, she grew up in a family that strongly identified with Catholicism and Democratic Party politics. In college, she majored in sociology and developed a strong commitment to social and economic justice. She found her way to Hershey circuitously, moving to accommodate her former husband's career requirements. She admits to feeling "like a fish out of water" when she arrived in the 1970s: "I was surprised moving to this area how conservative it is. People around here tend to be anti-union, anti-abortion, Republican." The "religious slant" of the region is reflected in the region's politics, she observes: Derry Township, which encompasses Hershey, has consistently voted Republican since the Civil War.[3] But politics have not inhibited her success as the leader of a domestic-violence shelter network. "I've been fortunate in the anti–domestic violence work I do. Politicians in Harrisburg have been very supportive on both sides of the aisle."

Nancy's ongoing anti–domestic violence efforts critically inform her observations about the Hershey Trust and Milton Hershey School. "About 85 percent of the kids at the Hershey School come from homes with domestic violence; that's why they're there," she explains. "Their mothers typically want a place for them to be safe and have opportunities. Our network of domestic violence shelters gives information about the Hershey School through the shelters." And yet the only anti-violence curriculum at the Hershey School takes the form of anti-bullying program directed mostly at girls, she observes; the school "doesn't recognize domestic violence as an important issue." This has less to do with school administrators' political or religious affinities than with trustees' distance from the everyday lives and experiences of students, she suggests: "There's something out of sync between trustees and the everyday of the school, and that's recent."

The attorney general's newly announced "probe" does not give Nancy confidence. That the trust board was recently chaired by a former state attorney general, and that the office of attorney general is practically the only authority with oversight of the trust begs the question of serious reform. "The trust truly is invisible," she reflects. "Sometimes it looks suspicious; maybe it's not. There should be public knowledge, but there isn't. It's just this small, closed network."

For my part, I take the attorney general's probe as an opportunity to "talk trust" with Hersheyites such as Nancy and her friends, to whom she introduces me. I have no special access to the board of trust. Nor do I have specialized training in the intricacies of charitable trust law and practice. My inquiry takes me to coffee shops and private homes across the town and township, and eventually to the corporate headquarters of the Hershey Company and the campus of Milton Hershey School. Along the way, I depend on local knowledge as my guide.

WHAT IS A TRUST, ANYWAY?

In American trust law, which is derived from English law, a "trust" is a property relationship in which property owned by one party (the trustor) is controlled by a second party (the trustee) for the benefit of a third party (the beneficiary).[4] Represented among diverse cultural and legal systems around the world, trusts are integral to common-law systems like the one in the United States. A trust can be created to benefit a few specific persons, as in a family trust fund, or a category of persons, as in a charitable trust fund. Family trusts are typically subject to the rule against perpetuities, a public policy that effectively limits their duration to a hundred years; charitable trusts are not subject to the rule and may exist in perpetuity.

In the case of the Milton Hershey School Trust, Milton and Catherine Hershey are the trustor; the Milton Hershey School board of trustees are the trustee; and officially enrolled Milton Hershey School students are the beneficiary. The board of trustees is composed of private individuals nominated and elected by sitting board members, and it serves two distinct functions. First, the board members act as managers for the school, charged with hiring and supervising key administrators and ensuring that day-to-day operation is consistent with the terms of Hershey's deed. Second, the board directs the Hershey Trust Company, a private bank that manages the school trust fund's investments (chief among them, the Hershey Company); local commercial real-estate holdings; and the wholly owned, for-profit Hershey Entertainment and Resorts Company, which operates Hersheypark and various lodgings, restaurants, and amusements in south-central Pennsylvania. Profits from these assets are funneled back into the school trust fund to support the ongoing operation of the school.

The Milton Hershey School Trust is one among nearly one-and-a-half-million charitable organizations recognized in the United States today. Excluding religious congregations, these charities control about $3 trillion in assets; perhaps predictably, they are sources of reverence and discontent (King and Roth 2007). Government oversight varies by state. The Internal Revenue Service, which grants federal tax relief to charitable organizations in exchange for public service broadly construed, is partly responsible for oversight. But the bulk of responsibility is shouldered by individual states. In Pennsylvania, the office of the attorney general oversees all of the state's charities, acting in the role of *parens patriae* (parent of the country); it represents the public's interest in preserving charitable gifts and avoiding waste. As a rule, neither the IRS nor state attorneys general interfere with the everyday governance of charitable trusts. For the authorities to interfere with the activities of trustees, attention must be drawn to evidence of harm to beneficiaries. Often the burden of drawing attention to harm falls on individual beneficiaries, activists, and journalists.

Historically, Americans have been uncomfortable with the large sums of money held by trusts and the power of private boards that confidentially dispense those sums. Long-standing anxiety over entrusted wealth is rooted in a tension between democracy and plutocracy that, as legal scholar Lawrence Friedman observes, can be traced to the founding of the country. The United States was, after all, "born in revolt against a system of inherited, dynastic wealth" (Friedman 2009: 21). Following the Revolutionary War, writes legal scholar Ray Madoff, "the charitable trust, associated as it was with privilege, the dead hand, and massive wealth held in perpetuity, was viewed with particular suspicion" (2010: 92). Jefferson warned against future generations of Americans being dominated by previous generations' contracts (Madoff 2010: 5). Madison expressed concerns about religious establishments perpetually controlling large amounts of property: "The growing wealth acquired by [ecclesiastical corporations] never fails to be a source of abuses," Madison warned (quoted in Madoff 2010: 92).

In the late nineteenth century, the predominant American view toward entrusted charitable wealth changed dramatically:

The late nineteenth century was a time when individuals in the United States began amassing wealth at levels never before seen in history. At the same time, it was an era of growing public awareness of larger societal ills, particularly those suffered by immigrants in the rapidly expanding American cities. In the end, the combination of societal problems in need of resources and the possibility of devoting a portion of this growing private wealth to the problems of the day outweighed earlier concerns about the unfettered growth of perpetual charitable organizations. This transformation was also eased by the simultaneous development of another entity with perpetual existence: the [business] corporation. (Madoff 2010: 95)

By the time the Milton Hershey School Trust was established, the United States "had grown its own crop of dynasties" involved in charitable organizations, writes Friedman (2009: 14). Unlike English dynasties, the new American dynasties were "not old, noble families"; they were, rather, "the descendants of men who made their money in business. To be 'in trade' was not a disgrace; it was one of the highest callings a man could have" (2009: 122). "A new American aristocracy of wealth had emerged—bankers, industrialists, captains of industry. Judges were, by and large, men who sympathized with society's elites. The doctrines [of trust law] catered to the needs and wishes of rich dynasts. These were men who were beginning to endow universities and create huge charitable foundations. They were often—not always—benefactors of society. The law reflected the conservative views of these men. It supported the wishes of founders and owners of great fortune" (120–21).

As the public image of entrusted wealth improved, so did the capacity of banks and trust companies to lobby for their interests in Washington: "The new professional trustees, the trust companies (or banks with trust departments), became, for the first time, significant players in the game of trust management" (Friedman 2009: 134). In the twentieth century, "they largely took over the business of trust management from private individuals . . . with regard to larger and dynastic trusts. And by the end of the twentieth century their influence on trust law was felt in decisive ways" (2009: 134).

Hershey's trust is an outlier among charities and thus a special case for regulation and oversight in one crucial respect: its controlling stake in a business corporation. The trust is a de facto "industrial foundation" through its control of the publicly traded Hershey Company. Such foundations were common in the United States until the mid-twentieth century. The Tax Reform Act of 1969—passed under the Nixon administration—prohibited tax-exempt foundations from owning a controlling share of votes in a business corporation. The legislation made it "illegal, with very few exceptions, for private foundations to own more than 20 percent of the voting interest in any for-profit enterprise" (Fleishman 2009: 98–99). This was intended to prevent the founding of charitable foundations as a "vehicle for retaining control of a closely held corporation" (98). A specific exception was granted for the Hershey Trust, however. Senior Pennsylvania senator Hugh D. Scott secured exemption from the act on the grounds that the trust is organized and operated for the benefit of a specific school and not primarily for the purpose of retaining control of a corporation (DiRusso 2006).[5]

Though rare in the present day United States, industrial foundations are common in northern Europe, as business scholars Hansmann and Thomsen report (2012). Nonprofit foundations own controlling interest in leading companies such as Bertelsmann, Heineken, and Ikea. In Denmark, foundations control a quarter of the hundred largest Danish corporations, including "Carlsberg beer (the world's fourth largest brewery group), A. P. Møller (the world's largest container shipping company), and William Demant (one of the world's largest producers of hearing aids)" (2012: 3).

An industrial foundation is typically governed by a board of directors; its purposes are set out by charter or deed. The purpose of the Carlsberg Foundation, for example, is to support a Carlsberg Laboratory (which researches the science of brewing) and to support basic research in natural sciences, mathematics, philosophy, the humanities and social sciences (Carlsberg Group n.d.). Its board is appointed by the Royal Danish Academy of Sciences and Letters.[6] Such foundations are "evidently chosen as protection for the company's one large donor—its founder," Hansmann and Thomsen observe:

> In most cases, presumably, the founder is effectively seeking a degree of immortality. He wishes to assure, as far as possible, that the firm he built will live on in perpetuity—often with his name on it. In short, he wants to perpetuate his control over the firm beyond the grave. Or, put differently, he is making an ongoing gift from his live self to his dead self. But clearly his dead self will be unable to police the fulfillment of any arrangement to this effect that his living self makes with the persons who will control the firm after his death. So the founder reduces the incentive for those persons to deviate from his wishes by constraining their ability to profit from deviation—which he accomplishes by giving ultimate control of the firm to a nonprofit organization. (2012: 6–7)

In sum, Hansmann and Thomsen speculate that the typical founder of an industrial foundation is seeking a degree of immortality through his business corporation, rather than through his nonprofit organization; the latter is a means for ensuring the perpetuity of the former. The situation is the opposite in the case of Hershey's founder. From what is known of his intentions, Milton Hershey aspired to immortality through his nonprofit, not through his business; the Hershey Company was a means for ensuring the perpetuity of the Milton Hershey School. But the intentions of the founder do not change the fundamental point: the Hershey Trust remains a de facto industrial foundation by virtue of its long-standing, customary control of the chocolate company. This institutional arrangement is the crux of modern Hershey's distinctive ecosystem.

TALKING TRUST WITH THE HILLARY GIRLS

When Nancy invites me to her home one evening for desert with friends, I eagerly accept, anticipating insights into the trust's evolving and, evidently, controversial role in the community. Inside a well-appointed dining room, I meet four local women who span two generations—the youngest in her forties, the eldest in her seventies. They tell me they have been meeting together at each other's homes for food and conversation since 2008, when each actively supported the nomination of Hillary Clinton in the Democratic Party's primary campaign. "We were 'The Hillary Girls,'" Nancy recounts. "We were going to have a big Hillary rally in Hershey." For whatever reasons, the rally did not happen, but the four women—Nancy, Rebecca, Lisa, and Jennifer— have become warm friends. They still revel in their group name, especially in a town and region that is, as they put it, "Republican through and through."

Each member of the "Hillary Girls" is a longtime resident of Hershey, invested in the community's improvement in at least two respects: more and better services and amenities within the town of Hershey, and increased community participation in local institutions, both public and private. Together, they have approached affiliates of the Hershey Trust about the use of space in downtown Hershey. They have publicly suggested to trustees that a former chocolate-factory be repurposed into art studio space, for example. In general, they see themselves as advocates for more community input into the trust's development activities in Hershey's historic core, which sits atop trust-controlled land.

"It's taking me some time to figure out exactly how the trust, school, company, and town are interlinked," I admit as we sit down at a large oak table set with coffee, tea, and apple crumb cake. This elicits chuckles: "Yes, they're very enmeshed! It's almost incestuous." Until recent decades, the women tell me, everyone who ran the Hershey Company and Hershey School lived in town and all were "accessible" to residents. "You could go down the street and talk to them," comments Rebecca, the most senior of the group. "They considered themselves neighbors." Most locals were Hershey employees or had some relationship to Hershey enterprise. "You were beholden to him for your job, so you didn't question the way things were done," she explains. Factory workers' wages were deposited at Hershey Bank; employees were never handed a paycheck. Electric, water, mortgage, telephone: everything was paid for at the bank downtown. The company made groceries available for purchase. A pharmacy, creamery, abattoir: "Anything you needed, Hershey provided."

The four women concur that the company town changed dramatically beginning in the mid-1960s. That was when the trust partnered with Penn State University to construct a medical research and teaching center just outside town, and new professional families settled in the community. "After the medical center came, people began to think the company town model was crazy," says Lisa. "It was as if the chocolate company had been saying, 'This is what's good for you, what you'll enjoy or need,' and people began to resent that kind of paternalistic thing. That's when you started to lose things." The people affiliated with the medical center were a new population: "Hippies, Jews, Democrats. They all had beards," Nancy jokes. They "didn't want anyone telling them what was best for them."

> *Lisa:* So there was a lot done for the community at one time, but it was all, "This is what is good for you." Noblesse oblige—that's the term. There were wonderful aspects of that—benefits the community had which we no longer have.
>
> *Nancy:* Sometimes I think it's a shame we no longer have those benefits. When it's done well, altruistically . . .
>
> *Jennifer:* I don't find anything wrong with Hershey having done those things. I'm not sure why people took offense to their saying, "This is good for you." It was good, wasn't it?
>
> *Rebecca:* But that's about the time the trust began to withdraw its support from the community. Because trustees were getting so much grief. Things became too costly. People came in from the outside—not just related to the medical center—and they wanted everything to be run in a more businesslike manner. "Enough of this taking care of everyone; we're not going to do this anymore!"

Other significant local changes followed, the women recollect. In the early 1970s, a fence was erected around the amusement park: "Before that you could just go in and buy tickets for the rides," Lisa remembers. As the decade unfolded, most of the amenities of the company town were sold off or closed: the drugstore, the community center, the Cocoa Inn—

a landmark of the town center. "The trust was divesting themselves of these things because they were draining off resources," Rebecca observes. "Things change. A new head of the board of directors comes in and they have new ideas."

The relationship between the Milton Hershey School and the surrounding community was also changing at the same time. Nancy remembers that when she moved to Hershey in the early 1980s, her home abutted a working turkey farm occupied by Milton Hershey students. The boys raised the turkeys and used them for food at the school; later, the unit was converted into a home for members of the school marching band: "You'd hear the drums and the horns. It was so wonderful having those kids in the neighborhood." Students would visit with local people for dinner on weekends—"a way for the community and the school to feel on the same page. It was very personal."

"The Milton Hershey students were more integrated in the community then," Rebecca observes. "Friday nights, the boys visited families in town for dinner. We used to take two boys every other weekend or so. Tyrone played hockey; we took him everywhere. He spent Christmas with us and everything."

"Now they're not really part of the community," Jennifer adds. Weekly visits stopped around the time the school centralized its campus and "'bottom-line profit' people" moved onto the board of trustees, Nancy recalls. "This would have been sometime in the '90s. They started to close the school in, and you never saw the kids."

> *Nancy:* [speaking to me] Peter, you have to figure out how to tell what is the trust, the school, the company, the town. . . . It is so, *ugh!* The attorney general disbanded the trust's board of directors after the attempt to sell the chocolate company in 2002. One of the trustees owned a construction company, and every construction job at the school went to him. A real conflict of interest. He wasn't the only case. The attorney general said, "You cannot have these conflicts of interest."
>
> *Lisa:* Trustees say they don't take money from the school to pay

themselves. They say they get it from the chocolate company, but . . .

Jennifer: And then there's the dinner at Mr. Hershey's mansion for Republican candidates . . .

Rebecca: There was an article in the newspaper a few months ago, "Is the GOP taking over the trust?" Because they have all Republicans at the trust. The good old boy network is alive and well!

Concerns about politicization at the trust are long-standing, I learn. Recent cohorts of board members have included influential Pennsylvania Republicans, as well as prominent businesspeople with close ties to Harrisburg, the state capital; and most of these trustees have been white men—hence the impression of a "good old boy network." Sitting among the "Hillary Girls," it is not hard to understand why community members say the trust board is made up of "all insiders" who are helping each other enrich themselves politically and financially.

As newspapers have reported, trustees enjoy generous compensation for their service to the school—a base salary of roughly $100,000 that grows according to responsibilities. Locals, as well as some outsiders looking in, are generally baffled by what they perceive to be excessively high pay. They point out that most trustees work only a few hours a week. For its part, the trust board draws a distinction between, on the one hand, duties performed as school managers and, on the other, duties performed as directors of the Hershey Trust Company. Technically, trustees are not paid for managing the school; they are paid for managing the trust company's assets, which includes oversight of the Hershey Company. Moreover, trustees regularly sit on other Hershey boards—the chocolate company and the entertainment company—for which they receive compensation on par with directors of for-profit businesses. A single Hershey trustee sitting on multiple "interlocking" boards may earn as much as half a million dollars a year for his services.

Among the local public, nuances of technical justifications for high compensation tend to get lost. It is common to believe, rather, that trustees are exploiting their beneficent positions for personal gain and, moreover, that they are helping their friends in high places do the same thing. In the view of community members, the evident self-interest of trustees is ultimately what led to the trust's decision in 2002 to sell its controlling stake in the Hershey Company—a radical break with custom that united all corners of the Hershey community:

> *Jennifer:* I think the time everybody came together was "Derail the Sale" in 2002.
> *Lisa:* Yes, it was as if we'd just had enough. When the company came up for sale, the community said, "That's it, we've had enough!"
> *Rebecca:* People got very upset that our town was going to go down the drain. Who knew what the new owners of the company would do?
> *Jennifer:* I still have the signs from our march. We used candy themes: "Hershey Trust is *NutRageous*! Hershey Trust is Sending *Reese's* to Pieces!" And my favorite: *Mr. Goodbar* saying, "Hell no, we won't go!" It was in the London *Times*—a picture of us holding up the signs. The signs got in the papers because they were fun. Everyone was honking with the signs while we had the rallies and were marching up to the trust's headquarters at the Hershey mansion.
> *Nancy:* Oh, my, I loved that—shades of the '60s. But you're marching with Republicans and staid proper people who were all doing the same thing. That was pretty awesome. I don't think you'd find that happening too often. And then we went to the courthouse for the hearing the attorney general was having. It brought people out. People got really protective of Hershey.

The expression "shades of the '60s" about the 2002 effort to "Derail the Sale" of the chocolate company lingers with me as conversation comes to a close. It strikes me as curious, given that it was not a protest in the name of rights per se—or was it? What kind of "activism" was this, in which stakeholders in a trust fund (who are not themselves beneficiaries) mobilize against trustees in the name of community?

At the end of the evening, the four women give me names and phone numbers of people possibly willing to "talk trust" with me. The list is made up mostly of male community elders who have insider knowledge of the trust, school, and company and who participated actively in "Derail the Sale." "If you get them talking," Nancy tells me by way of goodbye, "these guys will tell you everything you want to know."

REMEMBERING "DERAIL THE SALE": 2002

"Derail the Sale"—the initials correspond to those of "Derry Township Schools"—is the single major public outcry over the Hershey Trust in local memory, uniting townspeople, chocolate company employees, and Milton Hershey School alumni, as well as local and state political officeholders. It implicates the legal rights and obligations of Hershey's trust, company, and school, as well as the social fate of the community in and around Derry Township, Pennsylvania. Its legacy permeates everyday talk about the past, present, and future of all things Hershey.

In the sunlit living room of a warm brick house on Hershey's esteemed Elm Avenue, I ask the homeowner to tell me how the campaign to stop the sale of the company got started. Arnold is thoughtful and careful with his words, both eager to tell the story and protective of it. Self-described as "Hershey through and through," he is a senior community member who spent his early years at the Milton Hershey School and his later years working in the management of several Hershey enterprises. He was one of a small group of village elders who—amid planning the hundredth anniversary celebration of the community—first received word that the trust was planning to sell the chocolate company.

"It was a July, Wednesday night," Arnold recalls. "I remember saying to the person who called me on the phone, 'Who would put out such a heinous rumor?' And his comment to me was, 'Well, it's going to be in the *Wall Street Journal* tomorrow.'" The next morning the news broke in the *Journal* ("Hershey May Go on the Block," 2002). Over breakfast, the hundredth-anniversary celebration group began strategizing: someone was tasked with communicating with town residents, someone else with affiliates of the Hershey Company and the Hershey School, someone else with press. Several former Hershey trustees in the group agreed to "go public" with their opposition to the sale, emphasizing potentially detrimental consequences for the local community and, by extension, the school. They had no portfolio, no standing to make decisions, Arnold tells me. "All of us had a common feeling about the negativity of this whole thing. And I forget what did we do, how did we do it—but it grew from that."

The campaign to "Derail the Sale" was publicized by national and international media. For many Hershey locals, it seemed as if the battle for Hershey was "everywhere." "My wife's calling on the phone ordering something from a mail-order place," says Arnold, "and the woman in Arizona says 'Good luck!'" Sympathies for the community coincided with tactical assistance to the campaign's primary organizers. Bellhops at area hotels reported on the comings and goings of representatives of potential buyers of the company. Documents internal to the Hershey Trust and Company and details of board meeting times and locations were leaked. At the same time, American and European press moved into town and painted a portrait of David versus Goliath. The community—described as "unique," "historic," "iconic," and decidedly "small"—was David. The trust—standing in for the interests of giant, indifferent, even hostile capital—was Goliath. "All the stars were aligned—legally, politically, everything," Arnold recalled. "It was providential."

In a climax of the campaign, a rally on the downtown plaza on Chocolate Avenue brought together school alumni and employees, residents of the township, workers at the factory, former company officials, and former Hershey trustees: all the Hersheyites who opposed the sale (Sherzer 2002). Both the Democratic and Republican gubernatorial candidates came out against the sale. The latter, crucially, held the office of state attorney general, with oversight of charities. Within a matter of days, his office successfully petitioned the local probate court—the "life cycle court" having to do with wills and estates, known in Pennsylvania as the "Orphans' Court"—to delay the sale, pending review by a higher court.

The legal decision to delay the sale "bought time," another participant in the campaign, Jeffrey, tells me as we sit down in his dining room a few blocks from Arnold's home. A recently retired chocolate company executive and longtime town resident, Jeffrey leveraged his marketing experience during "Derail the Sale" to help wage a public-relations battle in local and national news.

"One of our challenges was making sure that this wasn't like a Flint, Michigan,[7] where news reporters would come in and report the sad news that another iconic community had been shuttered because of the greed of capitalism. So we devised a strategy to make the campaign entertaining," he explains. "That way we could prolong the stays of all the newspeople and build up the pressure upon the social responsibility of those that were irresponsible and hopefully break their backs." Over three weeks of sustained press coverage, the town's capacity for punning on associations with chocolate, nuts, and sweetness was deployed as a public-relations weapon to great effect.

Portfolio diversification was the trustees' motivation for the sale. In their understanding—which, they believed, reflected the U.S. legal community's consensus on what it means to be a prudent fiduciary of a charitable trust—the Hershey Trust's function was not to protect the company or community but to prudently maximize the revenue stream of the Hershey School Trust fund. They were following the logic of "portfolio theory": the idea that "a good trustee will invest in a variety of stocks and bonds. . . . If the portfolio as a whole is 'prudent,' then the trustee has done its job and should not be open to criticism (or to lawsuits)" (Friedman 2009: 123).

The assets of the trust appeared obviously undiversified to trustees: if Hershey Company stock tanked, what would happen to the endowment of the Hershey School? Selling the company seemed to make good fiscal sense. Furthermore, trustees claimed their attempt to sell the company came at the behest of the Pennsylvania attorney general—a claim the attorney general publicly denied. The attorney general's office may have suggested the trust diversify its assets, a spokesperson acknowledged, but it did not advise selling the company outright.

"Derail the Sale" campaigners rejected trustees' claims that prudent management of the Hershey School Trust fund necessitated selling the company. The sale was not a matter of "fiduciary responsibility" to the charity; on the contrary, trustees were "misguided [by] their own interpretations of what Mr. Hershey intended," as Jeffrey puts it. The problem was that the board of directors was made up mostly of "outsiders." "Some of them didn't live here. They came here from outside. They didn't have the sense of community." The logic of financial diversification did not consider the Hershey School's need to be situated in a safe and secure community—a community built around the Hershey Company.

The probate judge who ruled in favor of the attorney general's injunction against the sale echoed campaigners' sentiments in his opinion (*Re* Milton Hershey School Trust 2002). The board of trustees was too "large" and too "distant and disconnected" from both the beneficiaries of the charity and the local community. The school, company, and community enjoyed a "symbiotic relationship," which is "common knowledge," the judge asserted. The trust's sale of the Hershey Company potentially would do harm to this "public interest," and therefore the attorney general was entitled to injunctive relief. This holding is remarkable for essentially establishing a public right over a private charitable trust if the trust's activity threatens the local community.

Before an appellate court would have the opportunity to hear the trust's appeal to the court's holding, the board of directors voted to abandon the sale—ten to seven. Trustees attributed their last-minute reversal in consensus to both local and state resistance, which had taken them aback. Victory was declared by residents of the community, employees of the company, alumni of the school, and local and state politicians. Press reports later confirmed that, had the vote turned out the other way, the Hershey Company would have been sold to the Wrigley candy company for $12 billion.

THE SOCIAL AND LEGAL AFTERMATH OF 2002

In the aftermath, the attorney general's office—exercising its *parens patriae* power to intervene on behalf of citizens in need of protection—moved to reconstitute the board: all those trustees who voted in favor of the sale, and a few others, would resign; ten in total were left. A former state attorney general—the first in the state to have been elected to office, in 1980—took over the chairmanship of the board of directors and pledged fidelity to the trustor's original intentions for the school. Though it was not an explicit stipulation of Milton Hershey's deed of trust, the new chairman vowed publicly never to sell the company. Concurrently, at the school, a new president pledged to restore morale and a more orthodox mission. Restoration was the order of the day.

With the board reconstituted, the Pennsylvania state legislature entered the scene, enacting a new law that seemed to bolster the prospects of the Hershey Company's remaining headquarters in Derry Township for a long time to come. Lawrence Friedman explains:

> [The new Pennsylvania state law] made it the duty of charitable trusts—if "a majority of its beneficiaries" lived at a particular place in Pennsylvania, and if the trust had as one of its assets "voting control of a publicly traded business corporation"—not to "consummate any transaction" that would give up that control, without notice to the attorney general—and to the "affected employees." In the "case of a charitable trust," a fiduciary making investment and management decisions was supposed to consider "the special relationship" of an asset, "and its economic impact as a principal business enterprise on the community in which the beneficiary of the trust is located"; and the "special value of the integration of the beneficiary's activities with the community" where the business might be located. The language is quite general, but obviously was aimed squarely at the Hershey Trust. (Friedman 2009: 168)

For a moment in the wake of "Derail the Sale," it seemed, as one campaigner puts it, that "everything was lovely and back to normal." That moment—in which local publics exerted power over the trust to enforce the status quo—did not last.

U.S. legal scholars have scrutinized the canceled sale of the company in terms of state power over charitable trusts—specifically the power of state attorneys general to interfere with trustees' exercise of fiduciary duties.[8] Evelyn Brody, for example, analyzes the Hershey case in terms of the parochial (or locally bound) conception of "public interest" inherent in charitable trust law, as well as the paternalistic role played by regulators of charities (attorneys general, legislators, and courts).

For Brody, the 2002 canceled sale is an instance of illegitimate "near-seizure of assets" by the state (2004: 3). "The Hershey case illustrates the lesson that the value of narrowly-confined charitable assets does not disappear—it just gets appropriated by those with power over their disposal," that is, the office of governor and attorney general in Pennsylvania. The state's appropriation of charitable assets comes at the expense of the beneficiaries of the trust—the students of the school—as well as Pennsylvania residents who, Brody speculates, might have enjoyed more employment opportunities had Wrigley's acquired the Hershey Company (28).

Legal scholars Klick and Sitkoff take the analysis of 2002 in another direction. The "ugly secret" of U.S. charities is that "their lack of clearly defined owners invites deadweight losses" arising from agency costs (2008: 750). Agency costs—the primary concern of corporate law—are the costs of delegating control of a principal's assets to an agent (830); in business, such costs arise when the incentives of managers diverge from the interests of shareholders.[9] In the case of the Hershey Trust, Klick and Sitkoff argue, the canceled sale of the Hershey Company—what they term, rather provocatively, "the aborted sale"—imposed roughly $850 million in agency costs on the students of the Milton Hershey School. Furthermore, the authors argue, it erased substantial gains in the value of the company that followed the public announcement of the sale: a sign that the true market value of the company had been long suppressed by trustees' control. "The $2.7 billion increase in the value of the Company on exposure to the takeover market is a damning indictment of the trustee's failure as agents of the Trust to maximize value," they write (831).

A portfolio valued primarily on the performance of a single business corporation is unnecessarily exposed to uncompensated risk, Klick and Sitkoff argue. This sort of risk is not offset by "improvement in expected return"; it can and should be avoided "costlessly" through diversification (2008: 766). Instead, the trust's retention of control of the company leaves the Hershey School at the mercy of the candy market. It also makes the company unnecessarily cautious—because corporate managers are anxious not to squander the Hershey School Trust fund; perhaps, the authors speculate, this is why the company continues to lack an international presence on par with its competitors, Mars, Nestle, and Cadbury (2008: 755). The trust's holding onto control additionally creates "an unfortunate expectation in the town of Hershey that the trustees will retain control over the Company indefinitely" (755). The sentiments of Hershey locals who agitated against the sale "obscures the sad reality of the Trust's exposure to uncompensated risk and the growing disconnect between the Trust's value and its mission" (755).

This view from corporate law has been challenged in business scholarship. Hansmann and Thomsen (2012), for example, suggest that industrial foundation arrangements such as Hershey's encourage foundation trustees to consider themselves "virtual owners" of a business corporation and to act with a clarity and an objectivity that come from "managerial distance." Where Klick and Sitkoff find inefficiency—high agency costs—in the industrial foundation arrangement, Hansmann and Thomsen find superlative economic performance: "If one considers the entire four-year period surrounding the brief event interval on which [Klick and Sitkoff] focus," the authors observe, "the foundation-controlled Hershey Company . . . strongly outperformed both the industry average and the overall Dow Jones Industrial Average" (2012: 5). In other words, trustees' responsibility to Milton Hershey students encouraged the Hershey Company to perform more efficiently and productively than the average corporation.

For their part, Hersheyites who recollect "Derail the Sale" regard the social and legal aftermath of 2002 as ongoing, if largely out of public view and out of local control. Several senior community members point me to a *Fortune* article that, in their view, best encapsulates the fallout from 2002. After detailing the efforts of the "citizens' militia" that organized in opposition to the sale, the article concludes on an antiheroic note:

> Now that the immediate euphoria of the town's victory has worn off, some wonder whether that victory was a Pyrrhic one. For these self-appointed keepers of Milton Hershey's flame, there's no

going back. The end of silent acquiescence is surely a good thing. But it's been replaced by endless chatroom conspiracy theories. One popular protest sign tells all about the new age of suspicion: HERSHEY TRUST IS AN OXYMORON. . . . The town emerged with its beloved company—but it can't truly regain its past. The quilt that is Hershey has frayed, and many of its threads have popped. Hershey long proclaimed itself "the sweetest place on earth." Now, it's bittersweet. (Helyar 2002)

The campaign to "Derail the Sale" "got to be something that I don't think can be duplicated, because I don't think the stars are going to line up like that—that there's going to be an election for governor at the same time there's that same kind of outcry," Arnold tells me, reflecting on *Fortune*'s conclusion. "People from 2002 are changed," he suggests: "I'm not sure that if the company went up for sale again we could get near the same kind of firestorm of outrage. Hundreds of chocolate factory jobs have been moved to Mexico and people could care less. The old plant is closing down. We don't have that same legacy feeling, I guess—a feeling of heritage. Or, it's still there, but leadership has changed a lot. . . . Whatever's going to happen next, it comes down to that trust board."

THE SCANDAL GROWS

To be sure, the "firestorm of outrage" over the trust in 2002 may have subsided in intervening years, but public attention has not waned; on the contrary, journalism, activism, and legal actions involving the trust have proliferated. It comes as no surprise, then, that as I make the rounds talking with Hersheyites about "Derail the Sale," my interlocutors and I are confronted with "breaking news": in an unprecedented move, an active Hershey trustee has filed a whistle-blowing lawsuit with the state attorney general (Associated Press 2011). The lawsuit alleges a variety of ethically unscrupulous, potentially illicit practices by fellow trustees: personally profiting through property acquisitions; luxury hotel stays and first-class airplane tickets; trust-backed, partisan political campaign contributions;

financial enrichment of relatives through contracts; and general negligence in the management of the school, including overlooking situations in which children were involved in sexual misconduct and abuse.

The author of this most recent lawsuit is a long-standing and well-known figure in the Hershey community: Robert Reese, grandson of the founder of the Hershey-based Reese's Candy Company. Reese's grandfather, H. B. Reese, was a dairy farmer and a shipping foreman for the Hershey Company. As local legend has it, he was personally inspired by Milton Hershey to establish his own candy business. In the 1920s, he started a company in the basement of his home in Hershey and began making Reese's Peanut Butter Cups—peanut butter candies coated with Hershey's milk chocolate. When he died, Reese left the successful company to his sons, who merged it with the Hershey Company in the early 1960s. Today, Reese's remains a subsidiary of Hershey's (it is the chocolate company's bestselling brand) and the Reese family remains closely tied to Hershey's entrepreneurial-philanthropic legacies. Such is the context for Robert Reese's sitting on the board of trustees.

Reese's lawsuit details publicly for the first time the escalation in trustees' compensation (disproportionate to monetary inflation) since the founding of Hershey's charity in 1909. Disinterested observers may find the escalation unremarkable, yet among concerned stakeholders, the escalation is taken as objective evidence of trustees' "self-interestedness" (see table).

HERSHEY TRUSTEES' COMPENSATION	
1909–1940:	$ 0
1941–1984:	Below $1,000 and [later] up to $2,000
1985–1990:	$12,500
1990–1993:	$20,000
1993–1996:	$30,000
1997–2002:	$35,000
2003:	$49,000
2004:	$65,000
2005:	$85,000
2006–2010:	$100,000 to $130,000

The Reese lawsuit is withdrawn within a couple months of being filed, with the petitioner citing health conditions preventing him from proceeding.[10] But by this time, the attorney general's probe has expanded to include an investigation of the allegations. The golf course purchase is whispered to be "the tip of the iceberg."

Gossip grows louder. Scandal accelerates. As I dig deeper into the history of the community and the mystique of the founder, I start to realize that trust is the heart of the matter.

CHAPTER 2

⇒ THE MAN AND THE TOWN ⇐

IN LOCAL LEGEND, "Mr. Hershey" is conjured as a weird fellow—in the sense of odd, strange, and connected with fate (the archaic meaning of *weird* [McKean 2005]). A "genius of a man," "benevolent and kind," Milton Hershey is also remembered as "vain," "controlling," a "dictator," and a "feudal lord." From what is recollected of his countenance and affect—a man of few words, an unremarkable humor, a homely appearance—he was not especially magnetic in person. Yet among Hersheyites—town residents, company employees, school alumni and others—he counts as a charismatic personality.[1]

The founder's biography has been written numerous times, yet there is tantalizingly little interpretation of his interior life, as he evidently did not write or keep personal letters or diary entries. Historians working in local archives have only fragments available to them. Reading in the Hershey Company's archives (in the Paul Wallace Research Collection, comprising local oral histories from the mid-1950s), I find curious bits and pieces of recollections from others. None can be added up to achieve a holistic account of the person, but they do complicate and embellish the legend:

⊚ "M.S. was terribly knock-kneed. His feet were eighteen inches apart when his knees were together," recalls a chocolate plant manager.

- "He was of the old school with a hard-boiled background. He was absolutely honest, but strict. His tendency was not to raise the rate of pay. That was the old school," recalls a dentist employed by Hershey at the industrial school.
- "Mr. Hershey would do a favor for you, but not too often," says a housefather at the school.
- "He talked in a high-pitched, eager, nervous voice," says a state senator. "Mr. Hershey, as far as English was concerned, was illiterate."
- "He did eat an enormous amount of candy," recalls his personal physician. "He was a deep thinker. He was really brilliant. I asked him, 'Where did you learn this chemistry?' 'Well,' he said, 'I never studied it.' He had something that you just cannot explain."
- "Mr. Hershey was a very fair-minded man, without bigotry," recalls a monsignor based in Lancaster, Pennsylvania. "He was a businessman, and he wanted to run religion on a business basis."
- "He told me his religion was the Golden Rule," recalls his personal nurse.[2]

Milton Snavely Hershey was born in 1857 on his family's farm in Derry Church, Pennsylvania—what is today called Hershey. The farm was situated in the heart of Pennsylvania Dutch country, the territory settled between the end of the seventeenth century and the middle of the nineteenth century by immigrants from Alsace, southwestern Germany, and Switzerland. Lutheran and German Reformed settlers—so-called Church Germans—made up one dominant segment of these settlers. Another segment consisted of smaller sects of Anabaptist or Brethren, commonly known as Plain Folk. Hershey's ancestors are counted among these Plain Folk. Though a diverse lot, they are "united by certain persistent convictions," observes historian Sydney Ahlstrom:

Above all, by the desire to reconstitute the Church as a community of earnest believers whose conversion had been sealed by adult

baptism (they rebaptized, hence Anabaptist). Behind this lay
their protest against state churches and their insistence that the
Church as a whole had "fallen" when it entered into cooperation
with rulers, identifying itself with whole peoples regardless of
their personal dedication. Almost universally these Anabaptists
were pacifists; personal uprightness and charitableness were the
constant conditions of good standing in their churches. . . . They are
best known in contemporary America as devout and sequestered
communities, archaic, simple, and prosperous. (2004: 82)

The Hershey family was Mennonite—one of those Protestant sects,
writes sociologist Max Weber, whose religious way of life is connected
with "the most intensive development of business acumen," whose "oth-
erworldliness is as proverbial as their wealth" (2001: 10). Indeed, Milton
Hershey's business acumen was evidently encouraged from an early age.
His first million dollars, arriving at the close of the first American Gilded
Age, was acquired by selling his Lancaster-based caramel candy company
in 1900. This modern fortune furnished a modern lifestyle set apart from
traditional norms.

As a wealthy young entrepreneur, Hershey rejected for himself the plain
living of his Mennonite kinfolk—his mother was "Reformed," his itinerant
father non-practicing—and he became something of a Victorian man of the
world. Not unlike his peers, he expressed strong distaste for urban industrial
order. In his early twentieth-century entrepreneurial efforts, he began, as did
other entrepreneurs of the age, "to approximate the old [nineteenth-century
republican] image of the businessman as family provider and citizen"—an
image, writes sociologist Robert Bellah, tied to the "often-sentimentalized
family farm" (1996: 43). Indeed, when Hershey returned to his birthplace
in 1903 to build a model industrial community, he incorporated as much
as possible of his former family farmland into the physical site.

In the early 1900s, the crossroads called Derry Church—"Hershey-
before-Hershey," as locals refer to it—was home to a small community of
Pennsylvania Dutch and Scots-Irish farmers. It was situated adjacent to the
Blue Mountain "anthracite region," commonly known as coal country. Be-

ginning in the 1870s, industrial coal mining ushered in a new social order to that region. "A big union and a cartel of coal, iron, and railroad corporations banded the diversities of religion, national origin, and social class together into a state within a state," writes historical anthropologist Anthony Wallace (1988: 367). Coal towns were strictly administered, buoyed by "a perception by both unionists and capitalists that a higher level of sovereignty, social control, and industrial discipline was required for mutual survival" (367). "Apart from being the economic mainstay of the entire region by virtue of direct employment and the purchase of local goods and services," Wallace observes, "the [coal] company wielded an enormous power comparable only to a state's right of eminent domain" (426). Land was appropriated at the will of the company. Social control was enforced by the state as well as by private police. Labor disturbances were quelled by secret police (i.e., the Pinkerton Detective Agency). Hershey's model industrial community both appropriated and countered the social order of these coal towns—establishing a model town adjacent to the anthracite region in farming territory.

Though geographically proximate to coal country, Hershey, Pennsylvania would be inspired less by coal company towns than by the "garden cities" of England, which Milton Hershey admired and presumably visited. These industrial towns can be identified with the latter of "two tendencies [which] accompanied modern capitalism through the whole of its history," observes sociologist Zygmunt Bauman (2001: 34). The first tendency is "a consistent effort to replace the 'natural understanding' of bygone community, the nature-regulated rhythm of farming and the tradition-regulated routine of the craftsman's life by an artificially designed and coercively imposed and monitored routine;" the second "was a much less consistent (and belatedly undertaken) attempt to resuscitate or create *ab nihilo* a 'community feeling,' this time within the framework of the new power structure" (34). Company towns expressing this second tendency "put a wager on the moral standards of labourers, their religious piety, the ampleness of their family lives and their trust in the boss-patron. . . . The bid [of such model towns]," Bauman writes, "was to recreate community centered around the place of work and, conversely, to make factory employment into a 'whole life' pursuit" (35).

Hershey's model industrial community was especially inspired by

Bournville, England—home of the Quaker-established Cadbury chocolate factory.[3] Quakers in England turned to chocolate making, among other business pursuits, in large part because they were banned from universities and restricted in professions such as law; they could not stand for Parliament; and as pacifists, they did not join the armed services (Cadbury 2011). At Bournville, George Cadbury paid relatively high salaries to women, limited working hours, established sick pay and a pension plan, and in lieu of passing his fortune to his children, established the Bournville Village Trust,[4] created to maintain and improve the community surrounding the factory.[5]

Like Bourneville and other "garden cities," Hershey boasted an assortment of company-sponsored health, welfare, education, and recreation resources, many of which no longer exist: the trolly system that brought factory workers and tourists in and out of town; the Hershey Hospital, which served as the community's health care center; the Hershey Junior College, built during the Great Depression to provide free education to locals. Hershey also had a sister town in Cuba: "Hershey, Cuba," established outside Havana in 1916 for sugar production. Its central sugar refinery was sold by the company a few years after Milton Hershey's death and the town lies mostly in ruins today.[6]

Other core components of Hershey's model community remain, including the amusement park, zoo, theater, hotel, gardens, golf courses, stadium, and ice rink with ice hockey team. Most of these are presently controlled by the for-profit Hershey Entertainment and Resorts Company, which is wholly owned by the Milton Hershey School Trust.

The story of how the model community was transformed after the death of the founder in 1945 is at the heart of local understandings of the Hershey Trust. Having inherited the founder's estate, the trust became the predominant entrepreneur in the community. At the direction of the trust board, and with minimal input from ordinary community members, former amenities of the company town were either sold off, demolished, or turned into profit centers to feed the trust fund. For better or worse, as Hersheyites tell it, the trust's new ventures in entertainment and resorts, as well as its unprecedented partnership with Penn State University to create a university teaching hospital, attracted builders, job seekers, new residents, tourists, and ever more car traffic. Modern suburban Hershey reflects, in large part, the trust's entrepreneurial efforts since the mid-1960s.

To better appreciate the historic role played by the trust in the community, I talk with longtime residents who have first-hand knowledge of Hershey's transformation from model industrial community into modern suburbia. I meet with faith leaders who speak to the ongoing influence of Hershey's entrepreneurial-philanthropic legacies on local religious life. I also engage "new" community members, associated with the university teaching hospital and other professional settings, who variously reckon with their place in the local social order and their values vis-à-vis "old" Hershey. My conversations begin with a discussion of Hershey's "golden age," in which, by all accounts, the community flourished as never before.

HERSHEY'S "GOLDEN AGE"

The 1950s and 1960s—the American baby boom years—are widely acknowledged as the "golden age" of the Hershey model industrial community, overlapping in large part with the civic renaissance and economic boom of the postwar United States. Town residents who grew up then recollect with special fondness the culture and entertainment furnished by Hershey's enterprises at no cost to the local public.

Everyone in the community could freely enjoy Hershey Park (not yet rechristened Hersheypark), which was more like a picnic area than a modern amusement park. One could walk through anytime one wanted—the zoo and the beautiful rose gardens likewise. There was the starlight ballroom, where men and women dressed up and danced to big bands, and the sunken gardens, where a fountain lit up at night and couples embraced when they tired of dancing. "Dutch Days," a Pennsylvania Dutch arts-and-craft fair, brought thousands of Amish and Mennonite people into town to sell trinkets, dolls, hex signs, and Pennsylvania Dutch delicacies: apple butter, chicken corn soup, shoofly pie. At the Hershey Theater, the Philadelphia Orchestra visited regularly and performed free of charge for townspeople. The Hershey Community Center organized dozens of games daily. And children regularly entered the chocolate factory at will. Inside, they followed the yellow line corresponding to the production sequence. Workers threw candy for them to catch. At the end of the line, their thermoses were filled with fresh, cold Hershey's chocolate milk. Here was American consumer capitalist culture at its most picturesque.

"It was like a little utopia for kids," recollects Brian, a lifelong resident with a warm countenance and softly graying hair who lives a few blocks from the house he grew up in; his sister and her family live down the street. "You didn't need any money," he tells me over coffee in his family kitchen, "and there was always something to do." Even when it was raining, there was the penny arcade, and pennies were plentiful.

Brian's parents are Pennsylvania Dutch. They grew up in nearby Annville and Lebanon County. His paternal grandmother spoke the Pennsylvania Dutch dialect; he did not learn to understand or speak it. His father was born "in the heart of Amish country," and Brian grew up with the influence of "plain folk" in his life—particularly through his experience in the Brethren Church. Each of his parents claim long-standing ties to the Milton Hershey School and Trust. His mother's family sat on the first board of managers of the trust after selling their farmland in neighboring Lebanon County to the Hershey Company. And his father is among the oldest living alumni of the Hershey School—enrolling there with his brother during the Great Depression after his own father died. Brian's sister's full name includes the name of M. S. Hershey's wife, Catherine—a way of honoring the family benefactor.

Many of Brian's classmates in the public schools lived on farms; he knew all their names. "It was a small town." Indeed, Hershey's population in the company town's golden age was less than half of what it is today. Protestant Germans—in particular Pennsylvania Dutch or "Dutchmen"—and Catholic Italians made up the primary social division in the community. Germans were those who owned and worked the farms in the region before the chocolate factory was built in 1905. The Italians were skilled laborers—many masons among them—who settled in the region when they were employed by M. S. Hershey to build the chocolate factory and company town. Both Dutchmen and Italians worked the chocolate factory floor; Hershey corporate officials were primarily Dutchmen through the late 1960s.

The Germans were "the whites"; the Italians were "the other whites." Germans ate meat and potatoes; they spoke English and some Pennsylvania Dutch dialect. Italians ate pastas with sauces; they spoke Italian and some English. "Blacks"—meaning African Americans—were few and far between; members of the township historical society remember the name and location of the house of the one African American family that lived in the township in the early twentieth century. Marriages between Germans and Italians, when they occurred, were known commonly as "interracial." Often they resulted in both bride and groom being disowned by their respective kin. "On the religious thing, you stayed apart," Brian recalls. He and his sister remember a young German-Italian couple who dated and made an appearance together at a local Presbyterian Church service sometime in the late 1950s or early 1960s: "All the youth of the town flocked to see if there would be thunder and lightning—if God would strike them dead."

During the lifetime of the founder—between the early 1900s and mid-1940s—the relations between Catholic Italians and Protestant Germans were evidently more antagonistic than in later decades. The social contact between Germans and Italians was minimal—the latter ghettoized in Hershey's own "Little Italy," organized around the local Catholic church. Among those who grew up in the postwar golden years, the play of Christian difference among Protestant German and Catholic Italian is recollected in terms of fun and friendliness: "The Italians lived on Areba Avenue [named after a cocoa-growing region] and the German guys would live on Cocoa Avenue," Brian recollects. "On weekends we'd have 'holy war' football games—the Catholics and the Protestants. We all went to school together. We were all friends."

Looking back, "Hershey was a good opportunity not just for Pennsylvania Dutchmen but for Italians too. . . . Each generation of Italians got more educated; they were all hard workers," Brian reflects, echoing a widely held local sentiment: "At one time Italians weren't particularly wanted real badly. Hershey Estates wouldn't even let them build in Hershey—because if you were Italian you were a little bit lower, you know? But they got around that. The kids started to go to college and doing better and better. Now if you look, a lot of them are legislators. Our district attorney is an Italian.

Judges are Italian. They got over that and it all worked out pretty well. Some of that bigotry, you know how it gets—it gets watered down. And by the time people are more educated, it goes away." In the company town's golden age, as Brian recollects it, the primary social division between Germans and Italians was overwritten by a shared sense of socioeconomic equality: "There were no rich people, there were no poor people. We were all pretty much in the same boat." After the death of Milton Hershey, the new chief executive officer of the chocolate company, Percy Alexander Staples, "was probably making more money than the rest of us—but it wasn't like he and his family were rich."[7] The "first family to become rich" in Hershey were the Reeses, Brian remembers. After the H. B. Reese Company was sold to the Hershey Chocolate Company for $25 million in 1963, the Reese family "had more money than anybody else, but they were good people. It wasn't like they were any different."

When Brian graduated from Hershey's public high school in the late 1960s, "leaving home to find [his] way" felt like the right thing to do. First he went to Texas for college—he had applied to only one school and did not know what he wanted to study—and then to Philadelphia where he trained as a health care professional. In Texas, he was "the Yankee" in a time when "Yankees were still different." In Philadelphia, at Temple University, he was "the Gentile." Both experiences were a "culture shock." But Hershey "always felt like home," and he was glad to come back in the early 1970s: "Just like my father who graduated from Milton Hershey—and he thought Hershey was a pretty special place to live—I stayed in Hershey because I remembered what a wonderful place it was." When he returned, the company town he grew up in had been transformed: the amusement park, now fenced, was expanding into an industry; and a new teaching and research hospital, the Penn State Hershey Medical Center, was attracting a differently diverse population to town. A new kind of community—more suburban, affluent, and "transient"—was taking the place of the old model industry community.

Today, Brian and his wife have four children together, each of whom is grown and lives in a different part of the country. He is "semi-retired"— "more retired than semi"—and enjoying himself: "Like Jane Fonda says, life is best at sixty." He is financially secure. His children have attended college and are trying to find career paths: "I'm kind of waiting for my kids to go to a different stage of their lives." He expresses the hope that someday soon he will have grandchildren. He does not expect, however, that those grandchildren will grow up in Hershey.

"Hershey did not stay as special as when I grew up," he explains. Growing up, his children "all thought this was no more special than any other place—a nice pretty little town, but so are a lot of other towns." The reason for this de-specialization, in a phrase, is money: "The powers of Hershey wanted to make more money, and they did it at the cost of kids."

When he observes that the profit motive of the "powers of Hershey" comes "at the cost of kids," Brian specifically means at the expense of children of the public town: children such as his own who—in the absence of distinctive memories of the company town and realizing upward mobility lay elsewhere—seemingly have no need or desire to return. Implicit in this observation is the knowledge that many of the changes introduced to the town have been carried out by the trust (the "powers of Hershey") nominally for the benefit of the students of the Milton Hershey School—the alma mater of Brian's father. Whether those changes have in fact benefited students is another matter of enduring local concern. For better or worse, the "golden age" of the Hershey model industrial community has come to a close, and the trust, as Brian and other senior townspeople recognize, has played no small part in its passing.

HOW THE TRUST CREATED HERSHEYPARK

When Milton Hershey died in 1945, his model community, chocolate company, and school for children in need were left in the hands of trusted business partners and longtime employees via the legal mechanism of the Hershey School Trust fund; for two decades, Hershey trustees oversaw these assorted enterprises as the founder had done—and by all accounts the community flourished. The town's utilities continued to be owned and operated effectively by company men. Residents paid a single service bill at the company department store for water, electricity, waste disposal, and groceries. Children living in town continued to attend school at the public school buildings built by Milton Hershey. Among the few modern buildings in Derry Township not built or owned by Hershey were an Italian grocery store catering to the palates of Italian American factory workers and a motel. Hershey, Pennsylvania, remained a company town through and through.

The transition out of the company town model into its present-day suburban incarnation begins in the mid-1960s. Locally during this period the Hershey enterprises, led by the trust, gradually withdrew its investment in the town's infrastructure, utilities, education, and recreation. For the first time, the public township formed a taxpayer-financed police force, taking over duties that had been assumed by private security at the chocolate company. A township building code followed. In the early 1970s, the first public school constructed with tax dollars was opened. And the township began paying for the electricity, previously paid for by the trust, that powers the Hershey Kiss–shaped street lamps running along Chocolate Avenue in the town center. While the Hershey enterprises withdrew services and infrastructure from the town center, the trust retained downtown property for future development projects—many of which remained largely unexecuted in the decades that followed. Commerce and real estate proliferated in suburban developments surrounding the town center, making Hershey "a town that has no town"—"a town without a town," some locals say.

Young villagers during this period of transition were perhaps most affected by the withdrawal of the Hershey enterprises' interests in public recreation and education. There was little public outcry when the Hershey community center—the primary alternative to church youth groups for socializing young people—was appropriated for office space by the rapidly expanding chocolate company, perhaps because many locals (young and old) felt they had no right to complain; so many benefits they enjoyed—recreation, education, jobs—came at the pleasure of the "powers of Hershey." There was some outcry, however, over the closing of the Hershey Junior College, the two-year community college built by M. S. Hershey at the height of the Great Depression, which promised free matriculation to residents of the township as well as students of the Milton Hershey School (Klotz 1973). Many students graduating from Derry Township's public high school had their sights set on the junior college, and when it closed its doors in 1964, people had to change plans quickly. Managers cited unsustainable annual shortfall in earned interest on the peripheral trust established to fund the college, the M. S. Hershey Foundation.

It was during this period that Hershey trustees began brooding over the future of the amusement park. Though it remained popular—frequented by "bus groups and picnic groups"—no substantial capital had been invested in it since Milton Hershey's death, and it made little money for the school trust fund. With maintenance cut down to once a week to limit operation costs, it was admittedly "a little shabby." Inspired by recent national developments in theme parks—led by the Disney Company[8]—Hershey trustees invited consultants to evaluate the property.

A multiyear, phased program was enacted to enclose the picnic grounds and transform them into a national amusement park operated by a newly formed Hershey Entertainment and Resorts Company, wholly owned by the school trust fund. Initially, park officials focused on attracting visitors from the surrounding region—termed the "hilly market" for its topography. Their long-term goal was to transform this previously minor center of regional tourism into "Destination Hershey: Come for the chocolate, stay for the fun." The trust financed the venture with money made from auctioning the company town's utilities and infrastructure, which apparently elicited raised eyebrows from Hersheyites but no substantial resistance.

The story of the park's journey since its commercialization in the early 1970s is oft told. Riding a wave of national-cultural interest in environmentalism,[9] the park became known in the 1970s for "clean and green family fun." This public image disintegrated when, in March 1979, a nuclear reactor at the Three Mile Island power plant, located a dozen miles outside town, partially melted down.[10] Hershey trustees directed the entertainment company to diversify its amusement assets outside the central Pennsylvania region "so that if something really did happen [at Three Mile Island], the whole company wouldn't be lost," recollects a former Hersheypark official. New hotel and resort ventures—in Philadelphia, Connecticut, and Texas, among other locales—were badly mismanaged and sold off within a decade, leaving the entertainment company near bankruptcy by the late 1980s. Crucially, the trust bailed out the entertainment company with a cash infusion, after which bank financing was secured to expand the park locally.

Through the 1990s, the value of the entertainment company and the size of the park's physical plant grew considerably. Trustees of the various Hershey entities opened legal avenues between the Hershey Company and the Entertainment and Resorts Company in order to introduce the Hershey brand into the park itself—a strategy of "synergy" that makes the park and brand generally synonymous in the eyes of today's visitors. Over the last decade, the entertainment company has added roller coasters and a water park; constructed a new concert stadium; invested heavily in area restaurants; and refurbished the Hotel Hershey—transforming the original Depression-era construction into a luxury spa resort. The park has won prestigious industry awards;[11] it is regarded as one of the best of its kind in the mid-Atlantic region. Speaking from firsthand knowledge, it is indeed a pleasure to visit when weather is accommodating.

Today's Hersheypark is part of a national amusement and theme park industry that includes five hundred businesses generating around $10 billion a year—half a billion of that in profits (Samadi 2011). At present, its marketing campaign is "100 percent family." The imagery in television commercials is designed to emphasize "the precious little time that families have together," a leader of the campaign explains to me inside Entertainment and Resort headquarters. Hersheypark is "an ideal environment where people can come and be totally immersed as a family." The "family unit" the park appeals to is not restricted to nuclear family, he explains: "It could be an extended family. It could be three families from the neighborhood. . . . Our mantra is family. The reason we do what we do is because of the family unit, and that's why business is going to stay strong. We don't do the biggest, tallest, or fastest of anything. We play it down the middle so that it's something everyone can enjoy."

Long-standing local families are decidedly ambivalent about the entertainment and resorts economy in Hershey. Some find the modern focus on family ironic given that the park no longer freely admits families of chocolate company employees; they have taken to calling it, cheekily, the "Hershey Entertainment Industrial Complex." The employment opportunities afforded by the Hershey Entertainment and Resorts Company are by no means negligible, everyone recognizes; but car traffic is a persistent nuisance, and, in general, there is a sense that Hershey has become less beautiful, more crowded, and more money-minded because of the commercialization of the amusement park. "The love of the place used to tie it together. The park was genuinely for the workers at the chocolate factory, the families in town, and for people around the region," a local resident tells me, echoing a common sentiment: "Today Hershey is more like a very expensive fantasy—a fantasy of familiarity. The tourists who come, they pay to be a part of the fantasy. But the park is no longer for the workers; the old swimming pool is closed down; and they're making Hershey's chocolate in Mexico! People get upset about that because it makes the place less special. But I guess in the end, that transformation from love and family to expensive fantasy is just evolution; it's bound to happen. You can't ask a company to be entrepreneurial and then stop."

HOW THE TRUST SPONSORED A MEDICAL SCHOOL

The story of the arrival of the Penn State Milton S. Hershey Medical Center, concurrent with the commercial enclosure of Hersheypark, implicates the power of the Hershey Trust in collaboration with the state of Pennsylvania. Longtime Hersheyites tell it with marked ambivalence.

The beginning of the story is set sometime around 1963 with a "$50 million phone call" made by the chairman of the Hershey Trust to the president of Penn State University (based in the city of State College, a hundred miles northwest). The chairman offered the university president $50 million of trust monies for the hospital's construction, provided it was carried out in Hershey and named after the founder. The money would be transferred from the trust to the university vis-à-vis the M. S. Hershey Foundation (the peripheral trust established initially to support the Hershey Junior College, among other community educational ventures). The money would be channeled through the Hershey Foundation "in order to gussy it up—to satisfy the court," as one Hersheyite tells me. The foundation's mandate to support local education legally justified financing the hospital.

In relatively short order, without public announcement, the local probate court—the "orphans' court" in charge of wills and estates—approved
the transfer from the trust to the state under a U.S. legal doctrine known
as *cy pres*:

> American law . . . acts to fulfill the donor's wishes by giving courts
> limited authority to modify the terms of a trust (rather than
> allowing the trust to fail). Under the doctrine of "cy pres" (the
> term derives from the French expression "cy pres comme possible,"
> as near as possible), if a charitable purpose becomes "impossible,
> impracticable or illegal" to fulfill, and if the donor expressed a
> general charitable intent, then a court can modify the terms of the
> trust to put in place an alternate scheme that will carry out the
> donor's original charitable scheme as nearly as possible. (Madoff
> 2010: 98)

When courts apply *cy pres*, "they tend to authorize only the most minor
changes to the donor's plan," observes legal scholar Ray Madoff (2010: 98);
however, in the case of the Hershey Trust, the courts authorized a more
major diversion of funds. The rationale for diverting $50 million from the
care of orphans to the construction of a university teaching and research
hospital was this: the trust had accumulated an excess of wealth. The Hershey Company was performing well in the years following World War II,
and the trust had a surplus. Instead of directing the surplus to the Milton
Hershey School, which at that time was serving around 1,200 students,
trustees settled on a previously unimagined alternative.

That the trust could have but did not spend its excess wealth funding
the locally beloved and endangered junior college was not lost on locals
at the time. Nor was the fact that the trust could have used the surplus to
dramatically expand enrollment and infrastructure at the Milton Hershey
School. In fact, one recent account of the founding of the medical center
suggests Hershey trustees had considered both possibilities but ultimately
decided against them (Lang 2010). Expanding the charity would mean taking children from "broken homes," which would undermine the core mis-

sion of Mr. Hershey's school for orphan boys, trustees reasoned. (The trust began admitting children from broken homes—"social orphans"—about a decade after these deliberations [see Chapter 4]). Alternatively, funding the junior college would attract too many "outsiders" into Hershey who wanted to take advantage of the free education, trustees speculated. Apparently, there had been "complaints" from townspeople about "outsiders," and trustees felt responsible to address their grievances.

Constructing a public university teaching and research hospital would be a service to the national interest, trustees agreed, and this was "as near as possible" to the donor's original intent. Indeed, the *cy pres* petition for a $50 million reallocation of charitable monies included statistics on the impending dearth of physicians in the United States relative to its growing population (Lang 2010). This novel "national interest" argument won over both the state attorney general and the orphans' court judge. The Pennsylvania governor was informed of the proceedings and gave his endorsement. Apparently, some members of the state congress, upon learning of the *cy pres* after it had been approved, were furious: first, because of the fiscal implications of funding a public university that had just acquired a teaching and research hospital, and even more because of the secrecy of the process.

"Can we bring back the family doctor?" asks a December 1967 *Boston Globe* feature (Rogers 1967). "The Pennsylvania State College of Medicine at the Milton S. Hershey Medical Center—just opened in September—is the home of [an] experiment which, in this age of specialization, aims at turning out family doctors." The experiment, the *Globe* reports, is funded by $50 million of "Hershey chocolate wealth" in combination with $21 million in "federal cash." It centers on exposing medical students to patients early in their training and focusing on "bedside manner," among other central components of general practitioner medicine. "I have absolutely no interest in being a specialist," comments one new medical student. "I want to be a family doctor who sees ordinary people in ordinary circumstances." Twenty percent of physicians in the United States are family physicians, the article notes, down from 30 percent at the beginning of the decade. The medical school at Hershey "feels a need to buck this trend." As a general practitioner, "you treat the patient as a human, not as a bag of interesting organs," comments one senior physician. "This program is binding us and the community closely together," comments the program's first dean. It realizes the "ideal family doctor concept . . . regarding patients as people, not cases."

Townspeople initially directed a certain suspicion and even hostility toward the medical center. Some claimed that the hospital performed experiments on patients and warned family and friends to avoid it. Others openly criticized the trust for driving the town's family doctors out of business, long-standing residents remember. Physicians who had staffed the former company town hospital were given the option of retraining and being employed at the new hospital or locating their practice elsewhere; a large majority chose the latter.

Over time, it seems townspeople started to recognize the benefits of having such an institution in their backyard, and they grew sympathetic toward its explicitly family and community focus. Moreover, the medical center provided job opportunities that some younger townspeople with credentials could take advantage of: "I walked right over to the medical center and got a job," recollects Brian, the Hershey resident who trained as a health-care professional at Temple University in Philadelphia before returning to his hometown. "Back in those days, if you came from Hershey and you kept your nose clean and you were of average intelligence—it didn't hurt to be white—doors opened up."

Among locals, the most ambivalent aspect of the medical center's appearance was the social capital it introduced and the reconfiguration of social relations it precipitated. The medical center recosmopolitanized the population of the company town and surrounding region by attracting novel varieties of high-skilled labor including highly educated nonwhite and non-Christian citizens and non-U.S. citizens. It introduced more or less permanent "newcomers" and "outsiders" to the community. First among the new population associated with the medical center were "hippies, Jews, and Democrats." (My own parents are associated with this population, having moved from the New York metropolitan area in the mid- to late 1970s and found employment with Pennsylvania state-affiliated health and education services.) This was followed in later decades by South and East Asian families. The expanding medical community established residence both in town and in suburban annexes, one nicknamed "pill hill" for its association with pharmaceuticals.

Today, the teaching and research hospital of Penn State University has become the township's primary employer—larger than the chocolate company. The medical center's research and development, direct delivery of health services, trauma center with an aviation component, and children's hospital make it "the most significant progressive project undertaken in modern times in south-central Pennsylvania," as a prominent Harrisburg politician put it to me. Its well-funded infrastructure and extensive campus coexists with Hershey's increasingly dense development of entertainment and resorts. The resulting preponderance of medical facilities and roller coasters might lead a tourist to speculate that roller-coaster riding is a widespread public health hazard; this is not the case. The link between these two disparate domains is Milton Hershey's trust.

HOW NEW STRANGERS CAME TO HERSHEY

In 1967, two decades after the death of the founder, the *Los Angeles Times* declared Hershey "strictly a company town" (Joseph 1967). In fact, that industrial identity already was in flux and would become increasingly unstable over the next decade. When *Newsday* special correspondent Ehud Yonay reported on Hershey in the early 1970s, he noted that "residents point automatically to the second-story company offices of Hershey's Estates, above the Hershey Drug Store and across the street from the Hershey Department Store, when asked to direct a visitor to the seat of their town government" (Yonay 1972). "There are some residents who grumble quietly, saying that the town is not what it used to be, that the company no longer cares for the people. The new management, they note, is trying to shove down their throats a huge amusement park." New residents tend to observe the change is for the better, Yonay notes: "I think that M. S. Hershey spoiled his people," one recently arrived resident tells him. "You can see it now, the way they don't know how to take care of their own affairs, or to stand up to the company."

New residents partnered together, Yonay observes in *Newsday*, to protest the Hershey Estates' decision to stop paying for street lighting in downtown Hershey and to move the cost onto township taxpayers. Were the street lamps—in the shape of Hershey's Kisses, installed in the mid-1960s—not actually advertising for and by the company? Such grievances are held by commuting suburbanites, Yonay notes, who are on the cusp of becoming the majority in town: "The newcomers not only bring into Hershey great numbers of Democrats and liberals, nonexistent here for many years, but an attitude toward the company which can at times be called rebellious. . . . Law-enforcement sources say that drugs, long an unheard-of element here, are available in Hershey schools as they are elsewhere," Yonay reports. The town apparently has become a "dropping point in the Philadelphia-Harrisburg dope route." As the estate divests itself of company town assets and sells off property to residents and real estate agents, "the company's grip on the town weakens, and the resolutions between the two gradually become dependent on goodwill."

By the mid-1970s, even the local sports team was becoming more "transient" (Cuniberti 1979). "In this chocolate-factory city that resembles the top of a huge birthday cake, the Hershey Bears of the American Hockey League once held the deed to the people's hearts," writes journalist Betty Cuniberti in the *Washington Post* in 1979. "Like almost everyone else in this play town of golf courses, amusement parks, and fragrant chocolate factories, the hockey players often worked for the Hershey chocolate conglomerate." Now, the article continues, after achieving unparalleled success in the American Hockey League—and being the oldest team in the league, dating back to 1938—the players are more interested in working "to get out of Hershey and up to the NHL." Fans are mad because the Bears have turned into a "development team." "What they used to care about in the days when there weren't 17 NHL teams and zillions of dollars floating around was Hershey—the team, the town, the tavern [and] the people," the article concludes. "Now it is hard for a minor-league hockey player to feel a part of anything."

By 1985, the Allentown-based regional newspaper *Morning Call* could declare, "Hershey No Longer One Industry Town" (1985). "The nation's self-proclaimed chocolate capital isn't much of a company town any more

. . . . The hospital that chocolate built played a role in transforming the community." The article quotes a chocolate worker and longtime resident: following the introduction of the hospital, "for the first time I saw people living in the community who did not owe everything to the power structure," he says.

The now-familiar local distinction between "Old Hershey" and "New Hershey" emerged at that time. Old Hershey people are characterized positively by their capacity to "talk in shorthand," explains another longtime resident: "Old Hershey is when you see everybody you grew up with and you know who you're talking about. You know who's related to whom. And everybody knows about you too—all your foibles, the stuff you did bad. That's the thing any place: they [locals anywhere] want to know, 'Who are your people?' They mean, go back a couple generations and tell me who you're related to. 'Who are you?' That gives them a frame of reference—to make up their mind about you or something."

Perhaps because they lack the capacity to reckon kin in shorthand and memorialize the community of the company town, New Hershey people continue to remain relatively anonymous and transient in the eyes of Old Hershey—despite the fact they may have lived in town for decades or raised a family there. Michelle—an urbane, distinguished woman who has lived in town for several decades and raised her children there with her husband, a physician—expresses a familiar sentiment among New Hersheyites: "We're still not considered original and we'll never be original. There is pride in growing up here and 'remembering when.' The impression I get is, 'it was better then.'"

Over coffee on the patio of her handsome brick and wood home, Michelle reflects on raising her children in town. Two of her three children—the youngest of which has just graduated from the public township high school—were not happy here, she tells me. They were "different kinds of kids." Difference is not celebrated in Hershey, she observes; it is "difficult to be different here." For example, one of her daughters enjoyed the taste of tuna fish, and she would get made fun of for eating it during lunch periods in school. None of Michelle's children wanted to stand out in terms of taste preferences or dress styles; they wanted to "blend in." It can be "hard to be yourself" in Hershey as the community "tends to be homogeneous." As another example, she points to the disappointing response of the community to the foreign-exchange students her family has hosted over the last couple decades. The most difficult part of hosting an exchange student is that "the phone never rings for that kid." Exchange students interact only with other exchange students and the immediate host family. Michelle questions why these children are not welcomed and introduced to local children: "Here's a kid from Thailand or Chile, we know nothing about their country or culture, and there is no interest in learning. Maybe that's just American" and not unique to Hershey, she speculates—"like our 'World News', it's all of a minute."

Despite the "homogeneity" and inward-looking quality of the community, Michelle appreciates her neighborhood specifically because of its diversity, by which she means class, occupational, and national diversity: "It's a mix: a truck driver, an older retired man, a chocolate factory worker, a physician, an electrician—from several different countries." She worries, however, that her children gravitate socially toward the town's most affluent families, who are the minority in this largely working-class community. Her youngest son is almost exclusively friends with children of physicians, she observes; he enjoys visiting their homes because they have big-screen televisions, pools, large basements, and so on. She tells her children—all of them now grown—that in their fortunate situation, others easily will assume they are "spoiled brats": "Assume that's where you're starting and keep that in the back of your mind. You have to be extra nice."

Michelle is a keen observer of status among parents active in the township school district. The back-to-school night is dominated by parents who make use of the forum to ask questions related specifically to their own children—to curry favor among administrators or otherwise gain an advantage, she observes. "Status" among these parents is related to "how busy you are": saying "I'm sorry, I'm just so busy" to other parents is a mark of high status. This is "the whole busy soccer mom thing." Such parents—she includes herself among them—are "overinvolved" in their children's lives. They want to be the "ideal parent" who does not miss a back-to-school night and is involved in all of her children's after-school activities. For their part, the "ideal student" plays a musical instrument, plays on the varsity sports team, is enrolled in a large number of Advanced Placement classes, and is in the process of applying to prestigious colleges. It is also "helpful" in status terms if students drive a high-end car (namely, a BMW or Mercedes); at the public high school, "you can tell the teacher's parking lot from the student's lot because the students have better cars." Talking about status issues in Hershey can be embarrassing when the township is compared to neighboring Harrisburg, which has yet to recover fully from loss of jobs in the 1970s and 1980s. Michelle adds, "We have so much, and we're only ten miles away from Harrisburg."

On the subject of Old Hershey and its seminal institutions—the chocolate company, the school for children in need, the long-standing families of Pennsylvania Dutch and Italian descent—Michelle "confesses," as she puts it, to not paying much attention. "It seems like the school was for the greater good. And it seems like the town worked out well. Milton Hershey provided for the townspeople and the townspeople benefited." Occasionally she reads about the trust in local newspapers, and "it doesn't sound great." She followed news of the chocolate company's potential sale in 2002 and was relieved when it did not sell.

Her chief concern about the trust relates to its control of property in downtown Hershey. The town's historic core been relatively underdeveloped and underutilized for decades. There are few shops and restaurants that are independent of the Hershey brand, Michelle observes. "I've had tourists stop me and ask, where is town? There are so many beautiful towns around. Hershey people like me who live in the town think, 'I wish we had a town.'" Periodic rumors suggest that the trust plans to substantially redevelop it. In the meantime, as Michelle says, Hersheyites keep "wishing for a town."

FAITH IN THE POST-COMPANY TOWN

Few institutions in present-day Hershey are untouched by the founder's entrepreneurial-philanthropic legacies, and houses of worship are no exception. Milton Hershey's Anabaptist Christianity informed his business practices, and vice versa, one might say, his business practices informed his Christianity. The founder was ecumenical when it came to religious life in his company town. Recognizing the mutually beneficial effects of spiritual harmony and labor harmony, he embraced—and financially supported—the prominent Protestant churches in the community as well as the Catholic one. As I learn in conversation with local faith leaders, that legacy of patronage lingers.

"Hershey was built around the Church of the Brethren," remarks Pastor Franklin, a lean, kindly gentleman in his early sixties who invites me into his study on church grounds. The original Brethren meetinghouse dates to before the Civil War. It was transformed into a modern facility in the mid-1930s at the height of the Great Depression through funds from M. S. Hershey. "Mr. Hershey's idea was, we have all these little churches in town, let's just build one great big church," the pastor recounts. "But his mother or wife said, 'It's not going to work!' So instead he gave about $20,000 to each of the five churches"—four Protestant, one Catholic.

The refurbishment of the original meetinghouse using Hershey money made the Brethren Church "look like other churches," he observes. A pipe organ was also installed using those funds. These transformations in building reflect the increasing "worldliness" of the Brethren throughout the mid-twentieth century. Photographs in Pastor Franklin's study show the early Brethren wearing plain clothing, plain coats and hats and bonnets. In the early 1940s, as the photographs depict, younger women began substituting more embellished dresses for their simple dresses and men gave up their black plain coats. Around that time, the Brethren transformed from a "free ministry"—in which elders were called out of the congregation to pastor—into a ministry that employed professionals such as Pastor Franklin.

The peak of membership in the Brethren Church in Hershey coincided with the golden age of the company town—the 1950s and 1960s—a time, Pastor Franklin recollects, when "everything Mr. Hershey built for the community was still for the community." The church included about 600 active members at its peak. Growing up locally during those years, the pastor remembers church activities blending with the exuberance of "Pennsylvania

Dutch Days," the fair hosted in the Hershey amphitheater and surrounding fields, which drew Brethren and other "plain folk" from around the region. "Culture has obviously changed" since those years, he observes: "Postmodernism—whatever you want to call it—we're living in a very pluralistic culture right now." Established churches such as the Brethren's struggle because of the "phobia to institutions of any kind and the individualism of our culture." Pastor Franklin attributes the decidedly low membership numbers in the church today to this larger-scale cultural transformation. The church has around 250 members, most of whom are senior citizens. "If we don't change the way we're going [about] things, ten, fifteen years from now we might not be here anymore. The building might be here, but there might not be any more of us."

Today, it is "tough times" for the Brethren and "scary times." The struggle and fear "hit home" one recent autumn, the pastor says, when the Brethren Church was excluded from participating in the organization of a community event—the Hershey Half Marathon, sponsored by the Hershey Entertainment Company in partnership with the Children's Miracle Network.[12] A month before the marathon, the church received a letter from the Hershey Entertainment Company explaining that the marathon's route would cut off access to the church on a Sunday. Specifically, access would be cut off on the day of Worldwide Communion Sunday—the first Sunday in October—which is one of the most highly attended services of the year next to Christmas and Easter. Pastor Franklin took away a lesson from the experience: "The church is not what is at the top of people's minds anymore. Sunday morning is no longer church time."

The church's exclusion from the organization of the marathon route led the pastor to reflect with his parishioners on cultural change in general and how the church ought to respond. "Culturally, going to church was the thing that you did" when many current parishioners—including himself—were growing up. Church was where people made business contacts necessary to professional work, and there was an expectation in the professions that employees would be involved in a church somewhere. Though this has changed, the church "is still living in the old Christendom paradigm where the whole culture revolved around the church and where churches try to influence government—almost like a theocratic kind of thing." One solution to this impasse is, the pastor observes, "starting a church from scratch" such as the neighboring Evangelical Free Church—but this is not an option available to the Brethren.

Pastor Franklin has become convinced, he tells me, that the church "needs to be out in mission and out in ministry in the community." In local terms, this means participating in events such as the Hershey Half Marathon. After the Brethren sat down with the entertainment company and Derry Township administration, an agreement was reached, Pastor Franklin explains: the marathon will be run mostly on Milton Hershey School property instead of township property, and the route to the church will remain open. The church will help with one of the water stations on the route. It also has volunteered to provide an opening scripture or prayer before the marathon begins. "We can fight or we can get out there and be a part of it. This year we're going to be a part of it," Pastor Franklin insists.

Whereas the once-dominant Church of the Brethren confronts generational decline and a collective sense of "fading away" in the eyes of the local public, the still-vibrant St. Joan of Arc Catholic Church confronts a different challenge: the "transience" of its parishioners. The Catholic church in Hershey originated with the Italian population that emigrated to the area in the early twentieth century to work in the chocolate factory and in nearby brownstone quarries; it has remained an important parish in the wider south-central Pennsylvania region. "Mr. Hershey thought the Italians made the best stone masons and they were the best to build his kingdom, if you will," the young and popular parish priest—Father Kevin—tells me over lunch in a local restaurant. The Italian population of Hershey is "largely a result of his entrepreneurship."

Today, the St. Joan parish is made up of two dominant groups: the descendants of Italian immigrants to the area, many of whom are senior citizens and live in the homes surrounding the church; and the group of Catholics who moved to the area beginning in the late 1960s—the families of physicians at the medical center, lawyers in Harrisburg, and other professionals. The boundary lines of the parish extend well beyond the local township. The parish is specifically challenging because of its size and diversity, observes Father Kevin. There are many families and individuals that must be ministered to who are "transient"—who seek care at the medical center's trauma center or children's hospital. There also are Catholic students at the Milton Hershey School who—"as long as their houseparents aren't anti-Catholic," he notes—are bussed in on Sunday mornings for mass and Sunday evenings for Bible classes.

Through reading on his own and talking with senior townspeople, Father Kevin evidently knows more about "Old Hershey" than many of his parishioners. St. Joan of Arc was his first assignment after being ordained as a priest about a decade ago and he has tried to educate himself about the history of the parish and town: "Milton Hershey wanted all the local churches to combine into one nondenominational church, but he failed to account for church history. You can't just be all one happy family that easily—it's not that idealistic of a situation. But that's what Hershey wanted: he wanted Hersheyism; he wanted idealism; he wanted houses to look alike and whatever—the all-American town." Father Kevin often refers to Milton Hershey in homilies as an example of perseverance, emphasizing the business failures that preceded financial success. Such homilies reach upward of a thousand people, he observes—many of whom know little Hershey history in general or the fact that Milton's wife, Catherine, was Catholic. He has also invoked stories about Milton and Catherine in messages about the meaning of marriage, as I witness while attending a wedding one Saturday afternoon at the church: "Marriage is a covenant, not a contract," Father Kevin tells those in attendance. "It's about the commitment you make before God, not the emotional feeling of love you experience for your partner or the legal, transactional aspects of your partnership":

> Let me tell you a story. Bishop McDevitt who was in Harrisburg in the early decades of the twentieth century found out that the boys at the Milton Hershey School weren't allowed to go to Catholic service. He brought this up with Milton Hershey at a meeting at High Point [Hershey's mansion home]. "Mr. Hershey," McDevitt said, "Why are you not allowing your Catholic boys to go to Catholic service? Don't you know how important it is for them to

receive the Eucharist? You must know how important this is, as your own wife, Kitty, was raised Catholic."

Mr. Hershey wasn't listening well to Bishop McDevitt. Hershey had in his mind that he would provide everything for the orphans at his school: their clothing, lodging, education, and church would all be taken care of inside the school by Hershey himself. At first he refused McDevitt's request to allow the orphans to attend Catholic mass on Sundays. But then he changed his mind. When McDevitt asked him why, Hershey responded: "Kitty made me do it." His wife, Catherine, made him change his mind. But here's the thing: Catherine had been dead for over fifteen years! She was speaking to Milton even after her death. Their covenant was still strong. That's the meaning of marriage.

In his time at St. Joan, Father Kevin has tried to bring Hershey history to people's minds because that history is "getting lost amidst the transience." Those in the congregation who do know Hershey history tend to be the older population of St. Joan—aged sixty and above. There is little these parishioners will say about the founder that is negative; indeed, Father Kevin observes, they tend to be defensive even at the perception of a slight to the Hershey name—for example, the suggestion that Catherine Hershey was infertile because of untreated venereal disease (as put forward in D'Antonio 2007). The mistreatment of Italian Catholic workers in the early decades of the enterprise is little recollected, he observes. Longtime Italian Catholic parishioners tend to criticize, if anything, the commercialization of recreation: "There is a sense in people's minds and hearts that the Hershey Entertainment stuff has gone over the top." Parishioners routinely complain about the high price of admittance to the local amusements. "Hershey is now nickel-and-diming people for everything"—tourists and locals alike. But the reverence for the name of the founder and his wife remains.

Whereas St. Joan of Arc Catholic Church strives to meet the traditional faith needs of an evolving demographic of believers, the more recently instituted Evangelical Free Church of Hershey strives to serve people who have exited established Christian institutions and who struggle with the place of faith in an evolving secular culture. An associate of the Minnesota-head-quartered Evangelical Free Church of America, the Hershey Free Church draws the largest number of people for Sunday services among the churches in Hershey today and plays prominent roles in the local public life of the township. The church building itself is enormous and modern in design, more reminiscent of a secular performing arts center than a conventional house of worship. The main auditorium is fitted with high-end audio-visual technology, stage lighting, and plush, cushioned seats.

I attend a Sunday sermon at the Free Church led by Pastor Ryan, a tall, dark-haired, young man and talented orator who, with a faint Western drawl, addresses anyone in the audience "unsure about the whole Christianity thing." He introduces the morning's teaching with a video clip projected on a screen behind him, showing images of computers, cars sitting in traffic, office work, and so on: "Are you tired of all the noise around you? Do you feel overwhelmed? Find solace through prayer," says the voice narrating the media presentation. Pastor Ryan follows with commentary on the resurrection and readings from Corinthians 15. Christianity is predicated on the reality of Christ's resurrection, he tells the audience of several hundred. If you do not understand resurrection as truth, then Christianity is just another "do-it-yourself, follow-your-own-path, whatever-works-for-you" approach to life that is morally equivalent to other paths. Only if you believe in resurrection can you be a true Christian.

The Hershey Free Church emerged in the early 1970s out of a home Bible study among a set of local families, Pastor Ryan tells me when we meet in his private office adjoining the main auditorium. Those original families were associated with leadership positions in the Hershey entities—the company, the charity, the amusement park—and in particular the state university medical center. The Bible study grew into a church as it attracted new Hershey residents, especially white-collar professionals who "invested their leadership skill sets into the life of the church in very creative and entrepreneurial ways." This is what gives the Free Church today a "cosmopolitan feel," the pastor observes. For example, in a Bible study group he facilitated the previous evening, half of the half-dozen participants were physicians who excitedly engaged in debate about the medical dimensions of an episode in the Book of Acts. "I'll never read that Bible passage the same way again," he smiles.

Pastor Ryan grew up in the south-central United States and attended seminary in the United Kingdom before joining the Free Church in Hershey a few years ago. During his studies in the Oxbridge system, he gained an important cultural insight that informs his preaching in Hershey. In England, he observed, Europeans born into low social rank were not expected to overcome their status to become leaders in industry or government. Americans, by contrast, thrive on the mythology of "rags-to-riches stories— you know, like a Milton Hershey who tries and tries again only to become a success." Americans have difficulty accepting the biblical concept of grace because, as Pastor Ryan puts it, "we have an almost unique sense of hard work, achievement, and transcending limitations." A hard-work ethic and responsibility are laudable, but the transformational work of Jesus Christ is about grace—"receiving rather than achieving." Grace is "countercultural and counterintuitive. So much of American culture says work hard and earn, but ultimately the gospel is about receiving the gift. It's the difference between being an employee and being a child."

Pastor Ryan preaches to everyone that God is in the process of restoring his creation through the work of Jesus Christ and that people have roles to play in that process that are unique and diverse. The Free Church's appeal in Hershey—the reason it is the "big boy on the block," in his assessment— is because of its strong commitment to this gospel. The typical religious background of people in the region—south-central Pennsylvania and beyond—has felt "legalistic or burdensome," he observes. The Free Church attempts to draw people from minimal church backgrounds, especially people with "a level of church memory from when they were a child and now they're a parent."

The congregation of the Free Church includes local families that span four generations. While this generational integration is highly desirable, it is a challenge to sustain. Generations within the church come into conflict over politics, he notes. Whereas most senior members of the congregation push to be associated with electoral politics and political institutions, church members under forty tend to avoid this kind of engagement: "We go from a generation with almost absolute confidence in certain American institutions to a generation where the default is skepticism and criticism almost to the point of cynicism."

At present, older members of the church are committed to producing a memorial to September 11 emergency responders. For older generations, not to commemorate September 11 emergency responders is "to be unpatriotic," he observes. But for younger members—the pastor counts himself as one—a "more exciting issue" or approach is "connecting with the community." The church participates in a food bank in Hershey, English as a Second Language instruction, and financial counseling, among other projects. Pastor Ryan hopes to expand the Free Church's charitable activities into neighboring Harrisburg in the coming year: "We're in this little rural area, but in reality we're suburban Harrisburg—and Harrisburg is looking for help."

In sum, across the spectrum of church life in modern Hershey—from the evanescent Church of the Brethren, to the enduring St. Joan of Arc, to the dominant Hershey Free Church, among more than a dozen other houses of worship—one can observe an arc of social transformation in local life since the pinnacle of Hershey's "golden age." At the Church of the Brethren, descendants of the "Hershey-before-Hershey" community of Derry Church worship alongside descendants of "Old Hershey" Anabaptist families who populated the company town in the first half of the twentieth century; their modern leadership is inspired and welcoming of revitalization, yet the number of souls they count grow fewer as generations recede and conversions to the faith wane. At the Catholic Church, working-class Italian American families of "Old Hershey" worship alongside white-collar, multiethnic professionals of "New Hershey" and the suburban region beyond; amid transformations in demographics and the economics of work and leisure, the parish continues to revere and find fresh significance in the social legacy of the Protestant founder and his Catholic wife. At the Evangelical Free Church, local families and individuals loosely joined by their lack of formal affiliation with the more established churches come together to worship in "New Hershey." Here, the social imprint of the former model industrial community is faint, and the overriding spiritual concern is related to salvation in a postindustrial, suburban, secular landscape.

Observations from other houses of worship in and around Hershey could be added to supplement this general picture of local social transformation since the mid-1960s. Each church confronts that transformation differently and creatively, finding in it unique challenges and opportunities for serving the faith needs of its parishioners; and yet, the overall arc of transformation is similar: from a twentieth century industrial community (which had been built atop an agricultural community) to a twenty-first century community of "services" (entertainment, hospitality, health care, and so on). In present day Hershey—as in any contemporary local place—aspects and elements of new and old, agricultural, industrial, and postindustrial, are layered, laminated, compounded; one might say, "confected" together. Such are the ingredients, variously combined, that produce modern Hershey's social distinctiveness.

PRIORITIES IN CONFLICT

The reconfiguration of Hershey's social order beginning in the middle 1960s sparked certain resentments between longtime residents and recent arrivals that have cooled in intervening years but have not entirely dissipated, I discover. For one, the appearance of white-collar populations associated with the medical center upset entrenched ideas about who in Hershey is "sophisticated" and who is "provincial." In the golden age of the company town, Protestant Germans occupied a sophisticated position in relation to Catholic Italians; yet in the post-company town, the historic population of Hershey—Germans and Italians taken together—found itself in a provincial position vis-à-vis new arrivals. This engendered some bitterness, as one longtime resident tells it: "A lot of people would come in associated with the medical center and ask where to get a decent haircut or suit as if it's Manhattan. These people who had lived in metropolitan areas, they'd say, 'My god, how do you live in such a place?' Well, we're living just fine, thank you very much."

In general, newcomers and outsiders who took up residence in Hershey beginning in the late 1960s and early 1970s characterize Hershey in terms of "small-town America" or "middle America." Despite the social claustrophobia that attends the small town—a place where "everybody knows your business," if not your name—newcomers seem to relish advantages over metropolitan living. As one recently arrived resident puts it to me, "Hershey's safe, it's clean, it's beautiful. The cost of living is relatively low. The schools are good. People aren't flashy. There's money but not like in Manhattan. There's less materialism." Such sentiments are commonplace.

Old Hershey residents—who may or may not claim some experience living in a metropolitan area—make similar observations about life in Hershey compared to city life, specifically New York City (about three-and-a-half hours by car or train). Yet for them, Hershey is not one small town among others; it remains, or ought to remain, distinct, unique—"one of a kind" on account of the founder's legacy. Because of Hershey's distinctiveness, Old Hershey residents say, "A lot of outside people are coming in and purposely investing in Hershey: They expect to get nothing but the best in terms of quality of life and education for their children." This expectation of "superior quality" of services can grate on longtime locals. "Today there are far more mandated requests from families than ever before and it's ugly," says a retired Hershey executive active as a volunteer in the public school district. For example, parents are increasingly petitioning the school district to place their children with specific teachers rather than accepting the district's internal process of assigning students to teachers. Such requests from newly arrived residents may seem benign on their face, but the assertive manner in which they are pursued can lead to conflict.

Some new Hersheyites characterize efforts to become "rooted" in Hershey as a struggle against inequality. Maggie and Rob, for example, are upwardly mobile professionals who moved in about two decades ago from the New York metropolitan area. I meet them in their living room a few miles outside town in a quiet, recently constructed suburban neighborhood. She is a devoted homemaker with employment experience in journalism and finance; he is a respected lawyer who works for a Harrisburg-based technology company. The two bemoan inequalities between New Hershey and Old Hershey "in every domain" of local community life. "If you aren't part of one of the families that is well known," Maggie tells me, "you are treated very unfairly."

Maggie and Rob, impressive in their knowledge of Hershey history, trace the roots of this inequality to the origins of the company town: "Milton Hershey had no heirs, so the people that have been here for a few generations think they own the place and can do whatever they want." Starting football players on the public high school team, for example, are often from "an old Hershey family name. It's like a dynasty, and it has nothing to do with whether you're good or not at football." In their daughter's dance classes, "it's the old Italian families whose children get assigned the lead roles. Something like that would never happen where we come from." The legacy of the company town is manifest in the "docility" of local people, Rob observes. If locals do not cause trouble, he says, they eventually can do whatever they want in terms of "control and power." Anyone who "rocks the boat" gets persecuted, ostracized. "There's something to admire about the company town: everybody is taken care of," Maggie suggests. "But," Rob adds with a note of melodrama, "there's a price to be paid, and that price is freedom."

Rob identifies as an "outspoken guy from New Jersey" who was raised to "stand up for what is right"—the opposite of Hershey people who, he says, "in order to get along, bite their tongue and never speak up." I ask him to elaborate, and he exits in the living room in search of something, coming back with a copy of a short essay he recently published on an internet discussion forum. The title is "It's All About Control and Those Who Have IT and Want to Keep IT":

> Let's face it, Hershey is a strange place. Historically it started as a captive company town. When the great Milton Hershey passed on, without heirs, the void fell to the Trust and the in-families to run the joint. So over the years, the Trust has controlled the town via the Hershey Chocolate Company, Hershey Entertainment and Resorts, local politicians, the Milton Hershey and Derry Township schools, and the Hershey Medical Center—but mostly the in-families have controlled the town. . . . To keep control and the preferred natural, traditional order, they need to keep everyone in

check—especially new-comers. . . . The realities in the "Sweetest Place on Earth" are played out every day in local politics, our schools and sports teams. It should all be on merit and by hard work, but many times it is not.

Maggie and Rob's first experience "speaking up and rocking the boat" locally was with the township school board. They came to the defense of a school board member who was being slandered for allegedly acting inappropriately in the context of a local sports league's governance. From then onward, they were known as "people who would speak their minds"—plus Rob was a lawyer. Recently arrived residents approached them with matters of concern, the primary one being the behavior of Coach Winter in his capacity as public school gym teacher and coach of the high school football team. Concerned parents reported to Maggie and Rob that Winter was bullying students, physically and verbally; commenting on girls' weight in class; pitting "Jews against Christians" and "Yellows against Whites" in dodgeball; and making racist comments at public speaking events. Maggie and Rob raised these concerns before the township school district.

Coach Winter was "old school," in a phrase used on both sides of a feud that appeared to divide Old and New Hershey. School board meetings ensued in which large numbers of residents and employees, including the bulk of the football team and many senior teachers, spoke out in defense of the coach's character and against school board efforts to reprimand or fire him. Maggie and Rob and their allies were labeled the "P.C. Police" (short for "politically correct") in local media and gossip. They experienced retaliation: Rob's car tires were slashed; a football player threatened him; and, he says, a police officer sent to investigate the threat attempted to smear him by insinuating an affair between Rob and the school board member he previously had defended against slander. Despite this, Maggie and Rob tell me, Coach Winter eventually resigned in response to the pressure they and their allies applied. They do not hesitate to claim victory in the feud. Their family has "paid" for the gains made in Hershey, in terms of making enemies, but "it's worth it." "We've made some enemies here, but we've never been ones to worry about fitting in," Maggie says. "When it's your own kids who are being disadvantaged, how can you not speak up and try to change things?"

Supporters of the coach were not limited to Old Hershey residents, just as his detractors were not limited to recently arrived residents. But in general, the affair seemed to polarize participants along those lines. Among his detractors, the coach's authentic identity is plain to see, as one New Hersheyite puts it: "You know, 'Good old Coach Winter, what a guy, he's just amazing.' People thought he was a great guy because he drove kids home and gave them uniforms—but he's a bully. A bully is what he is. The outpouring of support for him was like, 'Coach knows how to make boys into men.' Maybe some kids respond to that kind of training, or whatever, but it's just not right." Among his supporters, on the contrary, Coach Winter is no bully. He is championed for "instilling children with confidence and hard work ethic" and for "working behind the scenes for kids that are less fortunate." As a general rule, his actions are consistent with the rubric of "tough love" he learned as a student of the Milton Hershey School.[13] The opposite of tough love is "coddling," an approach the coach's supporters were quick to condemn. A longtime Hershey resident puts it this way:

> If Coach yells at you, screams and rants and raves—get a grip! You're going to run into this shit all your life. And that's the problem [with those who moved into town and criticized the coach]. The problem is they're coddling kids in this sort of perfect little world, and then they fly and get knocked down when they get out in the raw reality of life and they have no experience behind them and get crushed. [Coddling] also promotes arrogance and certain qualities of aloofness—a condescending attitude. The fact is if kids don't have a little tough love along the way, they will turn into prima donnas just like their parents.

The fact that Coach Winter is a "homeboy" from the "old days" of the Milton Hershey School who married into a longstanding local family is critical to those who came to his defense. He is understood to be "very physical," especially with members of the football team, because of his experience at Milton Hershey School. His corporal techniques—variously described as pushing, shoving, "yelling in your face," and so on—are part and parcel of his "old school mentality," as another one of his supporters relates: "'Old school' is the mentality of the Milton Hershey School before blacks came and long before girls came. Coach Winter was operating under an entirely different set of rules that he had grown up in. Politically correct, not really; he was nothing of the sort. He was good-hearted. And there's no meter for that." As for the substance of the accusations against the coach, the supporter explains, "Those people who moved in and made a fuss were probably right the coach wasn't conforming to the letter of the procedures for public school teachers. But who gave a rat's ass? He's a good old 'home-boy' doing the best he can. We know where he used to come from, and we were just going to say 'he's our guy.' He decided to retire I guess because he didn't want people like that down his back all the time."

The coach's quiet retirement marked the end of a chapter that residents call "the Coach Winter thing." By the time his daughter was hired as a coach for a different local sports team, tempers and rhetoric in the community had cooled, and Hersheyites both old and new embraced the daughter's coaching arrangement—but clearly the affair has not been forgotten.

The feud between the coach's supporters and detractors was less a clash of values per se than a clash of priorities among values shared in common. No one, not even his supporters, defended reports of the coach's blithe racism and disparaging remarks toward girls; everyone agreed, in principle, some sort of action had to be taken. The more fundamental disagreement was over the process for achieving a reasonable and fair outcome. Supporters—many longtime residents who felt loyal if not indebted to the coach and who were motivated by their own sense of community pride—put a premium on saving face; they preferred informal, backchannels for reaching a resolution. Detractors—many recently arrived residents who felt outraged at what they perceived to be a threat to their children's welfare—put a premium on public shaming; they preferred formal, public channels. In the end, both sides walked away with the sense that they had won something and lost something: disappointed in the coach's coerced retirement, supporters could take comfort in the fact that he was not fired or officially found liable for any bad behavior; successful in their efforts to oust the coach, detractors were left feeling insulted that a large part of the community dismissed their legitimate concerns.

The "Coach Winter thing" reveals a more general community dynamic that, while not unique to Hershey, is highly relevant to its future fortunes. In any community, one can expect to observe a dynamic between informal and formal, backchannel and public-facing processes for resolving disputes. Such a dynamic is predictably more volatile in a community in transition, in which conventions of dispute resolution are unsettled and new norms and routines have yet to be firmly established. In early twenty-first century Hershey—a community in transition—this dynamic is likely to play out in disputes between community stakeholders and the town's longstanding institutions. Whether future disputes among town, company, school, and trust will mainly be resolved informally or formally, in private or in public view, quietly or loudly is impossible to forecast. But one thing is certain: there will be disputes. In this respect, the disagreement over how to fairly resolve the "Coach Winter thing" bears on the fate of Hershey's entrepreneurial-philanthropic legacy.

CHAPTER 3

≋ THE COMPANY ≋

At one point everything *about* Hershey was *in* Hershey. The interests of the
Hershey Trust and its various components and subsidiaries were pretty much
intertwined. That love relationship, that marriage, got fractured in 2002.
The trust level—everybody's trusting Hershey—changed after that.
The Hershey Company is well beyond being the patriarch of the community.
That's why there's friction. The former golden years, up to and including
the 1960s—the local predominant role of the company began to wane after
that. That's attributable to the global economy. You can no longer function
as an insular, locally based, locally popular company.

— Longtime Harrisburg politician, conversation with author

DEEP IN THE LIBRARY ARCHIVES of Princeton University lies an undergradu-
ate thesis written in the Department of History at the tail end of the Great
Depression. "The Story Behind a Hershey Bar: The History of the Founda-
tion and Subsequent Growth of the Hershey Chocolate Corporation, and
the Simultaneous Development of the Model Industrial Community of
Hershey, Pennsylvania" is authored by Richard Wallace Murrie—son of
William F. R. Murrie, who served as the president of the company (M. S.
Hershey's right-hand man) from 1908 until 1947.[1]

"The story of our time is in its essence the story of industry," Murrie's thesis begins. "No scholar of the future will be able to describe our era with authority unless he comprehends that expansion and concentration which occurred during the last half century, the great benefits of this change and the great excess" (1939: 1). "The growth of the Hershey Chocolate Corporation is a perfect example of the rise of big business in twentieth century America," but it is not only a big business, Murrie continues; it is also an idea (2). "We shall attempt to evaluate the whole Hershey Idea, and find out whether we have an Arcadian paradise for chocolate workers set up by an altruistic and benevolent employer; or whether we have merely a sugar-coated feudalism benefitting only the highest paid workers, and established to conceal the real ends of a thoroughly evil employer" (3–4).

At the end of more than one hundred pages exploring the geographical origins of cocoa, the chocolate production process, the biography of M. S. Hershey, and the physical site of the chocolate factory and company town, the thesis culminates with an analysis of the labor question: "The spirit of cooperation with its employees exhibited by the Company shows us the great advantages to be gained from the fair treatment of labor." Murrie concludes:

> The story of the Hershey Chocolate Corporation is important as an early and obviously imperfect example of the spirit of perfect employer-employee cooperation, which seems to be the ideal of the future. Only when we have achieved a perfect understanding between capital and labor, together with a more equitable distribution of the profits derived from business endeavors and a less selfish attitude on the part of both parties concerned, will we achieve any semblance of economic peace and stability, both of which are essential to the continuance of our democratic, capitalistic philosophy of life. (1939: 130)

With Murrie's thesis on my mind, I make the rounds among factory workers, labor union leaders, and current and former executives at the Hershey Company. I am curious to find out what persists of the spirit and ideal of perfect employer-employee cooperation. I also want to learn how the company conceives of its relationship with the Hershey community and Milton Hershey School—especially after the attempted sale of the company in 2002. Moreover, I want to know how the company envisions itself in a global context, and whether its control by the Hershey Trust is considered an asset or liability. My conversations take me to the first chocolate factory built in Hershey, the offices of the Chocolate Workers Local 464, and the company's corporate headquarters. My starting point is the not-so-secret secret process behind the iconic chocolate bar.

THE HERSHEY PROCESS

The Hershey Company's success was made technically possible by M. S. Hershey's turn-of-the-twentieth-century innovation in processing. Nominally, the "Hershey process" remains a trade secret; however, it is widely speculated the company puts the milk in its chocolate product through a process of controlled lipolysis (Moskin 2008). Lipolysis breaks down fatty acids in milk. It produces butyric acid, which stalls fermentation—key to the shelf life of the product—and gives Hershey's chocolate a characteristically tangy, sour flavor profile.[2] The characteristic taste of the Hershey's bar is the taste of this process, as it were; it has remained largely consistent over the last century.

"We ask people, 'Why do you eat candy?'" a recently retired Hershey marketing executive tells me over breakfast at a restaurant not far from corporate headquarters and the downtown chocolate factory. "And people tell us, 'Because I like it.' Period. That's all they say." I ask him to elaborate on what accounts for the candy's good taste, and he offers a biocultural explanation:

> Humans are born with a sweet tooth. . . . Mother's milk is sweet. It's in our genes. It's in our makeup to enjoy and to like sweet things. Chocolate happens to be one of those. Mr. Hershey didn't know this when he developed the Hershey bar. He basically traveled Europe, saw this great thing called chocolate—very expensive—and said, "I'm going to come back and I'm going to figure out how to make chocolate that's affordable— because

people like it, and I know people like it because I like it." And he did. There's no magic formula. We innately like sweet things.

There is no magic formula: perhaps the fact that humans innately like sweet things is itself magical. "Indeed," anthropologist Sidney Mintz writes in his cultural study of sugar, "all (or at least nearly all) mammals like sweetness. . . . That milk, including human milk, is sweet is hardly irrelevant" to modern cravings for commodified sugar products such as chocolate. "On the one hand, that the human liking for sweetness is not just an acquired disposition is supported by many different kinds of evidence; on the other, the circumstances under which that predisposition is intensified by cultural practice are highly relevant to how strong the 'sweet tooth' is" (1986: 16). The "sweet tooth" is irreducible to either biology or culture alone—as Hershey marketers understand well.

Sweetness, and sugar in particular, has "unusual symbolic 'carrying power'" that has evolved over time, Mintz observes. "[Sugar had] a symbolic weight that endured among the rich and powerful until sucrose became common, cheap, and desired, when [beginning around 1650] it spread widely through the working classes of all western nations, carrying with it many of its older meanings but also acquiring new ones. The affective weight of sweetness, always considerable, was not so much diminished as qualitatively changed by its abundance. The good life, the right life, the full life—was the sweet life" (1986: 207). The Hershey Company played no small part in bolstering the affective weight of sweetness by making sweet eating chocolate available in abundance to American consumers.

Prior to the introduction of the five-cent Hershey's bar in 1900, chocolate had been known as a European luxury.[3] In European society, chocolate "figured as a food of luxury and fantasy," providing a "rich field of symbolic associations," in particular an association with the feminine—in contrast to masculine-identified honorific foods such as tobacco and alcohol (Barthel 1989: 431–33, following Veblen 2007 [1919]). It was associated with acts of patronage from men to women and adults to children (Barthel 1989). It was also recognized in the nineteenth century as a healthful foodstuff, endorsed by English temperance advocates (Lamme and Parcell 2013: 200). Hershey furnished this socially virtuous and fantasy-rich European foodstuff to the American hoi polloi.

In the early days of the company, Hershey's chocolate was promoted as a food—comparable to contemporary "health foods" such as breakfast cereals.[4] Hershey's cocoa was a "food to drink"; Hershey's chocolate was a "sweet to eat." "Cocoa is a food and a good food is Hershey's" was one popular tagline. "Hershey's for health" was another. During World War II, American GIs became a market for a more substantial foodstuff, with their diet often including Hershey's Ration D bars manufactured to withstand high temperatures and to serve as a six-hundred-calorie meal if necessary. Evidently these bars tasted more like a boiled potato than like chocolate and were not popular with the troops; however, standard Hershey's chocolate bars became valued as currency among troops and civilians during the war, commonly traded for cigarettes among other goods.

In the postwar era stretching into the new century, the Hershey brand name has become "iconic," as the retired Hershey marketing executive puts it: "The Hershey bar has become part of Americana, emanating from World War II in particular, where Hershey bars could buy you just about anything in Europe. It's become part of our culture. It's Chevy, it's apple pie, and it's a Hershey bar. Unless somebody says one of its ingredients is bad for you, the Hershey bar is always going to be a Hershey bar—and hopefully it's always going to taste that good."

Just as the Hershey's bar has become iconic, so too has "the town that chocolate built." The Hershey industrial town, a.k.a. "Chocolatetown, USA," a.k.a "the Sweetest Place on Earth," is itself a part of Americana. Chocolate candy bars continue to be manufactured here, as well as in other locations across the United States and internationally. Whether this arrangement will last and for how long is a perennial matter of concern among the factory employees I meet.

INSIDE THE FACTORY AT "19 EAST"

In June 2010, it was announced that the "original" Hershey's chocolate factory—the first to be constructed in town, named "19 East" for its address on Chocolate Avenue—would be closed; a new, modern facility would open outside town—not abroad, as many had speculated and feared—and long-standing jobs would be lost in the transition. The announcement made news nationally, becoming the subject of a story on National Public Radio, among other media outlets. "Imagine Google wrapped in chocolate," the NPR story begins:

> What the Internet giant [Google, Inc.] is to its employees today— the extra benefits, the comfy workspace—Hershey was a hundred years ago. A theme park, a theater, low-rent housing and cheap public transportation were all things Milton Hershey brought to the dairy region of Pennsylvania when he created Hershey, the chocolate center of America. At the heart of the town was the chocolate factory, a brown brick building nestled in the shadows of two smokestacks, where cocoa goodness wafted out into streets and homes. That factory on the corner of Chocolate and Cocoa avenues, however, will soon be closing, and the chocolate making will move to another facility being built just outside the town. The Hershey Company says it needs to close the historic factory, and cut 500 jobs, to remain competitive in the global market. (Tarabay 2010)

As Hersheyites tell it, the closing down of 19 East is the "natural" next step in a process of optimization that has been ongoing for the last four decades. Optimization has made the company more efficient in market terms and more profitable for its controlling shareholder, the Hershey Trust. But the trust and state have also placed limits on this optimization, maintaining since 2002 that the company will remain headquartered in Hershey and will continue to manufacture products there, even as the Hershey brand name globalizes.

The total chocolate production operation in Hershey today employs about 1,100 factory workers—down from a peak of around 3,300 in the late 1960s. Many of the jobs lost in recent decades relate to cocoa-bean processing. When 19 East was constructed, cocoa beans arrived in railroad cars or trucks. The beans were deposited into silos where they were stored until being roasted, shelled, milled, and pressed. Cocoa powder, cocoa "nibs" (beans separated from their husks and crushed), and cocoa butter (vegetable fat extracted from the beans) were the result. To facilitate bean processing, a central shop employed machinists, plumbers, millwrights, and electricians, among others. Machinists fashioned additional parts for production equipment; electricians repaired motors; millwrights installed equipment. Many of these positions have been phased out and no longer exist, though the factory continues to employ maintenance staff that fix production equipment when it breaks. Today the company purchases cocoa derivative products from third-party vendors rather than processing cocoa in house. The 19 East facility retains only one cocoa-processing treatment—deodorization—in which cocoa butter procured from a vendor is refined to remove "impurities" such as shell parts or dirt.

It is early winter 2011, just months before the original factory is slated to close, and I have been granted the privilege of taking a guided walking tour through its interior. The 19 East building has been closed to tourists since the early 1970s, when the company constructed a simulated tour adjacent to the Hershey amusement park called Chocolate World. Visitors to Chocolate World take a ten-minute Omnimover-style[5] tour through a fantasy chocolate factory in which they observe a cocoa bean's elaborate transformation into a piece of Hershey's chocolate. Riders follow the beans from tropical rainforests to the end of a factory conveyor belt; a free sample of the product concludes the experience. Less high octane than Chocolate World though more dazzling, the walking tour of 19 East follows a now-faded yellow line printed on the factory floor tracing the production sequence from room to room.

My tour guide, Phil, a senior factory manager, tells me I will see only a fraction of the facility—"5 percent." The entire plant encompasses some twenty buildings, each with around half-a-dozen floors—the most famous part of which, the "conching rooms,"[6] are apparently off-limits to visitors. This is not an especially busy time; there will be more activity in the spring, Phil explains, when the factory has access to "true springtime milk." Springtime milk—procured from dairy farms in Pennsylvania and Maryland—is the "good stuff." Even though cows can be artificially induced to produce fat-intensive milk—they can be "tricked into thinking it's always springtime," as my guide puts it—true springtime milk remains the fattest and most delicious of the year. The factory will utilize as much of it as possible before closing its doors.

The tour emphasizes innovation and improvisation at the plant throughout its one-hundred-year history. In its beginning in the early 1900s, workers hauled wheelbarrows full of chocolate through the factory. The labor in those days was especially long and hard, though it was considered better than the other employment opportunities in the region: farming, coal mining, and—in northern Pennsylvania where Phil's family comes from—lumber. It made good sense to build a company town around the factory, Phil tells me: "It was a way to keep the workers happy," simply put. Later in the factory's history, steam pumps to transport chocolate were introduced, followed by electric pumps. Electric pumps made the labor of transporting ingredients less physically demanding, though the work never has been easy.

The wheelbarrows and steam pumps are gone, yet production equipment from the early 1900s remains in use, with parts added and taken away to produce new products. Phil points me to a machine he and his coworkers retrofitted: it was built to make metal cans for chocolate syrup, and now it produces plastic bottles for syrup. Other modifications have been made to more recently acquired equipment—for example, a machine that wraps palm-sized chocolate bars. When the wrapping machine was first installed, chocolate bars were falling off before reaching the end of the line; factory engineers added metal chutes on the side of the machine to funnel the candy—"a $75 adjustment that saved millions of dollars," as Phil puts it. This was an "in-house" innovation. Other innovations at the plant have been introduced from outside, for example, a tool organization system developed originally by the Toyota Company. Color-coded outlines of hammers, screwdrivers, spatulas, and other instruments are printed on walls and countertops throughout the factory, designating the place that tools are stored when they are not in use. The organization system means that "everything goes in its place." There are no superfluous instruments on the factory floor—maintaining efficiency and serving as a boon to worker safety.

Roughly two hundred workers will be laid off in the move from 19 East to the new facility outside town. Most of the physical plant will be knocked down, but some segments already have been refurbished into new Hershey marketing offices. Most production here will be relocated to the new facility; some production lines will be moved to other Hershey Company plants across the United States, Canada, and Mexico. The idea is to produce in each of these plants a small number of products on a large scale rather than many products on a small scale. The Virginia plant, for example—one of the company's largest facilities in the United States—will be dedicated to all products with peanuts and almonds; this reduces concerns about nut contamination at other plants and in general streamlines production costs.

Along our tour route, my guide exchanges nods and waves to employees, one of whom hesitantly approaches and inquires into the new plant: "Am I going to like it?" he asks. Phil assures him he will and that more information is forthcoming. The closing of 19 East comes on the heels of an antagonistic time between labor and management, Phil explains to me. In the early 2000s—after the attempted sale of the company by the trust—the union had an opportunity "to put their foot down" in negotiations for health care, but, he says, they ended up resigning themselves to cuts. It was around this time Hershey executives decided it was not going to invest any more in the original Hershey plant; it was "done innovating" there.

As Phil tells it, the company's announcement of the closing led to a collaboration between plant managers and union leaders to "discover efficiencies" at the plant and to continue production there as long as possible. The collaboration led to the purchase of a rather expensive ($5 million) wrapping machine that was installed in recent months. An agreement was reached in which factory workers could elect to work on the machine for a pay cut or take a layoff and be replaced with temporary workers. The temporary workers were employed for eleven dollars an hour instead of fifteen dollars. According to Phil, the arrangement benefited both company and labor union—allowing the former to cut production costs and the latter to create new jobs at 19 East. However, it will not last beyond the closing of the factory, he tells me, as the company determined that the cost of outsourcing production for the time it would take to move the machine to the new factory is too high. The recently acquired machine will remain in the factory after it closes and eventually be sold, and the machine that will replace it at the new factory will wrap even faster. "If you can save a little time on something—if you can produce more quickly—that's the name of the game," Phil tells me as the tour concludes. "We're not a charity. It's all about profit."

LABOR'S LOSS

Members of the Chocolate Workers Local 464 found out about the closing of 19 East when company executives called in union officials for a meeting in spring 2010. Ensuing contract negotiations between company and union took place daily over the course of several weeks in a Harrisburg hotel. During those negotiations, the company shared two sets of plans with union leaders: one set for a new manufacturing plant in Hershey, and one set for a new plant in an anonymous other location. The message from management to labor was clear: vote "yes" to the company's contract and production will remain local—though jobs will be shed; vote "no" and production will be moved elsewhere. The union voted nearly unanimously in favor of accepting the company's contract, under the assumption that the company would at some point "add on" to the new building.

Executives did not want the story of the closure of the original Hershey chocolate factory to leak to the press in advance of finalizing negotiations: they anticipated, correctly, a news event. When the announcement became official, television crews and reporters encircled the Local 464 union hall. Journalists crafted a well-rehearsed story of the precariousness of labor and community in heartland America. One example appeared in this CBS television news segment:

> Milton Hershey started his chocolate empire here back in 1903.
> Since then Hershey, Pennsylvania, became known as "The
> Sweetest Place on Earth." Even the lamp-posts are wrapped like
> chocolate. But hard times have come to Hershey. . . . More than
> 200 jobs were moved to Mexico in 2009. And now Hershey

will lay off up to 600 more people this year, as the company modernizes its plant. Workers without enough seniority . . . could lose their jobs.

The story here in Hershey is by no means unique. It raises the questions many small community towns are struggling to answer. What happens when these decent-paying manufacturing towns simply disappear? It's just that here [the segment cuts to a visual of Hershey's Kiss lampposts along Chocolate Avenue in downtown Hershey] the reminder of the importance of this company seems everywhere. (Doan 2011)

The story told by national news might have been crafted otherwise. "Hard times" have not come to all of Hershey, after all. White-collar employees enjoy relative affluence and security as the number and quality of local corporate jobs continue to grow. Hard times have hit blue-collar laborers, specifically young factory workers whose jobs are less protected than senior employees. A majority of jobs lost in the transition between 19 East and the new factory will be young persons' jobs. The loss is attributable to technological innovations. In the new plant's chocolate syrup department, for example, a new piece of equipment will run twice as fast as the current equipment. Only two shifts of labor will be required in the department compared to three in 19 East.

The story of the Hershey Company as told by corporate leadership and reflected in popular media has always focused on the special relationship between company ownership and labor. The company has consistently claimed a bond with factory workers that is rare if not unique in the history of American business corporations. In fact, labor in Hershey has always been in tension with this narrative—alternately recognizing itself as part of and not part of the company's official story.

As workers tell it, the town of Hershey remained a company town until a 1937 sit-down strike. The strike turned violent when factory workers came into conflict with dairy farmers, who were prevented from selling milk to the company because the factory was closed. A historical marker on Cocoa Avenue not far from union headquarters memorializes the site of the conflict. The strike inaugurated the Chocolate Workers Local 464 and, by all accounts, precipitated M. S. Hershey's first stroke.

The factory workers I meet at union headquarters—a former firehouse across the street from 19 East—refer to Milton Hershey as "Milton" instead of "Mr. Hershey." They use this informal appellation in the story they tell about the formation of Local 464. It counters some of the mystique and authority around the founder and brings him down to earth: "The story has it that when the union organizers were here, Milton showed up. They allowed him to speak," a union member recollects. "He said he won't be able to afford to operate if a union gets in, because it costs him $1,000 per student at the Hershey School. And somebody got up at the meeting and said, 'How do you think I can afford my two kids? I don't make $2,000 a year from you!' And that was the turning point. Milton made that statement and it backfired. He thought workers would be sympathetic to the kids at the School but it backfired."

Before the strike of 1937, Hershey's factory workers—many of whom resided in town (and others who commuted on the company-built trolley system)—were prone to seasonal layoffs from factory work. Some may have devised a way around this by appealing to Milton's economizing nature, as one union member relates: "People used to say that if the workers thought it was going to be slow and there would be a layoff, they would go buy something at the [company] store. Milton won't lay you off because you owe him something at the store." In general, workers were subject to the whims of the boss patron. They knew Milton as quick to anger and to fire people for minor infractions, and they understood that the benefits and amenities they enjoyed came at the pleasure of the company.

The 1937 strike resulted in a Congress of Industrial Organizations (CIO)–backed union that associated Hershey chocolate workers with bakers, confectioneries, tobacco workers, and grain millers. Today the Chocolate Workers Local 464 represents grain millers and flour millers (specifically pretzel flour makers), as well as many of the employees of Hershey Trust–affiliated operations. Full-time maintenance workers in the Hershey Entertainment and Resorts Company are represented by Local 464. So are employees of the Milton Hershey School. Houseparents at the school joined the local in the early 1990s after a successful organizing drive that focused on issues of favoritism by the administration (the time of the "Twenty-First Century Initiative"; see Chapter 4). Cooks, groundskeepers, electricians, and janitors at the school followed. After its success at Milton Hershey School, Local 464 organized cafeteria and custodial workers at other schools in the region.

"I'd hope the success rate [for organizing] would be better, but we get people. We have our victories," remarks Roger, a longtime official in Local 464. Tall, lean, eloquent in speech, and fiercely devoted to the constituency that elected him, Roger has been working at the Hershey plant since the late 1960s. He lives in neighboring Annville and speaks in the distinct accent of Pennsylvania's Lebanon County (pronounced "Leb'nin"), where he grew up. Roger talks about his work at the union in terms of a vocation: "Helping people, I've always enjoyed that." He started in the plant on the second floor of the Hershey Kiss department, which until the mid-1970s was occupied almost entirely by women—most of them older than him—whose job was to hand-wrap Hershey's Kisses. He heard about their insurance problems, and, when they had a complaint, he would research the problem. Over the years, he gained a reputation among factory workers as the "insurance guru." This reputation followed him into the union hall, after which he began attending all the union's negotiations with the company. As he has moved through various official positions in the union for nearly three decades, he retained his current office space in the union's headquarters.

Most of the recent negotiations between Local 464 and the Hershey Company have been oriented around health benefits. The price of benefits has soared over the last couple of decades, and the company has, in large part successfully, scaled back its financial commitment to cover the costs of employee health. "Bottom line is, the company tries to change the plans to save money. It has only one thing in mind: passing on a little bit more of the cost to either the retiree or the employee," Roger explains. "Our job at the union is to minimize that heartache for the retirees and the workers." Local 464 is essentially negotiating benefits for Hershey plants across the country, he explains. Hershey workers everywhere in the United States, from Virginia to California, enjoy similar benefits as Local 464 members—even those who are unsuccessful in unionizing or who historically have not unionized (such as employees of the Reese's factory, just down the road from 19 East).

Health benefits were the subject of the union's most recent major strike against the company, which lasted forty-four days in 2002—before the attempt by the trust to sell the company had become public knowledge. The strike, the longest in the union's history, was called in response to the company's attempt to raise the cost of employee contributions to their healthcare plan. A compromise was achieved between the union and company that eventually ended the strike; this was quickly followed by the trust's attempt to sell its control of the company. Following the strike over health benefits, the union took an active role in the local coalition of several publics to "Derail the Sale." "We were right in the thick of it," Roger recounts. "We didn't want it to be sold because what would a new company do? Would they just close it and operate somewhere else? We didn't know."

The early 2000s marked the point of the corporation's transition "from a family" into "just business, period," Roger explains: "Basically, the company used to have ties to the community. It used to be that people went up through the ranks and they were from around here. Some of the CEOs and chairmen of the boards even went through Milton Hershey School. They were tied to the school more. When they started bringing people from the outside to run the company, the company stopped caring about the community."

The corporation "has been in downsizing mode ever since" the introduction of outsider management and the attempted sale in the early 2000s. Products and the jobs that correspond to them gradually have been moved out of Hershey's production facilities. Seasonal peanut butter cups—produced in the shape of a pumpkin for Halloween, Santa Claus for Christmas, and eggs for Easter—were the first to be relocated; they went to the Virginia plant. About two hundred people were employed in Hershey at the peak of that operation; they were laid off and have not been recalled. Hershey's miniature candy bars were the next operation to relocate. Though the union expected production of miniatures to expand in the new Hershey plant, the production line was moved instead to California. This resulted in another round of layoffs. Then, "on Valentine's Day 2007," Roger remembers, the company announced it was building a plant in Monterrey, Mexico; six hundred jobs at the Hershey factory eventually were shed.

Although Hershey had manufactured chocolate internationally for years—maintaining a facility in Canada, for example—the opening of a production facility in Mexico was directly linked to a loss of jobs locally. It is regarded as the corporation's inaugural "offshoring" effort. "It took them a long time to decide to go outside the country to Mexico—it wasn't like Hershey was first [among U.S. corporations]—but they decided to go," Roger says. "Now they're doing the same thing that other businesses do":

> The stuff they make in Mexico—Peppermint Patties, Miniatures, Pot of Gold—what they did is they moved the stuff that is highly labor-intensive because they don't pay them hardly anything down there. I think this thing is going to go in cycles: eventually workers overseas are going to say, "Hey, why should we keep doing this for nothing?" At some point these things change. Companies aren't going to manufacture overseas if it ain't cheap. Look at Nike: they move from country to country in Asia. As soon as workers get disgruntled and say, "Hey, I want more of the cut!" they close the factories and move to the next country. Eventually they'll run out of countries, I guess.

The company encountered "a little glitch in Mexico" that may have benefited Hershey's local workforce, according to another union member I meet: the company intended for a subsidiary to produce the chocolate for the milk-chocolate miniature candies produced in Monterrey, but the chocolate did not taste like Hershey's. "Real" Hershey's chocolate uses liquid milk—a process that begins with transporting milk from dairy farms and pasteurizing it before water is removed and sugar is added. The condensed milk and sugar is combined with cocoa-bean "liquor" (derived from cocoa beans) and run through dryers, resulting in a powder which, when refined, is mixed with cocoa butter and other ingredients prior to baking. The subsidiary company in Monterrey was using powdered milk in its chocolate product—a different production process and a different flavor. The Hershey

Company ended up having to ship milk chocolate from Hershey to Monterrey at significant expense.

This hiccup in production reminded the company that keeping some chocolate production in Hershey—at least for the time being—is crucial. And yet long-standing union members clearly share a sense that local production matters less and less: "Nationally, manufacturing is booming, but they don't need any more workers. The same thing is happening here in Hershey," Roger observes. "Technology is good, but in manufacturing it's a loss of jobs all the time."

CORPORATE GENERATIONS

Hershey union members narrate company history in terms of strikes and layoffs; Hershey corporate managers talk in terms of generational distinctions. The late 1960s, when the company inaugurated its first national advertising campaign, are one marker of generational distinction; the year 2002, when the company was briefly considered for sale by the trust, is another.

After the death of the founder in 1945 until the late 1960s, the corporation "had been complacent about making money," a senior manager explains. "Hershey was technically public, but the trust always had a majority ownership. Through the 1960s all the company really cared about was keeping the trust happy, and they were making enough money to do that." As another manager puts it, "We had a lot of the old tenured Willy Loman-ish type of salespeople at that time. They were very polite, very personable, but they weren't ambitious to move things forward."[7]

Beginning in the 1960s, the company experienced a "cultural transformation" that led to a "cultural renewal," managers remember: "Hershey was getting clocked by M&M Mars. The company realized it had to become more marketing oriented and more competitive. Finally, there was a senior management decision that we had to catch up to become more contemporary and more relevant in today's society—because we had these wonderful icons but we weren't leveraging them." One *Newsday* article from the period (Brown 1969) declared, "The kids in the orphanage are fed up with trailing earnings, so the chocolate king will soon have a new image."

Hershey "tries first ad campaign, spurs acquisition effort, introduces new products," reported the *Wall Street Journal* (Morris 1970).

The success of Hershey's new direction in the 1960s was largely attributed to a graduate of the Milton Hershey School—William Dearden (after whom the school alumni campus is named). Dearden joined the chocolate company "in order to repay his debt to Milton Hershey for making him what he is today," a manger tells me. He is credited with introducing a dual class of Hershey stock in the mid-1980s, which raised money for the company while keeping it in control of the trust (Klott 1984). He is also held responsible for the introduction of national marketing practices, including what eventually would become one of the most famous product placements in American advertising history: the trail of Reese's Pieces in Steven Spielberg's film *E. T. the Extra-Terrestrial* (1982). The company grabbed the title "Number-One Candy Maker" in the nation from M&M Mars under Dearden's tenure as CEO. A colleague of Dearden's recounts, "Dearden was the visionary—the contemporary visionary—for Hershey. He basically grew up through the success of Hershey when he was a boy [through the school]. And he was very passionate about making Hershey number one again and restoring its prestige. He brought in lots of people, remolded the whole sales department, sophisticated it, and basically made it what it is today."

Throughout this phase of heightened competition and success, the company still felt "like a family," senior managers tell me. The scale of the company was small and intimate relative to other American business corporations. "The thing that made us good is that we were all pretty familiar with each other. It was kind of—I hate to use the word in today's corporate atmosphere, but I will—a family. Everybody kind of got together and did the things that had to happen," a manager reflects. "And we were successful." The corporation stood as an example of a "successful medium-sized company" with "integrity relative to its community and relative to society," says another manager. "It fulfilled its social obligations to the community."

As profits rose through the next several decades, the Hershey Company "became more visible to the world," observes a manager with experience in the marketing department. "There was a lot more pressure from the stock market, as well as the trust, to continue to grow and make more money."

The company made some tactical and financial missteps in its effort to expand into non–candy-related product lines (pastas, for example); yet it continued to grow in marketplace value and generate high returns for the trust through the beginning of the twenty-first century.

The year 2002 marks another generational shift, though it remains somewhat taboo to discuss inside the company. The trust's attempted sale is considered "a rough patch"—"past history," as one middle manager puts it to me: "I have a lot of connections and impact on the Hershey community and would hate to see our company get acquired by somebody, but I work for the company who's paying me to do my job. Ultimately, the Hershey Trust is responsible for funding the Milton Hershey School in perpetuity, and the Hershey Company is responsible for maximizing shareholder value." Former managers are at greater liberty to speak their minds. If the late 1960s were the years of "cultural renewal" at the Hershey Company, the early 2000s were a "cultural cleansing," a retired executive says. The installation of an "outsider" CEO in 2001 (the first time a CEO from outside the corporation had been hired) and the attempt to sell the company a year later were clear efforts to "break up the family" and "go large." The new CEO, arriving from the rival snack-food company Nabisco, "came in like a jackal." He and his "cronies . . . didn't really give a rat's ass about Hershey, its people." The mentality of the new guard was "to not give a shit about what happens to Mom as long as they get their wallets full."

The CEO hired by the Hershey Company in the early 2000s did not necessarily agree with or endorse the prospect of the trust's sale of the company; he initially came out against the sale. But the fact that the company was considered for sale soon after his arrival made him controversial among rank-and-file employees from the beginning of his tenure. And it did not help that during his first days, he reportedly removed historical images from the walls of his office: pictures of Milton Hershey's homestead and the first chocolate factory. Though he achieved some success improving the company's performance in his first few years, he ultimately struggled with the rising cost of dairy ingredients and competition from Hershey's archrival, Mars. Apparently feeling hemmed in and frustrated by his employers at the Hershey Trust, he stepped down in 2007 (Jargon 2007).

The Hershey Company is in the midst of "re-identifying what its true roots are," former executives tell me. In the wake of the Great Recession of 2008, current executives are "reestablishing themselves and trying to pull themselves back into what was Hershey's culture for over a hundred years." Sales volumes have decreased over the last several years. The company is now charging pennies more for its product and investing in national advertising to stimulate demand. Also it is introducing novel products with less expensive ingredients, for example, whipped chocolate products that use less cocoa—the most expensive ingredient in milk chocolate. Other recently introduced products include Hershey's "drops" (small, circular-shaped chocolate candies) and Reese's "minis" (miniaturized peanut butter cups sold in resealable pouches).

The company's reidentification with "true roots" entails several components, according to former managers at liberty to speak. One component is a return to familiar, "core" ingredients, such as peanut butter or nougat; the company had experimented with more niche products in recent years—macadamia nuts, for example—which were unsuccessful. Another aspect is a return to marketing products in terms of "reasons and seasons." "Reasons" are rationales for purchasing candy relatively independent of calendrical considerations ("Because I deserve to treat myself after a long day of work" is a "reason" for consuming a chocolate bar). "Seasons" are times of the year in which candy is commonly consumed, such as holiday celebrations like Halloween and Christmas. Apparently, the "reason and season" approach to marketing had been neglected in recent years with negative effects on returns; officials were hoping to reintroduce it.

A third component of the return to roots entails a "return to taste standards," which implicates the company's use of cocoa-bean varieties and cocoa butter, respectively. Hershey purchases cocoa beans from multiple markets, officials explained to me. Indeed, the cocoa-bean "varietal" developed by Milton Hershey in the early 1900s was a means of maintaining a consistent product taste despite an unstable global cocoa-bean market.[8] Beans of both "low cost" and "high flavor profile" varieties are "blended." In recent years, the company has reduced the number of beans in its blend and depended more on low-cost varieties; it is apparently reversing that trend at present.

Hershey is also "recommitting" to standards of cocoa butter. Cocoa butter makes chocolate smooth and slippery. It gives chocolate its "snap" when broken in half. In recent years, the company has increasingly substituted far less expensive vegetable oil for cocoa butter.[9] As vegetable oil is substituted, the chocolate becomes dry; instead of snapping, it bends. "There's a point at which you take too much cocoa butter out—you can tell," a retired executive remarks. "Six months to a year ago [in 2009–2010], the taste wasn't very good. Today it's pretty good."

The company continues its longtime strategy of marketing Hershey's chocolate as both a "kid's product" and an adult "snack—a sweet, wonderful snack." A single child consumes a larger quantity of chocolate than a single adult; however, adults consume most of the Hershey's chocolate in the United States—and adult palates are changing with the times. In the last decade or so, "haute" European chocolate has become big business in America. This "new chocolate" economy centers on dark chocolate with cocoa contents far higher than those of familiar mass-production brands such as Hershey's (Ferguson 2008). The marketing strategy of boutique dark chocolate appeals to adults by combining chocolate's association with passionate indulgence on the one hand and health benefits on the other.

In response to emerging markets for more healthful snacks, the company is developing a portfolio of products that are more nutrition focused than its primary line. Hershey has a connotation for being an "indulgent product line," a manager tells me, "but if you go back to the Incas and the Mayans, they were using cocoa-based items as medicinal products to fix a lot of ills." Some new products highlight the high antioxidant properties of cocoa. These are sold under various brand names: ReGen, a milk- and cocoa-based sports recovery drink is one. Eat.Think.Smile, a granola-based product line with "heavy cocoa content," is another.

Still, executives acknowledge, the large amount of sugar and fat in Hershey's products remains a liability. Sugar "has always been a problem, something the industry has been concerned about." The founder himself recognized a relationship between excess sugar consumption and tooth decay. He had rotten teeth on account of eating so much of his own product, and he commissioned dental research on the effects of sugar on teeth. In more recent decades, the company has attempted to produce sugar-free chocolate, but the artificial sweetener did not perform as a "bulking agent" as effectively as cane sugar—and it did not taste very good, managers tell me. Hershey continues to experiment with "sugar-free technology."

Like sugar, fat "has always been an issue for snack companies like us, and always will be," a manager explains. The company takes a firm position on the obesity epidemic in the United States and maintains that food manufacturers are not primarily at fault: "Our position has been and continues to be that there is a place in a healthy diet for consumption of our products, but it has to be in moderation," a current manager tells me. "We haven't and don't promote our products in a way that encourages overuse. You need to incorporate our products into a balanced and healthy lifestyle." A retired manager is blunter: "Chocolate is a treat. It's a darned enjoyable treat that people deserve to have periodically when they want to. It's up to individuals and parents—in particular, parents—to set examples and not overconsume sweets in general. It's not just candy that people overconsume. It's you-name-it. Why do some people weigh 300, 400 pounds? The issue is bigger than candy."

HERSHEY'S SOCIAL RESPONSIBILITY

I sit in an executive office at the Hershey Company's sprawling, modern headquarters, perched on a hill above the Hershey Country Club between the Hotel Hershey and Hershey Cemetery. I have waited several months for this official meeting with Victor, a longtime manager recruited several years ago to lead the company's new Corporate Social Responsibility Department. Corporate social responsibility (CSR) is among the distinctive features of Hershey's new generation of corporate management. Distinct from philanthropy, CSR is an attempt to "enhance corporate reputation" and to "build positive goodwill for the corporation," Victor explains to me when we finally meet. "The Hershey Company's been based on the premise of good corporate citizenship all the way back to the founder, but the mind-set of corporate social responsibility is different. It's about creating more space for corporations to be bragging about themselves—and we were never a company to do much of that."

From its beginnings, the Hershey Company recognized itself as "responsible" to society—particularly to the community in and around Hershey and to the wider region and nation-state from which the needy children of Milton Hershey School are drawn. One might say Hershey's was a "socially responsible" business corporation before the term existed. But the new practices of CSR are both more global in outlook and more carefully calibrated to generate returns on investment. Hershey's CSR encompasses the surrounding Hershey community and the Milton Hershey School, yet it situates the company in a much broader context than in the previous century. In this sense, CSR displaces older discourses and practices of corporate philanthropy and charity.

"There's very little we do in the area of CSR that actually is a cost or that negatively impacts the shareholder value we're ultimate trying to create," Victor tells me. "We believe positive goodwill for the corporation ultimately enhances shareholder value." CSR is really about the company's reputation in the mind of consumers, investors, employees and the general public, he explains:

> The company is the brand, is the town, is the whole mind-set of Hershey. Anytime our corporate reputation is affected, it has an effect on the reputation of our brands. And when the reputation of our brands is affected, it has an effect on our overall business. That's why it's really important that we do everything we can [inside and outside the Office of Corporate Social Responsibility] to protect our brands and protect our corporate reputation. We see corporate reputation as being an extension of brand and, vice versa, brand as an extension of corporate reputation.

Corporate social responsibility is not unique to the Hershey Company, of course. It rose to prominence in the late 1990s (Welker 2009). Its rise and consolidation were spurred in no small part by transnational activist campaigns that targeted badly behaving corporations with boycotts, shareholder resolutions, and other methods (Keck and Sikkink 1998, cited in Welker 2009). Anthropologist Marina Welker observes several common features of

CSR in today's business landscape: an emphasis on voluntary as opposed to mandatory state-led regulation, an emphasis on potential profits that flow from ethical behavior, and a link to international development practices, grounded in the "growing belief that corporations alone have the power to catalyze development" around the world (Welker 2009: 146).

As it happens, the Hershey Company's corporate reputation and brand is under attack at this time in 2010–2011; perhaps this is why it has taken some time to schedule this morning's meeting. Victor is understandably cautious in his responses to my questions about "Raise the Bar, Hershey!" an anti–child labor campaign organized by an international coalition of human rights, labor rights, and child rights organizations. The activist campaign focuses on the company's alleged complicity in child labor exploitation in West Africa (specifically, the Ivory Coast)—the source of most of the world's cocoa.

Cocoa products used by Hershey's and other chocolate companies are made from cocoa beans, which are harvested from the pods of cocoa trees.[10] Typically, beans are fermented and dried before being sold on international commodities exchanges. The U.S. Department of Labor estimates more than 1.8 million children are involved in their harvesting (Bertrand 2011). Seizing on this evidence of child labor, "Raise the Bar, Hershey!" has encouraged concerned consumers to sign a pledge to boycott Hershey products. It has been successful in recruiting Whole Foods retailers to remove Hershey's specialty organic chocolate products—sold under the acquired brand name Scharffen Berger—from its shelves. It has also organized, among other things, an online "brand jamming" contest[11] that invites campaign supporters to create "mock taglines, print advertisements, and commercial videos that reveal the reality behind Hershey Chocolate products." Some of the winning taglines from the contest include "Hershey: Sweet Chocolate, Bitter Story" and "Exploitation never tasted so sweet" (Green America 2011). Ultimately, the campaign is demanding that the company commit to using "ethically sourced" cocoa in all its products: "While Hershey's commercials, print advertisements and brand slogans emphasize joy and happiness, farmers in West Africa who produce the majority of the world's cocoa continue to live in poverty. The cocoa industry has been plagued for years by abusive child labor, forced labor and trafficking. . . . Hershey lags behind its competitors in sourcing cocoa that has been certified by independent, third parties to meet international labor rights standards"[12] ("Hershey Brand Jam Video Contest" 2011).

Responding to this campaign falls largely within the purview of Hershey's CSR office. "Child labor is a very serious issue for us," Victor tells me flatly. "We don't promote it." Publicly, the company stresses that it does not buy cocoa beans directly from cocoa farmers, implying that it is not directly responsible for child labor. Hershey purchases derivatives of cocoa products—chocolate-liquor cocoa butter, cocoa powder, and cocoa "nibs"— from processing companies, namely, Cargill, ADM, and Barry Callebaut. The responsibility to eliminate child labor is, as Victor puts it, a "shared responsibility" among industry, governments, and cocoa-growing "families themselves." "The majority of cocoa is grown on small family farms, on four to seven hectares of land that's owned by the family, and the kids are involved in the family, so . . . you see child labor happening all the time. Whether that's abusive child labor or imported [trafficked, forced] child labor is sometimes difficult to figure out. Hershey's approach has been, let's fix the social issues out there that have caused child labor in the industry and see if we can make it go away by those means."

The company's efforts to address child labor on cocoa farms are part of its ongoing "holistic approach" to CSR, he explains. Comparable to other major corporation's programs,[13] Hershey's CSR program is framed in terms of four "pillars": environment, community, marketplace, and workplace. The environment pillar emphasizes energy and water conservation, waste reduction, and recycling programs. These are essentially cost-reduction or profit initiatives that align with consumer interest in "green" business practice. For example, manufacturing and distribution facilities have been "re-bulbed" over the last several years—light fixtures have been replaced with relatively less energy-intensive ones—so that the cost of lighting these facilities has been reduced by half.

The community pillar involves monetary donations made in the name of community outreach. Donations are made to support a U.S. Track and Field Games program, for example; to support medical facilities for children near the corporation's offshore offices; and to support community schools and training programs for teachers and farmers in rural, cocoa-cultivating regions of West Africa. Further donations are made in support of charitable institutions with which individual Hershey employees are associated. The Milton Hershey School is included in this community pillar. The company organizes a business management course at the school; it also supports a fellowship project in which student homes are "adopted" by corporate employees who organize recreational events for students.

The marketplace pillar emphasizes "touch points" along Hershey's supply chain. This pillar includes, for example, efforts to equip cocoa farmers with cell phones, which furnish agricultural-educational material by text message. It also includes investments in the CSR projects of corporate customers such as Wal-Mart Stores, Inc.—an effective way of deepening ties with priority clients. Lastly, the workplace pillar emphasizes the health and safety of company employees. The CSR department sponsors "wellness challenges" in which employees are encouraged to substitute walking for television watching. This pillar also supports "affinity groups" that organize women, African Americans, Asians, Latinos, gay and lesbian employees, and junior-level employees under a rubric of employee diversity.

Though folded into the community pillar of Hershey's CSR program, the Milton Hershey School is uniquely publicized by the company. Indeed, it has become a marketing asset like no other Hershey CSR initiative. The history of the decision to publicize the company's special fiduciary connection with the school is a long one, as Victor tells it. After the death of Milton Hershey in 1945, the leaders of the various Hershey entities expressed concern about violating the stipulation in the deed of trust that monies dedicated to the Milton Hershey School cannot be used to advertise Hershey Company products. They also worried that publicizing the company–school connection could appear "exploitative" of the students. Apparently, the founder did not publicize the charity when he founded it because he did not want the news to read as a "publicity stunt" for chocolate sales. But as decades passed, attitudes altered.

A few years ago, Victor tells me, Hershey Company executives and

Hershey trustees resolved that the hundredth anniversary of the Milton Hershey School (celebrated in 2009) was "a milestone worth promoting. . . . We anticipated some halo effect on our brand equity as well." Graphics were introduced on Hershey's candy packaging that illustrated an association between the school and company, a website was created (thehersheylegacy.com), and a thirty-second television commercial was aired. The commercial, which premiered nationally during the 2010 Academy Awards, features young children from the school taking turns narrating an encapsulated version of the story of Hershey's beneficence: "There was this really, really nice man, and his name was Milton Hershey—like the candy bar. He couldn't have any kids. So he gave all of his money to make the Milton Hershey School where he could help children in need. It's way more than a school. It gives you a place to live. A home. This school helped thousands of kids. Thousands and thousands of kids who don't have as much as other people. They care about you. They love you here. He changed my whole life practically. I love it here."

Since 2010, the text on the back of Hershey chocolate bar wrappers reads, "Every Hershey's product you've enjoyed has helped support children in need through Milton Hershey School. Thank you for making a difference." The text directs consumers to a website that tells "Hershey's History of Happiness" in four parts: "The Man," "The Company," "The Legacy," and "Timeline," showing significant dates beginning with the birth of Milton Hershey in 1857 and concluding with "Today: Hershey's is still making people happy—in 90 countries around the world" (Hershey Company 2010).

Hershey managers were surprised when consumers responded to the publicity by sending personal checks to fund the school, Victor tells me. Those checks had to be returned in accordance with the deed of trust, which does not allow for monetary donations of any kind. The letters the school sends in response to consumers who write checks advises "two avenues": "We suggest you take your money and reinvest it in your own community in a way that helps support kids. Or if you want to help the Milton Hershey School in some other way, you can buy Hershey products—because if you buy Hershey products the majority of our proceeds from the Hershey Company will feed into the trust that supports the school." Here, the long-standing relationship between company and philanthropy—scarcely acknowledged in public over decades—is made in terms that explicitly connect the consumption of Hershey's candy with the care of children in need. This marks a significant strategic shift inside the company, which coincides with a generational changing of the guard.

HERSHEY'S SHAREHOLDER VALUE

In addition to a comprehensive CSR strategy, the new generation of leadership at Hershey prioritizes the maximization of shareholder value above older notions of company mission. Inside the company today, shareholder value is, to borrow anthropologist Karen Ho's characterization from her study of Wall Street, a "mission statement, a declaration of purpose, even a call to action. Creating or reclaiming shareholder value [is construed as] morally and economically the right thing to do" (2009: 125). That the social orphans of the Hershey School are by right the controlling shareholders of the Hershey Company heightens, perhaps, the sense of rightness and virtue in the pursuit of shareholder value.

Broadly speaking, the logic of shareholder value coincides with the fall of "the notion of the company as an ongoing social organization, an institution with multiple stakeholders and roots in particular communities" (Ho 2009: 124). Until as recently as the 1980s, paternalistic corporate and state policies and regulations shielded U.S.-based businesses from the claims of shareholders. Such policies and regulations were conceived in the immediate postwar period, when the business corporation "was dominantly understood as a social institution": "[The business corporation was considered] an organization with constituents and responsibilities well beyond the individuals and institutions that owned stock in the corporation. The primary concern of the corporation was the maintenance of the integrity of the organization over and beyond what was dubbed as the 'derivative' claims of the shareholder— which might have to be sacrificed for the good of the corporation itself" (124).

Beginning in the 1980s, the dominant understanding of business corporations has shifted from "complex, bureaucratic, social firms" into "liquid networks of shareholders." As a consequence, traditional publics of the corporations—workers, for example, but also the communities in which particular corporations have been historically based—have been reconceptualized "as components of individual and institutional stock portfolios governed by an ideology of instant liquidity and convertibility into cash" (Ho 2009: 125).

From the perspective of Wall Street, the Hershey Company remains an outlier because of its relationship with its primary shareholder, the Milton Hershey School Trust. In terms of ownership structure, the company is comparable to family-controlled firms: publicly traded business corporations "in which the founder or a member of his or her family by either blood or marriage is an officer, director, or blockholder, either individually or as a group" (Villalonga and Amit 2009: 3057). Such family firms—also known as "closely held" corporations—are powerful corporate actors globally and nationally. "Even in the United States, where ownership dispersion is at its highest, founding families exercise a significant degree of control over a third of the 500 largest corporations . . . and over more than half of all public corporations," write business scholars Villalonga and Amit (2009: 3048).

Most family firms are controlled by family trusts, which tend to use so-called dual-class stock mechanisms to leverage control over and above equity stake in a firm. Dual-class stock mechanisms typically divide a company's stock into A and B classes: A stock pays higher dividends; B stock enjoys more voting privileges. By amassing B stock, family trusts become "the only blockholders whose control rights on average exceed their cash-flow rights," Villalonga and Amit write. "Dual-class stock enhances founding-family control by creating a wedge between the percentage of votes owned by the founding family . . . and the percentage of shares it owns. The wedge is due to the superior voting rights associated with the shares held by the family with voting power, and will exist even when all shares are held with both investment and voting power" (2009: 3,088).

Dual-stock mechanisms were first established by firms like General Motors in the early 1900s; the majority were set up in the "dual-class recapitalization wave" of the 1980s (Villalonga and Amit 2009). The Hershey Trust retained a majority of common stock in the Hershey Company until the mid-1980s. Since then, the trust has divested itself of A stock in favor of B stock. It owns around one-third of company shares and commands around three-fourths of votes.

The crucial difference between Hershey's dual-class arrangement and the arrangement of typical family-controlled firms is the Hershey Trust's charitable status. Though there is no language in the Milton Hershey School deed of trust that mandates the trust retain control of the company in perpetuity, the trust has nonetheless retained control as a matter of custom—an Old Hershey tradition, as it were—and as a response to public pressure. The attempted sale of the company in 2002 revealed the extent to which the public and state are invested in perpetuating this arrangement. By essentially stopping the sale dead in its tracks, Pennsylvania government affirmed the Commonwealth's interest in the trust's ongoing control of Hershey's.

Veteran Hershey employees tend to regard the trust's control of their company as an enabling constraint. The company remains "the right size" because of it, a manager reflects: "It's prevented us from being sucked up by other large conglomerates. It's prevented us from becoming just another brand in a large consumer goods portfolio of companies." Another manager observes, "The only reason Hershey is independent today is because of the trust; otherwise the company would be merged. The trust wants Hershey to be an independent company and not controlled by somebody else."

The trust's control has not prevented Hershey's from merging in recent decades with smaller-scale companies such as Scharffen Berger, a boutique, West Coast confectionery. The point is to "be on the ownership [side] of the merger—not the acquired side," employees say. Indeed, it appears the trust's control has consistently shielded the company from hostile takeover attempts. Employees undoubtedly understand that most takeovers liquidate corporate assets and, in the words of sociologist Paul Hirsch, jeopardize "existing social arrangements such as plant and headquarters locations; product lines and services offered; union contracts; pension and retirement benefits; and contracts with local suppliers, banks, and other community [businesses]"—resulting in significant benefit-related and family problems for employees of the liquidated corporations (Hirsch 1986: 801, quoted in Welker and Wood 2011: 62).

Whether the trust's control conflicts with Hershey's capacity to compete globally is a matter of debate within and outside the company. The story Hershey tells at its 2011 annual shareholders meeting is about the "fundamental advantage" of the corporation over its national and global competitors in the second decade of the new century. The confectionery industry is large and growing globally—a $147 billion industry. The U.S. snack market—including snack and nutrition bars, bakery snacks, salty snacks, and cookies and crackers—accounts for half of that value. Hershey remains a leader in that market—accounting for nearly half of all sales (followed by Mars and Nestle); globally, Kraft Cadbury, Mars/Wrigley's, and Nestle dominate. The Hershey Company stresses that its "global footprint"—quantified in terms of sales outside the United States and Canada—is growing: Hershey's Kisses have been introduced in China, marketed during the New Year gifting season. And new brands have been acquired abroad, for example, Nütrine in India— producers of the popular chocolate-coated crispy wafer ball Choco Rocko. The company's overarching goal is "winning globally" in the confectionery market, in the language of its shareholder report (West and Bilbrey 2011).

Some former Hershey managers confide to me that they are skeptical about the company's global strategy. They point to Hershey's abandoned effort in 2010 to acquire the U.K.-based Cadbury Company, which they regard as misguided from the start. The Cadbury deal would have meant "biting off more they we can chew," says a recently retired executive. It is difficult to penetrate global markets because of long-established national and cultural flavor preferences, he explains, and moreover it is unnecessary: as an American chocolate company, "you don't have to own the world. You can be successful owning a few markets."

Such a mentality tends to irk Wall Street. In the view of many finance professionals, the point is not to stick to the markets a company knows best but to "make markets." In the case of Hershey's, this means cultivating a taste for the product among new categories of consumer, even if those consumers' conventionally preferred "flavor profiles" are incompatible with current brands; and it means implementing an aggressive global strategy. The lack of a substantial international presence relegates Hershey to a "mere domestic niche," critics contend (Merced 2010).

From the perspective of Wall Street, an aura of protectionism and insularity surrounds the Hershey Company. "It's amazing being at the company headquarters," a financial journalist tells me by phone from New York City. "They are tucked away and out of the gulf stream of corporate America, stuck there in their own little world. It's operating at a different speed and mentality." The journalist recollects his first visit to town, on assignment for his news organization: "I expected Hershey to be much more Disney-ish. That's the preconceived notion. But it's its own thing—more a protected thing than a produced thing. They're protecting their lifestyle. There's a whole lot of engineering that goes into it. There's a sort of fakey-feel to it—to protect it from the outside world—but it's not a replica of something else." Because of the trust's control of the company, he says, Hershey is regarded as "a company that can't do things as a company would." It is seen as constrained in the domain of mergers and acquisitions thus handicapped in the global market. Common A shareholders in the company—investors who enjoy higher dividends but have fewer voting rights—are "second-class citizens along for the ride," the journalist tells me. They are "holding out hope the trust breaks" in anticipation of a surge in Hershey's stock value—but they recognize this is unlikely to happen soon. "Smart money" pegs the company as a long-term investment, he observes.

In general, Wall Street (i.e., American financial markets and the professionals who work in them) hopes for the trust to "break." It is convinced the stock market value of the Hershey Company is suppressed because corporate leaders are constrained by their responsibility to the Milton Hershey School trust. If the trust relinquished control, the thinking goes, corporate leaders would no longer have to take account of how their actions impact the school trust fund. The company would be free at last to take bold risks and grow exponentially; its stock would rise accordingly. On the other hand, Main Street (i.e., stakeholders in the Hershey community, company, and school) hopes for the trust to "hold." It is convinced of the social benefits of the trust's control and does not accept Wall Street's analysis of the financial drawbacks. If the trust relinquished control, the thinking goes, the company likely would be acquired by a firm with no substantial interest in keeping Hershey's in Hershey. The new controlling shareholder would relocate or even liquidate the company, resulting in a loss of local jobs, a depression of property values and tax revenues, etc., to say nothing of the effect on community spirit; Hershey's stock might rise but the fortunes of the place and its people would fall.

Of course, in practice, this dueling dynamic plays out in less neat and less predictable ways. The opinion of Wall Street on the subject of the Hershey Company is not homogeneous, nor is the opinion of Main Street; alternative views abound. Nevertheless, the conventional thinking and received wisdom on both sides have real effects on the everyday lives of individual Hersheyites, who find their own allegiances divided between market values and community values, between the Wall Street status quo and the Main Street status quo. The future of Hershey's entrepreneurial-philanthropic legacy may be determined by how they navigate that gap.

CHAPTER 4

⇛ THE SCHOOL ⇚

SUNDAY MORNING ON THE CAMPUS of Milton Hershey School. Students, school employees, and visitors gather in the marble rotunda at Founder's Hall, in front of a bronze statue of Milton Hershey placing a fatherly arm on the shoulder of a young boy. The words inscribed on the base of the statue read, "His Deeds Are His Monument. His Life Is Our Inspiration." Beyond the statue, doors open onto a large, modern auditorium that seats around six hundred. There is no sign of the cross, no Bibles, no pews. Scores of young people shuffle in—an equal number of boys and girls ranging in age from six to eighteen. They are ethnically diverse: Latino, African American, white. Some of their faces and bodies bear traces of hard lives: scars, disfigurations. The majority look vibrant and spirited, laughing with friends before taking seats. Houseparents—married couples who supervise student home life—take seats among them.

The service is led, as it is most Sundays, by Pastor Bill, a kindly man with short-cropped salt-and-pepper hair and a German last name not uncommon in south-central Pennsylvania. Brass orchestral music, performed by a "middle division" student band, marks the start of the service. Elementary-aged students read brief, assorted Bible passages, and then the pastor begins to speak. The theme today is gratitude—"being grateful and saying thank you." The pastor gives examples of what he is thankful for: the assistant pastor, who chose the students to recite the Bible passages; a "bodybuilder" who is his friend and not his enemy (a light joke that elicits some laughter). He illustrates the importance of saying "thank you" with a passage about Jesus's cleansing of the lepers (Luke 17:11–19). Jesus healed the lepers without their having to do anything, he explains. The lepers walked on after being healed and did not thank him, except for one out of the ten. When the one leper thanked Jesus, his response was, "Where are the other nine?"

Pastor Bill directly addresses the audience, which includes senior students with less than one month remaining in the institution: "Most of you, once you graduate, will never express gratitude," he tells them sternly. "Nine out of ten of you will leave when you graduate and never look back. But that's not what God wants you to do." He continues, delivering what I am told is a typical Sunday-morning message at Milton Hershey School:

> God wants you to express gratitude. You can express it in words, by saying "thank you"—to your houseparents, to your teachers, to Mr. and Mrs. Hershey. Or if it's a little weird to say thank you to Mr. and Mrs. Hershey, you can show your gratitude in your deeds, by what you do for others. Remember there are always people who have it worse than you, and you can help them. Remember that you are fortunate to be a student at the Milton Hershey School. An observer might not notice that you're fortunate— because a lot of the time I look out and I see dour faces and I hear complaints that you have it hard. Sometimes I wish you'd just get over it. Sometimes I wish you'd just smile. You have been given an opportunity, and you should feel grateful for it. Now my message for today is coming to an end, and you can feel grateful that chapel is ending a little early. [Cheers from senior students in attendance]

The Mennonite faith of Milton Hershey's upbringing—what might be called a "social gospel"—is the reason the school was created, Pastor Bill explains later, when we meet for coffee. For Milton and his wife, Catherine, "it was obedience to faith, the call of God to serve the poor and serve the needy. They couldn't have kids so they helped kids in need—that was Milton

Hershey School." The pastor feels empowered by the current administration to carry out the original intentions of Milton Hershey and his wife when they founded the institution in 1909. In Pastor Bill's words,

> In 1909, the world of central Pennsylvania was Christian. One might not have been a follower of Christ, but Christianity was pervasive in the culture of that day. When the Hershey School started, it didn't begin as a Christian school. It was a home and a school that had a religious program, which was Christian—that's just the way it was. Over the years there has been a lot of tension because we didn't begin as a Christian school. People say, "If Mr. Hershey was alive today, he would have wanted us to be multifaith." But that's wrong. If Mr. Hershey were alive today, he would say, "We're going to teach kids the Christian faith. We'll welcome kids of any faith background and allow them to practice whatever faith they choose, but what we're going to teach them here is the Judeo-Christian faith of the Old and New Testament"— which is what we're doing today. We're not forbidding kids to practice a faith that is not Christian, but on our campus, in our chapel service, and in our religion classes, we're teaching the Christian faith.
>
> Now, the deed of trust says the school shall be nonsectarian and that we shall show no favoritism to any particular sect or creed. One might be inclined to think we're in violation of that because today "nonsectarian" means showing no preference to any faith or religion. But in 1909 nonsectarian meant nondenominational. We believe the best way to understand the language of the deed is to interpret it in the context of the world [in] 1909. We believe nonsectarian means nondenominational; that our religious program will be Judeo-Christian but we will show no favoritism to any particular denomination in the Christian faith.

The school's admission of children on a rolling basis, and the unpredictable termination of a student's enrollment for wrong behavior or withdrawal by legal guardian, makes it hard to determine the faith background of students. Pastor Bill figures about 65 percent of children at the school have "no faith background"—meaning they grew up without regularly attending a specific religious service. The other 35 percent are Catholic or Protestant. The number of children practicing non-Christian faiths is small: about five or six Muslim children, one Buddhist, and two Jews among nearly two thousand students. Pastor Bill tells me that Wicca—a cult of modern witchcraft claiming pre-Christian pagan origins—is not counted as a faith background, though he and his colleagues recognize it has become increasingly popular for children to identify with it. Wiccan-identified children at the school insist they practice white magic—"magic that we do for good," students say—in distinction to black magic; but as the pastor explains, the school explicitly prohibits the practice of any variety of witchcraft or Satanism on campus under the premise that it is harmful to the self and others.

Though more than a third of the school's population is figured to be Catholic or Protestant in background, Pastor Bill tells me most of those children "don't have a clue about faith." They do not know what a rosary is, for example. They have never been to confession. They know they are Catholic likely because they have been told so. For many students, the pastor explains, their church background is the food bank or the clothing bank—"which is what the church is supposed to be about, by the way: the church is about serving the poor," he adds. "But what I'm saying is, if the Baptist Church in Philadelphia has a food pantry and their family went there to get food, that's their church. When they fill out the papers, they're Baptist. They don't know what it means or the name of their pastor."

The Hershey School is generally the students' first introduction to the Bible and to "the fact that Christianity is not so much a label as much as it is a lifestyle and a practice," Pastor Bill explains. The school frames introductions to Christianity in terms of "having to do with the choices you make." Faith in Jesus Christ is central to chapel service, yet there is no public calling to Christ. The acceptance of Jesus Christ into one's life is construed as an informal, private act, involving a process of "crossing over," in which a child initiates a conversation with an adult follower of Christ. Though this does not happen at chapel service, the pastor tells me, it happens "in private every day."

I ask Pastor Bill about the "gratitude" theme of the chapel service I attended, and if he really thinks it is "weird," as he said in his message, to say thank you to Mr. and Mrs. Hershey. All the good the school does for its students produces a negative effect, "an entitlement attitude," he responds. The school gives food, clothing, education, a safe environment, a college scholarship, and health and dental care—"we'll even take out your wisdom teeth." This leads to an attitude among students that they are entitled to these goods: "It leads them not to be thankful, not to be grateful."

Students' entitlement attitude persists after graduation, the pastor observes. He tells me that, among those students who go to college, some return to Milton Hershey homes during break and want to eat the school's food. They do not understand why the school will not let them eat. The pastor elaborates: "They say 'we've got billions of dollars in the bank, why won't you help me?' Our response is, 'We have already helped you. We've helped you to be independent and to learn to help yourself. Now you've got to do it.'" Softening his tone, he adds, "We want to be there for them after they graduate, but at the same time we wish there were somebody else they could go to." All too often, apparently, there is no one else.

Pastor Bill's reflections strike me as curious, as I do not associate asking for food with an entitlement attitude. It seems natural to me that Hershey "family" members—heirs to the dynasty, as it were—would be welcome to return and eat at the homestead. But school management draws a bright distinction, I learn, between current and former beneficiaries of the trust fund. Whereas enrolled students receive all the resources Milton Hershey has to muster, alumni—after their college tuition has been partly paid for—receive mostly well wishes. The pastor, by preaching gratitude as an anecdote to entitlement, is in his own way preparing students for this transition out of beneficiary status.

I suspect that Milton Hershey students are keenly aware of their status as temporary beneficiaries of philanthropy, and that their "entitlement attitude" reflects, in part, a normal response to being subjects of charity. I do not have the chance to verify my hunch, however, as my interactions with enrolled students are strictly limited by school officials who are concerned, appropriately enough, with student privacy. But I am free to engage with staff and alumni willing to speak with me, and I find myself drawn toward their own attitudes about their employer and alma mater, respectively. These conversations take me across campus from administrative offices to student homes, and across town from coffee shops to Hershey's own "Chocolate Ballroom." Wherever we meet, our discussion tends to start at the same place: with the founders, their intentions, and their deed of trust.

THE DEED OF TRUST

The founders of Milton Hershey School—their acts of love and law—are central to the modern institution's understanding and presentation of itself. Theirs is a "story to remember," as one of the school's brochures tells it:

> The story begins with Milton and Catherine Hershey, a fortune
> made in the chocolate industry, and a deep concern for children.
> Unable to have children of their own, the Hersheys used a portion
> of their wealth from their chocolate business to found the Hershey
> Industrial School in 1909. The School opened its doors with just
> four young boys who not only lived at The Homestead—Milton
> Hershey's birthplace—but also attended classes there. Sadly,
> Catherine Hershey died just a few years later at the age of 42. In
> 1918, Milton Hershey gave virtually all of his personal fortune to
> the School to provide for its continuation throughout all time.

The most commonly told story of the school's origins focuses on a comment reportedly made by Milton Hershey that the orphanage was "Kitty's idea." The eldest of four children of Irish Catholic immigrant parents, "Kitty"—Catherine Hershey—had been active in charity since the early 1900s following her marriage to Milton. While Milton oversaw the chocolate factory and town in Hershey, Catherine participated in a charity society in neighboring Lancaster with, among others, F. W. Woolworth, the five-and-dime store founder (McMahon 2010: 12). The charity society was dedicated to "the elevation of the moral and physical condition of the indigent, and for the relief of their necessities," which included training for industrial jobs (2010: 10). Catherine's involvement in the Lancaster charity society extended to the orphanage that would become the Milton Hershey School. When the Hershey orphanage opened in 1909 with ten boys, Catherine planned their home life—including their meal menus, clothing, and social activities. She is remembered for inviting the children to have meals with her at High Point, the mansion she shared with her husband. In her final years, she was almost completely incapacitated. A practicing Catholic for most of her life, she embraced Christian Science shortly before her death in 1915.[1]

At its founding, Hershey's school was similar to contemporary philanthropic endeavors in that it was oriented toward social betterment; however, the deed of trust that established it was less akin to the modern foundation charters of Rockefeller, Ford, or Carnegie than to the nineteenth-century deed of Girard College, in Philadelphia. Girard's deed, which first raised the question of the oversight of charitable trusts before the Supreme Court in 1844 (*Vidal v. Girard's Executors*), was authored by French-born, naturalized American banker Stephen Girard—best known for financing the United States in the War of 1812. Like Hershey's deed, it establishes a charitable trust for the purposes of funding a school in perpetuity. Legal scholar Lawrence Friedman recounts:

> Girard . . . was looking for a kind of immortality; and his device for achieving this goal was through setting up a permanent and perpetual charity, in this case a school. Girard's aims were, however, in a kind of tension. The urge to set up something that would last forever tends to clash with an urge to specify, in minute detail, exactly how this something was to operate. In both regards, his charitable trust was an extreme example of the dead hand at work. . . . [Girard's will] left his vast estate to be used to build a "permanent college, with suitable out-buildings, sufficiently spacious for the residence and accommodation of at least three hundred scholars." The college was to be located on land that Girard owned. The estate would pay the teachers and supply the college "with decent and suitable furniture as

well as books and all things needful" to carry his "general design" into
effect. (2009: 146–47)

The "general design" of Girard's deed was extremely specific, including
provisions for how the school building should appear, the kind of food
served, the kind of curriculum offered, and where the residents will be
drawn from. It also included a restriction on residents' race, which eventually would be eliminated in *Pennsylvania v. Board of Directors of City Trusts*
(1957), a landmark Supreme Court decision that held that Girard's board of
trustees was "an agency of the State of Pennsylvania" and that the refusal to
admit African Americans was a violation of the Fourteenth Amendment
(Friedman 2009: 146).

Hershey's deed is similarly specific. Its purpose is to found and endow
"in perpetuity" the institution known today as the Milton Hershey School,
entrusting a wide tract of farmland in Derry Township for this purpose. The
deed of trust document, which is held in Harrisburg in the office of the Clerk
of the Orphans' Court of Dauphin County, provides that the school "shall be
permanently located" in Derry Township. Its text, which has been revised
to eliminate race and gender restrictions, instructs the school's managers to
admit "as many poor, healthy children as . . . the extent, capacity, and income
of the School will provide for. . . . Only a child deemed poor and healthy by
the Managers, and who . . . is not receiving adequate care from one of his
or her natural parents, is of good character and behavior, has potential for
scholastic achievement, and is likely to benefit from the program then offered
by the School . . . shall be admitted." The deed gives priority of admission to
students based on their place of birth: first, to those born in Dauphin County,
Pennsylvania, and its neighboring counties (Derry Township is situated in
Dauphin); second, to those born elsewhere in Pennsylvania; third, to those
born elsewhere in the United States. The deed does not make provisions for
children born outside the country. The key provisions include the following:

All children admitted to the School shall be fed with plain,
wholesome food; plainly, neatly and comfortably clothed, without
distinctive dress, and fitly lodged. . . . They shall be instructed

in the several branches of a sound education, agriculture, horti-culture, gardening, such mechanical trades and handicrafts as the Managers may determine, and such natural and physical sciences and practical mathematics as in the opinion of the Managers it may be important for them to acquire, and such other learning and science as the tastes, capacities, and adaptability of the several scholars may merit or warrant, to fit themselves for the trades they are to learn, and a useful occupation in life.

Each and every scholar shall be required to learn, and be thoroughly instructed in some occupation or mechanical trade, so that when he or she leaves the School . . . he or she may be able to support himself or herself.

The School shall be non-sectarian, but the moral and religious training of the scholars shall be properly looked after and cared for by the Managers. No favoritism shall be shown by the Managers to any particular sect or creed.

The deed of trust makes provisions for expelling a child if he should become "incompetent to learn," "insubordinate," or unfit in some other way—or if he has become competent enough in his chosen trade such that he no longer requires support. It also makes provisions for the appointment of future managers by those presently sitting on the board of directors of the trustee. Furthermore, it allows trustees to incorporate as a corporation at some future date; this occurred in 1919 under M. S. Hershey's tenure as chairman of the board of trustees and managers.

In its one-hundred-year history, the deed has been modified numerous times—occasionally controversially. The first of many minor and major alterations came about during the donor's lifetime: in the early 1930s, the definition of *orphan* was modified to allow for the enrollment of boys with a single living parent. A few years later, the deed was modified to establish the M. S. Hershey Foundation, designed to support education in the local township. (This foundation became, in the early 1960s, the mechanism through which the construction of the Penn State Hershey Medical Center was funded in Derry Township.)

In 1970, a modification eliminated racial restrictions on admittance; six years later, a modification eliminated sex restrictions. Both modifications were spurred by new legal precedents set through state and federal court actions involving peer institutions across the country. At the same time girls were admitted, the definition of *orphan* was modified again, this time to enroll children determined not to be receiving adequate parental care at home. Such "social orphans" (in distinction to what school administrators and alumni call "true orphans") make up the majority of children at the school today.

"TOUGH LOVE": THE SPARTAN SYSTEM

In marketing and public relations, the Hershey School emphasizes the cultivation of productive citizens. "Our main goal for all of our students," school publicity proclaims, "is that they leave the School well-prepared to enter society as productive citizens. We want all of our graduates to be good students, but we also want them to be good people, good employees, and responsible members of their communities" (www.mhs-pa.org). In brochures and on the Internet, publicity describes Milton Hershey School as "the country's largest pre-kindergarten through grade 12 home and school for boys and girls from families of low income and social need."

Students live under the supervision of married, opposite-sex couples—"houseparents"—in one of 150 student homes across campus, with about a dozen students of the same sex and relative age occupying each home. Tuition, housing, education, clothing, food, and medical, dental, religious, and psychological services are provided to students at no cost. Basic qualifications for admission are listed:

- Come from a family of lower income.
- Be 4–15 years old at the time of enrollment.
- Have the ability to learn.
- Be free of serious behavioral problems that are likely to disrupt life in the classroom or student home life at MHS.
- Be able to participate and benefit from the school's program.

The average household income of a student accepted into the school is around $15,000, according to school literature. (The median income of U.S. households is about $50,000 a year [DeNavas-Walk and Proctor 2014]). Nearly three-fourths of accepted students come from the state of Pennsylvania. Preference is given to the counties that immediately surround the school, in accordance with the deed of trust; the remainder of students is drawn predominantly from the U.S. mid-Atlantic region. Today over half of currently enrolled students are students of color. A little more than 50 percent are female. Nearly half of students have a brother or sister enrolled at the school—the effect of revised enrollment practices following the elimination of gender restrictions in the mid-1970s.

The technical and agricultural educational components of the academic curriculum are prominently featured in school publicity, which points out that a majority of students continue their education at a two- or four-year college or trade school. Enrolled students are given the opportunity to "earn" college tuition dollars through academic performance and good behavior—up to $80,000 in recent years. The modernity and comfort of the institution—both its physical plant and social body—are likewise emphasized. Advertising features the bright faces of young girls and boys of various ethnicities and body types and the beauty of the sprawling rural-suburban campus. Students are photographed at work in the classroom, in front of computers, playing instruments, and on tennis courts. Enviable campus amenities are prominently featured: centers for fitness, visual arts, performance, library resources, and student associations are highlighted, along with sports teams, choral groups, and service organizations. The school's presence on social media elaborates a vision of productivity and responsible citizenship. Its official Facebook page includes testimonials from students and snapshots of everyday life: students tapping maple trees to make syrup, walking to raise money for cancer research, playing basketball, and so on.

The regimentation of students' days is not a feature of the school's publicity; however, it becomes obvious when entering the institution. The dress of students, for example, is regimented. With minor variations, it consists of navy blue or khaki pants and pullover shirts with a collar. The daily schedule of students is, likewise, routine. Generally, it proceeds as follows:

6:00 a.m.: Rise and shine. Toilet. Morning devotionals at breakfast table. Student performs domestic chore—dusting, vacuuming, cleaning bathroom, setting table, etc.

7:00 a.m.: Breakfast, followed by table and kitchen cleanup. Dressing for school. Van transportation or walking to school.

8:00 a.m.–3:15 p.m.: School hours [on campus]

3:15 p.m.–6:00 p.m.: Extracurricular activities (athletics, drama, tutoring); relaxation time before dinner.

6:00 p.m.: Dinner, followed by cleanup.

7:00 p.m.–8:00 p.m.: Quiet study time.

8:00 p.m.–9:30 p.m.: Relaxation time (television, games, etc.)

9:30 p.m.: Lights out.

. . .

Saturday morning: "A deep cleaning day—washing the windows or, instead of washing the silverware, cleaning it with cleaner to make sure it's not getting spotty or the dishes getting stained. Cleaning the bathroom a little better, a little deeper," in the words of a school employee.

Saturday afternoon: Optional return to "home of origin" with legal guardians or other authorized visitors. Return by bedtime.

Sunday morning: Mandatory chapel service, followed by optional second church (transportation to town for students to attend churches). Optional leave again. Return by dinnertime.

Regimentation and routinization are, of course, common features of large-scale residential education institutions (i.e., the English boarding school). Milton Hershey administrators are eager to speak on this subject and correct a public misperception of the school's being "strict" or "harsh." One senior administrator—who is also an alumnus, as are many administrators—explains, "People who don't understand who the students are or what they're coming from, or don't understand what the Milton Hershey 'product' has been over the years—those people have difficulty" with what they perceive as strictness or harshness; in fact, strictness and harshness are forms of care—what some might call "tough love." The administrator's use of the term *product* is not official, though officials use it internally to describe what the school is meant to achieve. I cannot help but hear it in the context of the model industrial town: the product of the chocolate factory is chocolate, and the product of the orphanage is worker-citizens (who, in the old days, may have ended up working for the chocolate factory). "We're trying to change young people's thoughts and minds and behaviors from all that they've ever known, and it's not a simple task," the administrator continues. "We're trying to pick them up academically. We're trying to pick them up socially. We try to get them to understand that you're going to get knocked down—you might even get flattened—but you've got to get up again, because that's what you do when you want to get ahead." He goes on: "We're really about the true middle-class values of trying to be a hard worker, trying to believe that hard work and diligence will get you ahead. Work hard, pay attention to the rules, and you'll be a success: that's been the mantra. You may never be the head of the company, but you're striving to be . . . something. You're striving to get somewhere. That's been the entire goal of Milton Hershey since he started the school. The majority of people here believe in that and, on a daily basis, that's what we're trying to get students to understand."

Among the most routine operations at the school is the evaluation of students in terms of levels in the "Spartan System."[2] The system, which encompasses households, classrooms, and playing fields, is composed of four levels, as one official explains: (1) Spartan, "the highest you can get in the house if you're showing above and beyond what is expected"; (2) Gold, "if you're doing exactly what we expect"; (3) Brown, which restricts some privileges; and (4) Novice, the lowest level. "If you're a novice, you're on restriction and you have to sit outside the door to the houseparent's office. If you want to go to the bathroom, you must ask. You go to bed thirty minutes early. You cannot go anywhere on weekends."

Levels are changed weekly based on aggregate daily markings by school employees. Markings are point deductions for nonconformity to standards of dress, chores, and time management. For example, after children leave the house for school in the morning, houseparents examine the house and deduct points for dust, soap spots on dishes, unkempt clothes' drawers, and so on. Deductions are also made for "incidents," for example, a physical altercation between two children in the house. Incidents are inscribed in a computer database. The database proscribes specific "consequences" based on the incident, selected from a list by houseparents. Employees themselves are subject to audits of the sort they perform on students—though consequences are differently qualified. Multiple times a year a home life administrator—typically a former houseparent—will audit houseparents by performing an inspection of a house. The emphasis of these inspections is above all physical cleanliness—the hallmark of adherence to the Spartan System.

Crucially in the Spartan System, the words *consequence* and *consequencing* are substituted for *punish* and *punishing*. As administrators explain it, students have been "punished" throughout their lives for no reason: they have been abused, in a word. "To consequence" a student is, rather, to respond in a standard (negative) way to an action the student has chosen to take. Administrators debate with each other about what counts as an effective consequence. Institutions will always need "carrots and sticks" to get people to change their behavior, but in today's Milton Hershey School, there are few "appropriate sticks," an administrator explains. "Where are the sticks? That's what we are fighting every day."

Corporal punishment is a primary "consequence" that is no longer available to caretakers. The origins of routine corporal punishment at Milton Hershey School are opaque; it is not clear that spanking, belting, and the like were regularly practiced at the school's founding. It is possible physical punishment was eschewed—as the well-known Pennsylvanian Mennonite educator Christopher Dock once advised.[3] Whatever the case, corporal punishment had become standard operating procedure by the mid-twentieth century. Through the 1960s, it was one of the primary "sticks" available to houseparents: a legitimate exercise of violence that was construed not only as discipline but also as care—"tough love." There is no substitute for the effectiveness of corporal punishment today, confides an administrator who is also an alumnus of that earlier era: "I believe corporal punishment has a place in raising children, whether they're your own biological children or the children you're in charge of, but in today's society it's just not going to fly."

Undesirable chores are another consequence to disappear in recent decades—specifically those chores associated with the school's dairy program, which, through the late 1980s, were a part of every student's daily routine. The primary value of the dairy program seems to have been its loathsomeness. Alumni who participated in the dairy program as students talk about "hating it then," when they were obliged to work in the barns, and "loving it now." As they tell it, dairy chores instilled in young people the understanding that certain tasks had to be accomplished regardless of one's desire to accomplish them. The cows had to be milked whether the boys liked it or not—and it seems most boys hated it. Conveniently, these dairy chores could be extended to individual students as consequences of bad behavior. Today, in the absence of the dairy program, which closed at the beginning of the school's reform years, the repertoire of loathsome tasks to assign children is decidedly narrower.

The restriction of "town privilege" was yet another "stick" in the old days that no longer exists; it was perhaps even more effective than the others. This was in effect a restriction on students' interaction with a public—specifically a gendered public—and it served as a powerful deterrent to bad behavior, as an administrator who is also an alumnus tells it: "The worst punishment you could get in the old days was 'student home detentions,' because if you were on detention you could not go to town on Friday night. And so that literally meant the only time you potentially saw a young woman was on a bus while driving through town. Home detention was an awful stick that never blistered you or bruised you physically, but emotionally it was awful. It wasn't just the girls, but it was that bit of freedom on a Friday night."

"Town privilege" and "home detention" were phased out of everyday practice amid the administration reforms of the 1990s—perhaps partly in response to a general decline in town visits for students because of complaints by local township businesses that Milton Hershey students were shoplifting during their weekly visits. "Now we have movies here on our own campus, and we have recreational places for the kids to go, and they're both boys and girls at those places," an administrator explains. "We can still 'ground' kids, but it doesn't produce the same effect."

In general, Milton Hershey School employees narrate a gradual loss of authority to correct bad behavior at the school. Strikingly, some have responded by attempting to revitalize the "native culture" of the school's founder. Over the last decade in particular—since the recomposition of the board of trustees after 2002—administrators have introduced the idea of a renewed "Pennsylvania Dutch Mennonite culture." As they see it, this is the culture of Milton Hershey; it values labor and humility, an administrator explains: "Mr. Hershey, he was Mennonite. He really believed in the power of working long and hard and together. The whole system at the school was set up around that: Everybody pulls their weight, whether it's milking or picking corn or baling hay. We don't go anywhere, any one of us, until it's all done. We work hard, we persist and persevere. That's the culture of Milton Hershey School."

INSIDE A MILTON HERSHEY HOME

Houseparents Denny and Missy occupy a spacious, modern residential unit in a leafy cul-de-sac on the Milton Hershey School campus. With aluminum siding, green lawn, and basketball hoop in the driveway, the house resembles a conventional two-story American suburban home. It is scaled up, however, to accommodate a dozen young children—in this case, elementary school–aged boys. On this warm spring evening, Denny cooks prodigious batches of hamburgers in the kitchen, periodically rummaging through the oversized refrigerator for fixings. His wife and coworker, Missy, is occupied with chores in the couple's apartment, annexed to the main unit. The gendered division of domestic labor in this context is typical across residential units: Denny performs domestic chores in the school's household, while Missy performs domestic chores in the couple's private household. As I sit with Denny, boys pass through the kitchen. One announces that a toy has been stolen by another boy; another asks about the meaning of the word *geography*: "That means a place," Denny responds gently. "Look out the window here. That's geography. The lay of the land. You know how the land rolls and hills? And the place where we are: we're in Hershey." "Like Hollywood?" the boy asks. "Hollywood's part of geography but that's way out on the West Coast. Does that make sense?" "Yes. So is Canada part of geography?" "That's right." The boy walks away, satisfied.

Denny confides that he rarely has a chance to reflect in conversation on his work as a houseparent. "This is the most I've talked probably in ten years," he says after responding to a few of my questions about everyday life at the school. He pauses and takes time responding when I ask how he came to be a houseparent nearly twenty years ago: "It's almost like a calling. You want to give something back." Denny grew up locally in Hershey and attended Derry Township's public schools. His father died when he was a young teenager. Friends' fathers took Denny under their care. His mother continued to work and was supported by Social Security. He did not enter the school—though he could have given the circumstances: "I was a mess for a long time," he confides. Denny was saved by Jesus Christ about a decade before becoming employed as a houseparent. A good friend from church worked at the school as a herdsman (responsible for care and maintenance of cattle) before becoming a houseparent; Denny visited his friend regularly and started to consider making a job application: "Both husband and wife get paid; it seemed like the right thing to do."

Denny and Missy started their work at the school with a division of senior boys. After fifteen years, they considered quitting, as new cohorts under their care seemed to be more antisocial. "I'm real close with the first ten years of graduates; they still call for Mother's Day," Denny explains. "But in the last five years, they're a different-type kid. They don't call, they don't come back to see me. Things have changed." Administrators offered the couple an opportunity to work with elementary-aged boys, and this convinced them to stay. "The younger kids appreciate you more," Denny reflects. "Problems in the house are resolved in ten or fifteen minutes. It's just nicer."

A day in the life of Denny and Missy's household begins in the early morning with bed wetters. The couple currently has two daily bed wetters. Denny gives them showers while Missy wakes up the other boys and prepares breakfast. Three times a week, Denny cooks a hot breakfast. On Saturdays, the boys "can have anything they want"—eggs, pancakes, bacon, potatoes; the food is hearty and plentiful. After breakfast the boys brush their teeth, change into school clothes, and complete chores. Everyone has a kitchen chore and a house chore, such as wiping down the countertops or vacuuming the carpet. The boys are permitted a few minutes of television before a bus comes to pick them up and shuttles them across campus to the elementary school.

When the boys return at the end of the school day, they finish homework, eat dinner, and complete evening chores. This time of year, daylight savings is in effect—there is light well into the evening—so they get to play on the lawn outside before sleep. Bumblebees have provided evening entertainment over these last few weeks, Denny tells me. The boys knock the bees out of the air and entrap them in cups and buckets, proclaiming to one another, "These are *my* bumblebees!" At the end of the evening, they bathe and brush teeth, with the youngest among them going to bed as early as 7:00 p.m. Denny and Missy are asleep in the adjacent apartment by midnight. "Each day's a little different," Denny remarks; keeping the children active is the priority.

Houseparents oversee a domestic life in which students assume a "pecking order," as Denny puts it. The uppermost slots are typically occupied by "bus babies": recruits who arrived in kindergarten, picked up by the school's officials from the bus station; they know the workings of the institution better than their peers and tend to dominate. Denny likens the social order of the household to a "wolf pack": "I'm the alpha male and the rest get in line behind me. But they're always nipping at my heels. Nobody wants to be the bottom, so if you had two or three kids of equal stature, they are always fighting to keep from being the bottom guy on the totem pole. That's where you have the unrest. If everybody else gets in line, you don't have problems. You get trouble when they are trying to change the pecking order."

Like many houseparents, Denny has developed "a look" with the children in his home that signals to them they must change their behavior or be "consequenced." "I try to teach them, 'When you see this look on my face, you're either going to stop what you're doing or something's going to happen.'" He has cultivated this technique over time, he tells me, learning through experience that the children are "great manipulators." "I explain to them I try to be a man of my word: this is what we're going to do and that's what's going to happen—it ain't gonna change."

The Spartan System formally dominates everyday routines inside the house; however, both students and houseparents try to exert as much flexibility as possible. "There are definitely people more strict and people more lenient. You all have your own style," reflects Denny. "You've got to have some leeway. It's your personal preference. All homes across the United States are the same way, right?" For example, devotionals are part of the morning routine, carried out around the breakfast table. Houseparents have leeway in what they might read aloud with the children. A houseparent who, for example, wants to emphasize "success and positive spirit" might substitute John Wooden's *Pyramid of Success* (2009) for Bible passages. Other houseparents may proselytize students during devotionals; this is officially prohibited yet reportedly commonplace.

Denny and Missy are clearly confident and effective in maintaining order inside the household; they are both gentle and firm with their wards. Yet they and other Milton Hershey employees brood over the "new level of issues"—social, psychological, and psychiatric—that attach to recent student cohorts. The psychiatric diagnosis of ADHD—attention deficit hyperactivity disorder[4]—is a prominent example of one such issue. ADHD-diagnosed students require much more "hands-on" attention. ADHD-diagnosed children are incessantly asking questions and demanding answers, houseparents say; the endless dialogue is draining and disruptive to other children. In years past, such behavior would have been "diagnosed" as disrespect or lawlessness; it would have treated with literal "hands-on" attention, that is, corporal punishment. "ADHD might have been around in the 1950s, but if the kid acted out, you paddled them, and houseparents were able to do that," remarks Missy. "You don't do that now. The kids of today, they have so much baggage coming into the school. A lot of the kids are on psychotropic meds. All we [houseparents] can do is make sure they take their meds."

Much of the "baggage" students bring with them, as Missy puts it, is manifest as emotional distance. Older-aged students in particular "have a wall": "They won't let you get close to them. They don't want to have a relation. They want to get in here, get this over with, get their education, and get out of here." In turn, houseparents put up their own barriers to intimacy. Verbal expressions of love between houseparents and students are uncommon in households with older students, I am told. Physical displays of affection like hugs are likewise rare outside of elementary-age homes. In general, legitimate physical contact of any kind is confined to the school's medical-hygienic and recreational routines. This bears significantly on what employees and alumni refer to as the "coldness" of the institution.

Houseparents tend to perceive Milton Hershey School psychologists as having the most control and influence over students. Psychological staff members have become a "force," they say, over the last half-century. The staff has expanded from one part-time psychologist in the mid-1960s to around forty or fifty full-time psychologists, including around a dozen college counselors. "They tell us basic things about the kids when we get them, like what scars they have, do they wet the bed, who their sponsor [legal guardian] is," Missy explains. "But some of these kids have issues—whether it's suicidal or they're cutters or whatever—that we'll never find out about." Medical confidentiality is itself a source of tension and anxiety: Some houseparents even express concern that their own biological or adopted children, who live on campus, could be subject to physical or sexual abuse by Milton Hershey students with confidential "issues." For their part, psychologists whom I approach on campus do not consent to speak with me, even in general terms, on account of concerns about violating student privacy.

HOW HERSHEY BECAME HOME TO "SOCIAL ORPHANS"

Many of the "problems" and "issues" reported by houseparents and other school employees attach to students who fall under the category "social orphan." This category is not unique to the Hershey school. The term initially gained currency in the former Soviet Union, referring to "a child with living family members [who is] separated from them either temporarily or permanently by social circumstances" (Dillon 2009: 19). The general causes of social orphanhood include "legal and social barriers that separate one or both parents from the child and individual adult choices by which they become unable or unwilling to provide consistently for the needs of the child" (Wardle 2005, cited in Dillon 2009).[5] Several "possible outcomes" confront social orphans, legal scholar Sara Dillon reports: "Family reunification, extended family care or guardianship within the extended family or community, institutional care (orphanages and group homes of varying sizes), domestic foster care, domestic adoption, international adoption, or a more ad hoc and chaotic option, such as living on the streets" (2009: 2).

Social orphans were introduced to Hershey through a *cy pres* reinterpretation of the deed of trust.[6] Senior employees remember that, as the 1960s progressed, the school had difficulty finding and attracting the traditional Milton Hershey student: the boy who lived in an "intact family" before his father or mother died.[7] Social Security, which did not exist at the charity's founding in 1909, was expanding through the mid-twentieth century, they explain. With the compensation of insurance, families who lost a breadwinner could more readily afford to keep their boys in the home and educate them.

Another factor in the difficulty attracting traditional students in the second half of the century was the moral reputation of orphanages, which had become compromised. The Milton Hershey School may have been especially "stigmatized," employees recount, for its association with the chocolate company and its dairy-dependent product. That the orphan boys' routines revolved around the twice-daily milking of cows invited a perception among outsiders of exploited child labor.

Moreover, since the 1950s, administrators recount, the school had become increasingly associated among the wider public with juvenile delinquency and penal-correctional practices. The board of trustees tried dispelling this reputation by changing the institution's name from the Hershey Industrial School (with the connotation of a correctional facility) to the Milton Hershey School. Concurrently, the school replaced contracts of *indenture*, which have connotations of peonage, with *in loco parentis* contracts ("in the place of a parent"), which grant institutions temporary responsibility for the care of a minor. None of these tactics seemed to draw significant numbers of new "traditional" recruits, however.

A senior employee who is also an alumnus sums up Hershey trustees' rationale for introducing "social orphans" in the 1970s as follows: "The idea was, we're having difficulty finding enough children who meet the deed's criteria and who have a sponsor that wants to send them, and yet there are thousands of kids in America who are just as needy, just as poor, just as ill-kept—*as if* they were an orphan. And so the term 'social orphan.'"

The difference between "true orphans" and "social orphans" matters to school employees and alumni, especially administrators, as they ponder the fate of the Milton Hershey School in the twenty-first century. As one administrator puts it, "scar tissue remained" among true orphans from the tragic incidents leading to their orphanhood, but in years past those students could "buck up and go on": "True orphans lived somewhere and life was good. Mom or dad died and then they were here at the school. Mom couldn't pay the bills and so they came here. There might have been a stigma attached to mom because she gave them up, but ultimately the school was a better place for them—and when they graduated they got great careers." Social orphans have "a different kind of scar tissue." Often they wear the open wounds of malnutrition; mental, physical, and sexual abuse; and generational poverty and ghettoization. In recent decades, the economy has been such that when these social orphans graduate, they tend to confront a hostile or indifferent labor market rather than the promise of a "great career." And in distinction from true orphans who experienced, in one administrator's striking phrase, "the clean sever" from their parents, social orphans often retain links to their home of origin.

As administrators tell it, social orphans have been living for years surrounded by crime and drug use, and often prostitution by their mother or siblings. They have been "more abused, less well-cared for, less well-nurtured and nourished" than the school's traditional recruit. They have "more exposure to violence, including on themselves," and perhaps "a greater feeling of abandonment." One longtime alumnus and current administrator, a fun-loving, exuberant man in his fifties named Ronald, frames the distinction in terms of his own experience:

> I came from a very unstable environment with a mom who was
> crippled and had a whole bunch of boyfriends, and every time
> that didn't work out, it was my fault; it was just a terrible life.
> When I came to the school—my mom was abusive but my dad
> was gone [deceased]. My mom's comment to me was, "This is

where you're going to be." And that was the end of my relationship with her. I remember getting to the school and I could relax: I wasn't on the streets anymore; I didn't have to prove myself every day. Today the school has kids with guardianship issues. There's so much happening in their lives and so much happening in society. The kids today still have to go through proving themselves—even though the school is a safe place.

Most current students return to their home of origin—their "so-called home," as one administrator puts it—to visit a parent or legal guardians during breaks in the school's academic calendar. Parents and legal guardians are known as "sponsors." Administrators are generally inclined to limit leave and visitation privileges between students and their sponsors. In their view, students who are restricted in their contact with a home of origin and who remain at the school year-round are more effectively "inculcated" with the school's middle-class values. They are mindful, however, that introducing additional restrictions may give the appearance of "pulling the family [of origin] apart." The opportunity for sponsors to visit and for students to return home often and for extended periods is considered a valuable recruitment tool. Long calendar breaks appeal to sponsors who otherwise are uncomfortable with "the sacrifice of giving up their child," as one administrator puts it.

The typical adult who sponsors a student has a reputation among administrators for interference in the essential process of "inculcation." She—the large majority of sponsors are women—maintains a complex alliance with the student, alternately assuming the role of friend and of rival guardian. The enduring alliance between sponsor and student—signaled by the sponsor's dispensation of luxury tokens of affection, such as fashionable shoes or expensive technology—is especially disruptive to disciplinary routines, administrators note. A sponsor often "goes against the school" and "sides with the kid" in cases of disciplinary action. She sometimes will remove or threaten to remove a recruit for various pseudo-legitimate reasons: because she is "more homesick for the kid than the kid is for them"; because she discovers that "if she brings her child home she will get more welfare dollars"; or because she intends to put the child to work as a wage earner.

Longtime administrators and alumni contrast the typical sponsor of social orphans with the typical sponsor of traditional Milton Hershey students. As a "working poor" person, the latter understood that travel and visitation would be restricted because of the school's agricultural and disciplinary routines. She acquiesced more readily to administrators' authority and remained effectively indebted to the school and grateful to its governors. By contrast, today's typical sponsor "plays the system," approaching the school as if it were a government welfare agency. "The system is what's all around [the sponsors]," an administrator observes. "And so even though Milton Hershey is not a government agency, to them we're a part of the system. And they think, 'How can we get the most out of this system and put the least in?'"

Arguably, the introduction of social orphans (and their adult sponsors) had more impact on the social order and administration of the school than the introduction of black and female students. Social orphans marked a subtle but distinct shift in the school's mission and mandate. In retrospect, it appears that the introduction of social orphans beginning in the 1970s marked the end of the "old days," as longtime administrators and alumni say, and the beginning of a new era—one in which the traditional moral authority of school would no longer go unchallenged.

THE STUDENT BODY, THEN AND NOW

Milton Hershey School employees convey love, affection, and respect for the individual students under their care; at the same time, they express ambivalence toward students collectively—the student body. Employees who are themselves alumni are especially critical of the "new breed" of student that has populated the school over the previous decade or two. Such students are perceived as disposed toward "bucking the system." They "fight against themselves about everything," as one houseparent puts it. "They constantly divide each other up, four against five, five against ten." Race, ethnicity, and geographic origin are the primary terrains of these divisions and conflicts.

Any new student is expected to resist discipline briefly at the onset, employees say. During that initiatory period, new students test and play against institutional boundaries and the social and personal boundaries of peers and caretakers. What seems to distinguish the "new breed" of student from past generations is protracted resistance. A single student who "doesn't care"—about the institution's goals, its metrics of evaluation, its authority generally speaking—will "ruin" an entire household. Such students "get some kind of intense pleasure out of making other's lives difficult," another houseparent says. The institution is supposed not to have tolerated such resistance in the past: it would have expunged these students. Currently, however, the school is trying to bolster retention rates. Employees share a sense that, as one puts it, "it might be better to keep our numbers lower and help the ones who want to be here"—but they perceive this would be intolerable to the attorney general, especially in light of recent publicity around the Hershey Trust. Under the post-2002 agreement with the state, the school is expected to boost enrollment over the next several years.

Maurice, a houseparent who is also an alumnus, expresses a widely held view that "the kids today are . . . completely different animals" than the students who passed through the institution in the last half-century. "We called it a home," Maurice tells me when we meet for coffee in town. "A lot of students now call it a school, and they might say their home is wherever—no matter their circumstances." An alumnus for nearly twenty-five years and a houseparent for the last several years, Maurice entered the school at ten years old. Originally from Philadelphia, he comes from "a background of drugs, alcohol, and violence. . . . I wasn't a dumb kid; it was my environment." He had gotten in trouble with the law and was at the police station when he heard about the school from the police chief. Maurice was accepted to Milton Hershey within a month of applying.

"Every Milt remembers his first day," he recounts. "I'd never seen so much grass and trees, the big marble building [Founder's Hall]. My mother dropped me off, one of the kids took me and showed me my room, and I was all alone in the strange place with people who were supposed to be my surrogate parents. It was scary." An African American who grew up in a majority black and Latino neighborhood, Maurice was initially struck by his minority status at what was then, in the 1980s, a largely white institution. It was difficult at first to embrace the "new lifestyle that was thrown at [him]," particularly pertaining to the food, clothing, and musical tastes of peers. The unfashionable school uniforms seemed especially ridiculous. Gradually, as he tells it, he began to understand the uniforms and the Milton Hershey way of life as a means of "sharing the same thing, living the same life." The color of his skin "wasn't an issue" after accepting this.

Maurice was lucky to have houseparents who were present when he needed them most, he tells me. His were a "classic 1960s couple": the housemother always had makeup and hair done; she was always dressed "no matter what time." Whereas she was a little harder in demeanor, the housefather was softer—"silent but reassuring"—and would sing in the mornings to wake up the boys. Crucially in Maurice's personal experience, the Milton Hershey School "stopped being a school and started becoming a home" when he decided not to return on vacations to the neighborhood in which he grew up. The peer pressure to participate in his old way of life was strong. In Philadelphia, his acquaintances were stealing cars; they felt he was "acting better than them" by not participating. For a time, he was conflicted: was he still a "tough gangster kid" or an "educated kid who had a future"? To end the conflict, he resolved not to return. The school became the center of his life until he left for college, which the school helped pay for. His mother did not drive but periodically traveled by bus from Philadelphia to visit him during these years.

There were times Maurice wanted to leave—escape even—but he always reconsidered: "What am I really going back to, as opposed to the green grass and the great education?" The years he shared with other students from Harrisburg, New York, and Pittsburgh is "where I saw a future": "I started studying, doing chores, making new connections. I started to see there was something else going on, and a chance for me. I was taught vernacular, manners, being polite, showing respect. All the things that have made me who I am today were instilled in me there. I can honestly say Milton Hershey School saved my life."

Maurice worked in marketing and banking, trained in the Marines, and worked as a prison guard before returning to the school as a houseparent—a career trajectory not atypical of Milton Hershey houseparents. As a house-parent, he tells me he tries to reintroduce some of the "old school" mental-ity—before the administrative reforms of the 1990s. "I know we can't go back to the old days, but there needs to be more of a struggle to be here," he says, echoing a common sentiment among his peers in the institution. "You need to earn your place. You need to earn that name, 'Milt.'" The honor, Maurice explains, relates to "Uncle Milton and Aunt Catherine—because if it wasn't for them, there wouldn't be us."

Maurice teaches the high school–aged girls under his care that partici-pating in community service is a way of reciprocating the gift they have been given by the school founders. He tells them community service can range from picking up trash in a local municipal park, to contributing time and money to national and international charitable institutions (Red Cross, YMCA, Big Brother, Head Start), to finding private employment in a business oriented toward "community" (like the Hershey Company, he points out). The typical student lacks an imagination for community services, Maurice suggests: "Go help someone!" he tells students, and they respond "By doing what?" "Find something you like to do," he tells them, and they plead, "Will you find something for me?" They must do it them-selves, he explains. They perform service grudgingly and without "positive spirit"—one of the five "sacred values" of the school. "Honesty, integrity, judgment, commitment to mission, positive spirit—most alumni would say, that's how they live their lives today." The current Milton Hershey School student body is construed as lacking in these values. Among the current student body, says Maurice, "there is no honor in being a Milt."

The suggestion that today's students take no honor being affiliated with the Milton Hershey School may not be all that novel or recent. My impression is that the accusation that students suffer from school pride–deficiency is long-standing. What is recent or novel, however, is employees' explanation of the origins of the current student body's anomie. Specifically, the story administrators tell about the current student body has to do with the distinc-tion between true orphans and social orphans. While social orphans make up the majority of students at the school today, the "ideal" Milton Hershey student remains the true orphan who loses one or both parents due to illness or in a stroke of misfortune such as an accident. True orphans harken back to the "golden age" of the Milton Hershey School and its original mission as set forth by the founders. Though everyone understands this age has passed, it continues to dominate institutional memory and influence the ideas and actions of employees, especially alumni who work inside the school.

THE LEGACY OF MILTON HERSHEY'S GOLDEN AGE

Milton Hershey alumni recollect the "golden age" of the school just as fondly and fiercely as Hershey residents and company employees recollect the "golden age" of the model town and chocolate company. In 1950s and 1960s, the school had an enrollment of 1,200 boys and had graduated more than 2,500 students since its start. White boys with one or no living parents were the exclusive beneficiaries of the Hershey Trust at this time. Industrial-agricultural routines—specifically those associated with the dairy program—organized the everyday life of the boys and their caretakers. When they graduated, many of the boys would go on to work for Hershey's enterprises.

A short essay published in 1965 in the *New York Times*, "The Hershey School and Its Philosophy of Dignity in Working with the Hands" (Rusk 1965), depicts this period at the school in terms many alumni recognize. The article describes eighty-eight homes, featuring gymnasiums and playrooms, "scattered over 12,000 acres in the foothills of the Blue Mountains." Between twelve and sixteen boys live in each home under the supervision of a pair of houseparents, who each morning drive the boys in a station wagon to classes in the school's instructional facilities. Student's educational programs are "individually tailored to meet each boy's need and desire based on scientific counseling and testing." Half the students are preparing to go to college or university after graduation, for which the school will pay the majority cost and loan the remainder at low interest; the other half are being prepared for vocations such as carpentry, plumbing, food service—"and of course candy making." "The real significance" of the institution, the article notes, is its "philosophy of dignity that it is just as important to do good and creative work with your hands as it is to have an academic degree." The boys training to become plumbers feel "the same pride" as those training to become physicists. "This is social rehabilitation in essence that brings a new dimension to dignity." The article concludes, "The community and school that chocolate built . . . serves mankind as a significant example of total community service in its true meaning."

Memorialized as the "old days," this golden age of Milton Hershey School came to a definitive close at the end of the 1980s, after the school received an alarmingly low grade by a regional state accrediting agency (D'Antonio 2007: 250). Hershey trustees—acting in their capacity as the Milton Hershey School board of managers—responded to the state review by scrutinizing the school's long-standing curriculum and administrative structure. Trustees began to consider that the industrial-agricultural skills taught at the school were less valued on the labor market than in decades past. They began soliciting input from teachers who observed that students did not have enough time to study academic subjects—chiefly because their days were organized around the morning and evening milking of cows.

In 1989, the dairy program became the first orthodox component of the school to be eliminated in a series of controversial reforms that would become known as the "Twenty-First Century Initiative." The fact that the dairy program was instituted a couple of decades after the school's founding bore little on its being taken as an orthodox component. Symbolically, the program was—and remains—representative of the school's origins. As alumni attest, the dairy program was the fulcrum of character education and an instigator of the agrarian work ethic. The new work ethic introduced by the Twenty-First Century Initiative would be a technological one, centered not in barns and farms but in classrooms filled with computers.

After shutting down the dairy program, Hershey trustees recognized a need for fresh leadership to carry out a more extensive reform program. They conducted several national searches for a new president. A non-alumnus, out-of-state education professional eventually was hired, assuming the newly created position of "School CEO." Beginning in the early 1990s, the president and his leadership team undertook "a whole new direction for the school over the next ten years—creating a middle-class boarding school instead of a home for orphaned or disadvantaged children," as one alumnus puts it to me.

The Twenty-First Century Initiative reworked the practical and ideological character of the school from industrial-agrarian and technical-vocational to informational and college preparatory, broadly construed. Hershey's "home for orphans" became a "community," in the parlance of the new administration; the geographical territory of the "homestead" became "campus"; and the young people admitted to the school were awarded "scholarships." The initiative included the introduction of new admissions criteria focused on the academic potential of applicants; new college-accreditation criteria for employees; defunding of agricultural and vocational training; investment in computer technology in classrooms and student homes; selling off or subleasing of trust-owned farmland and consolidation of buildings; pluralization of religious programming; and expansion of psychological services. It coincided with the precipitous firing of several longtime, revered employees and the unionization of houseparents (under the Chocolate Workers Local 464 [see Chapter 3]).

In parallel with these reforms, the new administration attempted to pass a *cy pres* petition through county courts, which would have allowed for the founding of a research institute focused on the education of children in need. The attempted *cy pres*, which possibly would have diverted monies outside of Derry Township to another part of the United States, led to the administration's becoming an object of scorn among alumni and employees who identified closely with the "old days" and the school's "original" mission. The progressive educator from the Midwest who was president of Milton Hershey School for most of the 1990s became a bogeyman in the collective imagination of alumni and employees and largely remains so today.[8]

HOW MILTON HERSHEY ALUMNI BECAME ACTIVISTS

Though they welcomed innovation, many alumni active in the alumni association of the early 1990s were dismayed the school was moving away from the agrarian, "homestead" lifestyle intended by the founders. They worried about the effects of students doing fewer chores. They were disconcerted to learn that the minimum IQ for admission had been raised, from around 80 to 100—disqualifying especially low-functioning children.

The financial threshold had been raised as well, from around $14,000 to $25,000—opening admission to less impoverished families. Even more troubling was the new leadership's focus on sending every Milton Hershey student to college: "a terrific mission—but it wasn't Mr. Hershey's," as one alumnus puts it.

Alumni were especially irked by the new leadership's use of the term *scholarship* as a student recruitment tool. Potential students were told they would be granted "scholarships" to attend the school, which suggested admission based on scholastic merit. The use of the term was meant to counter the school's reputation as a remedial institution, leadership explained at the time; yet, many alumni felt it betrayed the spirit of the deed of trust which, in their understanding, was intended to recruit children who could benefit from programming regardless of demonstrated scholastic merit. The new leadership's description of the school as a "community" in lieu of "a family and a home" likewise drew the ire of alumni. "This isn't a community, where you opt to come here. This is a home," alumni insisted.

In an effort to push back against top-down reforms and make room for their own innovative ideas, members of the alumni association pursued legal counsel for the first time in the history of the association. The association did not enjoy legal standing to sue the Hershey Trust (it eventually appealed for standing in the Commonwealth Court of Pennsylvania and lost in 2005). Yet this did not stop intrepid members from approaching the Pennsylvania attorney general's office and detailing what they considered to be a long history of negligence and self-dealing by Hershey trustees.

These activist alumni drew the attorney general's attention to what they regarded as gross misappropriations of school assets, including using trust money in the 1960s to fund the Penn State Medical Center in Hershey; selling off or transferring of school properties to the Hershey Entertainment and Resorts Company; and abandoning and demolishing historic buildings across ten thousand acres of trust-owned land. Moreover, they pointed to the substantial drop in school enrollment numbers as the value of the Milton Hershey School Trust skyrocketed and trustee compensation increased dramatically. The attorney general responded to alumni activists' pleas by officially inaugurating a preliminary investigation. That investigation continued without resolution for a decade. Meanwhile, reforms at the school proceeded apace.

Had it not been for trustees' deciding to sell the Hershey Company in 2002, the conflict between the alumni association and school leadership "would probably still be happening," an activist alumnus tells me. "The community joined forces with the alumni, and we all got in lockstep against the board—just as the attorney general was deciding to run for governor."

In the collective effort to "Derail the Sale," school alumni, town residents, and chocolate company employees recognized each other as allies: "The townspeople didn't in general care about Milton Hershey School," an activist alumnus recounts. "It's kind of its own enclave and when you go to [townspeople] and say these kids aren't going to get the right training and aren't being admitted the way they should be—townspeople had an empathy for it but not a full understanding. But then someone [at the trust] said, 'Let's sell the town, let's sell the company!' and land prices and jobs and all that stuff begins to look like it's going to change. And man, people went like 'boom!' overnight."

After the success of "Derail the Sale" and the state-led reconstitution of the board of trustees in 2002, members of the alumni association were recruited into leadership positions at Milton Hershey School. Intent on bringing the school in line with what they understood to be the original intentions of the founders, they emphasized the institution's identity as a "family" and "home" rather than a "community" and "prep school." Likewise, they downplayed efforts to recruit young people with scholastic talent and collegial aspirations in favor of vulnerable youth who stand to benefit from Milton Hershey's full range of academic and nonacademic programming. "Preparing kids for college is not the school's role today," a post-2002 administrator explains to me:

> It's the school's role today to take the threes and fours of the world and make them sevens and eights. Somebody who's already a six or a seven will probably become a nine or a ten. Leveling the playing field is what we're supposed to be doing. We want our kids to become the guy next door. We want them to become the person

you can call when you need help—somebody that takes care of their property, somebody that takes care of their family. If you look at what Mr. Hershey said in the deed of trust, it was more about creating the guy next door. The school focuses more on their character than going off to college.

Post-2002 efforts to revitalize a more orthodox mission include introducing a lower economic threshold and lower IQ requirement for applicants; expanding enrollment; recruiting and retaining rural white students—males in particular—under a commitment to "racial-cultural balance"; explicitly Judeo-Christian religious programming; merit-based incentives for financing students' postsecondary education; "iconic" construction projects signaling the legacy of the founders; construction of additional student homes to accommodate a larger number of students; and property acquisitions that will accommodate future expansion (i.e., the controversial acquisition of the golf course [discussed in Chapter 1]). Administrators are intent on restoring nonacademic tracks to the curriculum: culinary arts, industrial technology, automotive mechanics. Above all, they are focused on restoring the home-life aspects of the school, convinced it "has to be a home" to best serve the needs of today's social orphans.

THE FUTURE OF ALUMNI RELATIONS

For all the efforts of the post-2002 administration to restore Milton Hershey School to its original mission, everyone I meet acknowledges the "old days" will never return. Indeed, they celebrate the improvements that have been made since the school's golden age in the 1960s, specifically the crackdown on bullying and elimination of corporal punishment. The "old days" live on, however, in the school's alumni relations programming, which is focused on cultivating a mutual sense of "home" among graduating students and longtime alumni. "Old days" are memorialized in recently refurbished buildings on campus, which serve as offices for alumni liaisons and social space for alumni association members. The Dearden House, for example, is a former student home repurposed as a meeting place that pays tribute to William Dearden—the 1940 graduate who fulfilled the express wish of the founder that "one day, one of the boys from the school will run the chocolate company." Dearden is "widely regarded as a legacy to Milton S. Hershey and his work" (Milton Hershey School Alumni Association n.d.). The physical office he occupied in the 1970s and 1980s as Hershey Company CEO is replicated in a room of the Dearden House, which serves as the school's office of alumni relations. Also replicated are several interiors of student homes from the 1950s and 1960s.

At an alumni association–sponsored event I attend—the "alumni-student fellowship dinner" hosted in a Hershey Entertainment and Resorts property aptly named the Chocolate Ballroom—the importance of Milton Hershey School as "home" is stressed across formal programming and casual conversation. The evening begins with an invocation led by the Alumni Association's chaplain, who thanks God for the food, the fellowship, and for Mr. Hershey and his wife, Catherine, whose actions were guided by the Lord. Among the headlining speakers is a locally prominent alumnus who was given the first name "Milton" as a tribute to the founder (Milton's elder brother preceded him as a student at the school). He shares an anecdote about his time in the institution, which clearly moves longtime alumni in attendance, among others: "One day me and some other Milts decided we didn't want to be here anymore. We wanted to run away. So we started packing our belongings and our houseparents approached us: 'Let us give you some food,' they said, and we agreed. So we left the house with brown paper-bag lunches and walked over the hill where our houseparents could still see us and where we could still see them. We ate our sandwiches, apples, and cookies, and then we wondered, 'What do we do now?' 'Let's go home!' somebody said. And we did. Those were the good old days."

After an awards ceremony—in which students are honored for academic performance and alumni for their commitment to the association—closing remarks are delivered by an alumni relations official. She speaks to the graduating students in the audience about her own fear of leaving the school before college. She encourages students to remain in contact with their houseparents, alumni sponsors, and peers: "Don't forget that you have nine thousand brothers and sisters around the country. Just remember that we're still here." I am surprised when her speech concludes without a request for giving back financially to the institution. The school's acceptance of donations is prohibited by deed, an alumnus reminds me.

At another alumni event, a lunch forum, I have a brief opportunity to talk with a few currently enrolled students—four African American young women in high school. I ask if they think of Milton Hershey School as home. "No, Milton Hershey is nothing like home," one young woman responds with a chuckle: "Here I live with all girls all the time!" I ask if most students like the school. They "like the school after graduation, but not before," one of the senior students reflects. "The rules are really strict. It used to be looser but the new president is stricter," she says. Another young woman expresses how proud everybody is to attend: "We don't boast about it but our families do. Our families tell everyone we're at Milton Hershey." "The best part of the school," says the fourth student, "is the scholarships we get to go to college." Indeed, I am told, this is the value of the Milton Hershey for most of today's students: the school provides an opportunity to go to college to those who otherwise could not afford it.

Decades from now, future Milton Hershey alumni such as these young women will probably have their own idea of the "old days" to impart on graduating seniors. Likely they will have a unique critique of upcoming generations of students, and a different way of thinking about what it means to "take pride in being a Milt." Whether they call the school "home" or not, they will feel impressed upon by the institution and, in some part, indebted to it. Among future alumni who participate in the alumni association, some can be expected to take on the role of stewards and protectors of the school's traditions; others, the role of reform advocates or activists for a new kind of Milton Hershey School. Perhaps they will read the Hershey deed of trust and interpret the founders' original intentions in novel and unexpected ways; or perhaps they will rally around the restoration of some earlier interpretation. In any case, future alumni who care about the legacy of Milton Hershey School are bound to find themselves, at some point in the life of their association, vigorously debating its fate. Whenever that debate happens, the higher learning they received by grace of Hershey's trust will undoubtedly serve the institution well.

CHAPTER 5

⇒ THE GIFT ⇐

We have to make sure we pass it on. Not live in the past,
don't want to do that. But we've got to make sure we
understand what we have: the community, the company,
the school, everything else. We were given a gift.

— A Hershey School alumnus, longtime Hershey Company official, Hershey
resident, and former Hershey trustee, conversation with the author

"THERE'S A LOT OF GOOD HISTORY HERE," Edward tells me as we duck our
heads to avoid the ceiling on the way downstairs. The basement of his home
in downtown Hershey is an unofficial, comprehensive museum of Hershey
history, filled with photographs and artifacts from the early years of the
company and model community. Admission is free. I have been invited here
this afternoon for the same reason I have been invited anywhere in town
over the past year: someone I meet during research reaches out to a friend
and makes an introduction on my behalf—in this case, a former Hershey
executive who rightly suspected I would be interested in Edward's basement
museum and that Edward would be willing to exhibit it.

A baby boomer of Pennsylvania Dutch ancestry who makes his living
as a hospitality entrepreneur along the U.S. eastern shoreline, Edward got
the idea to start a collection at a summer block party in Hershey a couple

of decades ago. In casual conversation, a neighbor asked him, "When did Milton Hershey die?" and when he realized he did not know the answer, he started doing research. At that time Edward's knowledge of Hershey history was limited, he observes. He knew about as much as his children, who were taught in Derry Township's public schools about "a man who failed and succeeded, who built this town and the park and the chocolate factory and the school." No one knew much more than this vague outline.

Edward started learning about Hershey history by collecting it. Beginning with a few postcards of early twentieth-century Hersheypark, he built up his basement museum by patronizing local antique malls and shops and buying anything branded Hershey's. With the rising popularity of online shopping and auctioning websites, he increasingly acquired memorabilia over the last decade. As his collection grew, he started to give talks about the history of Hershey Company advertising for historical societies around the south-central Pennsylvania region. Today Edward has countrywide networks with collectors of Hershey memorabilia—all of whom, he tells me, are "fascinated by the whole story of this poor, young Mr. Hershey who, learning through trial and error, failed and then succeeded."

Edward has presented material to the marketing division of the Hershey Company—correcting the common misunderstanding that the founder, during his lifetime, did not advertise his product. This misunderstanding is rooted in present-day associations of advertising with broadcast media. It is true, as Edward points out, the chocolate company did not engage in national print, radio, and television until the early 1970s, when it inaugurated a national advertising campaign. But Milton Hershey advertised variously and vigorously: for example, purchasing the first automobile in the central Pennsylvania region and driving it around as a billboard for the company.

In its early years, the company promoted itself through inserts in national trade publications such as the *Confectioner's Journal*. One insert, which Edward pulls out of a neatly organized display case and shows to me, touts the Hershey model town and its products under the tagline "A Step Ahead"—a salute to Hershey's turn-of-the-century progressivism. Providing free samples of chocolate was another means of promotion in these early days. Samples were available at the factory where people were invited to visit and make "inspection tours." Grocers' associations regularly picnicked in the nearby park, toured the factory, and sampled the goods.

The town itself was perhaps the most effective advertising for the company and was featured in playbills on Broadway in the early 1900s. Chocolate bars included postcards of the Hershey company town. Edward guesses "no town Hershey's size printed as many postcards of itself as Hershey." Similar to trading cards, which had become popularized around the turn of the century, these postcards traveled wherever the chocolate traveled. Edward's personal favorite features an image of Milton Hershey's mansion with text that reads, "This Is Milton Hershey's Home, The Man Who Owns This Town." "He was kind of a benevolent dictator," he observes, echoing a common refrain: "Loyalty is probably the quality he valued most in people."

Recent scholarship in advertising history shares Edward's interpretation of the founder's penchant for innovative, alternative advertising. What makes Milton Hershey "unique," write Lamme and Parcell (2013), is his "eschewing paid-placement consumer advertising in favor of creatively promoting his utopian town . . . which, indirectly, promoted his chocolate products" (199). Hershey's early approach favored "promotional strategies that conveyed . . . complex ideas to employees, consumers, and visitors about the value of quality, community, harmony, purity, and social compassion," values that, in turn, "reflected well upon the company, the brand, the town, and the man" (206).

Hershey's business practices, in particular the company's indirect approach to promotion, were "aligned to traditions of Mennonite principles" (2013: 200). As Lamme and Parcell suggest, the founder's style of business hewed more closely to his Mennonite contemporaries—agriculturalists, poultry processors, trucking business owners—than to more famous robber barons of the Gilded Age. Early company managers were hired from among the surrounding Anabaptist communities; employees were drawn from about a dozen families in total. Mennonite values of stewardship, hard work, community integrity, and individual economic security eventually "extended to the product, the brand, and the company, even to Hershey himself" in the mind of the public (201). Promotions in trade journals featured "messages and images that conveyed self-sufficiency, purity tied to proximity of dairies and ingredients," but they also referenced "technology and industrial power"—two decidedly non-Mennonite values (202). As the town of Hershey grew, the company shifted to "more complex layers of promotional messages and imagery that were designed to attract to the Chocolate Town potential employees and their families looking for a workplace and quality of life, and then, later, visitors seeking a wholesome vacation destination" (203).

Though his Mennonite background may have been uncommon among U.S. industrialists in the early twentieth century, Hershey was not alone in combining Christian principles with business acumen; indeed, Hershey's chocolate company participated in a wider movement among American businesses toward customer and community "service," which blended liberal republican values with Christian values (Leach 1993: 118). For consumers, "service" meant lines of consumer credit, new pleasurable spaces in which to consume, and highly affective labor by workers hired to serve them; it was essentially a "strategy of enticement," writes historian William Leach, comparable to new uses of color, glass, and light in attracting consumers (147). For employees, "service" meant productive work environments coupled with corporate-sponsored welfare programs. Macy's department store in the early twentieth century, for example, included a hospital and a school along with a publishing outlet for employee prose. Such an arrangement was intended to foster a sense of "family" among workers and ameliorate some of labor's conventional antagonism toward management (Leach 1993: 118–19). Wanamaker's stores likewise boasted employee musical choirs and bands, as well as "employee restaurants and medical clinics, branch public libraries, pension plans, and clubs for language instruction and debates on women's suffrage" (121). An open-air, rooftop gymnasium—perhaps the country's largest at the time—crowned Wanamaker's flagship store in Philadelphia.

The turn toward service among American businessmen "marked something of a turning point in industrial capitalism, which in the minds of many had for so long invoked only dark, satanic mills and undying penury," writes William Leach (1993: 112). It directly addressed the "image problem" of turn-of-the-twentieth-century industrial capitalism:

Between 1895 and 1915, when merchant enthusiasm for service
reached its highest point, many Americans were reacting
against what they perceived to be the repressive, sometimes
violent practices of the new corporations. Industrial workers,
badly treated, revolted against industry, and farmers organized
a populist uprising against the railroads, the banks, the land
speculators, and the utility companies for price-gouging and for
robbing the country blind of its lands and forests. . . . Businessmen
revamped their public image [through service] to try to prove that
they were operating in the best interests of all. (117)

Christian-inspired service remains a significant aspect of the Hershey
brand name and internal company culture; it also furnishes grounds for
criticism of the company among Hersheyites such as Edward, who laments
the gap between Christian values and contemporary corporate practice. As
we conclude our tour of his basement museum, Edward reflects on Milton
Hershey's original "ethic of fairness in making money" and how it has
collapsed under market forces as the business grew. In the early 1900s, he
explains, Hershey had an employee profit-sharing plan in place. Hershey
allowed employees, including women, to purchase property and a home
at a reasonable cost. But after the company's initial public stock offering
in 1927, the founder and his company became "beholden to stockholders."
"The drive for profit," Edward says, subsumed other values associated with
the model industrial community—in particular religious values. Today, "the
all-mighty dollar" rules. "When does the drive for profit turn into absurdity?"
he asks. It strikes me that Edward's investigation into Hershey history, which
started innocently enough at a block party decades ago, has led him to this
point: pondering the ethics and rationality of the corporate profit motive.

Edward is not alone among Hersheyites in his critical reflections. The
hometown pride and sense of good fortune that local citizens share is mixed
with ambivalence toward the growth of Hershey's for-profit enterprises and
uncertainty over whom that growth benefits. Many local families are themselves stockholders in the Hershey Company and thus benefit financially
when the company performs well in the stock market; yet it is not obvious

how growth in the value of company stock benefits the public welfare of the community at large. In fact, some Hersheyites hasten to point out, increases in company stock value tend to coincide with decreases in local, blue-collar, living-wage jobs, which creates even more distance between the corporation and the historically working-class community in which it lies.

Recent scandal involving the Hershey Trust adds another dimension to local citizens' concerns about corporate practice in Hershey: it raises the specter of individuals acting in bad faith. Public allegations of self-dealing among Milton Hershey School trustees gives reason to suspect "corruption" throughout the Hershey ecosystem, and to wonder if the "drive for profit" is primarily serving the self-interests of a powerful, unaccountable few.

The publicity around the trust's purchase of an insolvent golf course and the state investigation and private litigation that ensued gives credence to the locally popular notion that Milton Hershey's entrepreneurial-philanthropic legacy is itself the object of a "hostile takeover." Among those who feel responsible and accountable to that legacy—those for whom investment in Hershey goes beyond stock holdings—the impulse is to take defensive action. But the sort of action required—legal, rhetorical, electoral-political, etc.—is not clearly prescribed. When it comes to advocating for and defending stakeholder interests and rights in private charitable trusts, Hersheyites are experimenting and improvising.

TRUST IN THE RUST BELT

Consider the larger national region in which south-central Pennsylvania lies—the so-called Rust Belt, stretching from the upper northeastern United States through the Great Lakes and Midwest—and it is not hard to understand why Hershey's legacy as a model of business in the service of community continues to be invoked and revered locally. Known through the immediate postwar years as the U.S. manufacturing belt, this broad region began emptying out in the late 1970s and early 1980s as businesses relocated in search of less expensive labor and skilled workers left to seek opportunity elsewhere. What remains today is "a proliferation of rusting factories, declining home prices, population losses, high unemployment, and general economic malaise" (Safford 2009: 3). One does not need to drive far outside Hershey to dwell among the physical and spiritual ruins of the postwar American industrial economy.

Industrial scholar Sean Safford offers some crucial background for understanding the political-economic conditions produced in the Rust Belt. Through the immediate postwar years, Safford writes, the central feature of the U.S. industrial economy was "the large bureaucratic company, itself organized within large industrial complexes":

> Industries were defined by their core products (steel, autos, textiles, and so forth). Manufacturing output was oriented predominantly toward mass production. Frontline workers were represented by labor unions organized, not by craft or occupation, but rather by industry. Economic policy was oriented toward social stability, with Keynesian fiscal programs aimed at achieving full employment and a welfare state that mitigated the social impact of cyclical layoffs. The federal government—particularly following the Second World War—took an active role in regulating a number of key industries, particularly transportation, communication, energy, and banking. The demise of this way of organizing the economy—leading to an extended period of what economists have referred to as a "structural adjustment"— produced the crisis of the rust belt. (2009: 5)

Key to this "Fordist" industrial economy—named for the mode of production pioneered by Henry Ford (with whom Milton Hershey was on friendly terms)—was the "close interrelationship that existed between industries and the communities they inhabited" (2009: 5). Cities such as Akron, Detroit, and Pittsburgh were capitals of the industries they housed. Likewise, industry leaders tended to reside locally and held prestigious positions in the local social order. Corporations depended on the cities for infrastructure, short-term financing, an educated workforce, and labor peace (13). Beginning in the 1970s, that close interrelationship became disaggregated:

The evolution of the American economy toward global supply chains, customer bases, and financing; the emergence of national markets for labor, talent, and financing; and the willingness of communities to compete against one another to provide tax breaks and infrastructure improvements . . . cleaved the economic interests of business leaders from their civic interests. . . . Diminished, downsized, rationalized, and globalized, industrial firms—and their leaders—no longer played by the same rules when dealing with their communities. And because so much revolved around the industrial firm, the redefinition of its identity within communities rippled out to affect the roles and identities of every other actor in these places as well. (2009: 14, 10)

This realignment of economic identities affected other varieties of identity, both inside and outside the Rust Belt. Over the last four decades, for example, creative expressions of a postindustrial ethos have proliferated in American arts and letters, cinema, and music.[1] The absence of industry at the heart of community life is an enduring theme in these cultural productions. Another expression of postindustrial identity—an unfortunate expression, in contrast to creative arts and letters—is what anthropologist David Harvey aptly characterizes as "the cultural nationalism of the white working classes and their besieged sense of moral righteousness (besieged because this class lived under conditions of chronic economic insecurity and felt excluded from many of the benefits . . . distributed through affirmative action and other state programmes)" (2005: 50). "Besieged" white working-class cultural nationalist identity, amplified by national broadcast media such as talk radio and cable news, has become a stubborn feature of U.S. electoral-political discourse in the years since the terrorist attacks of September 11.[2]

No single U.S. community is immune or resistant to political-economic and cultural shifts as powerful as those that produced the Rust Belt, yet the effects are retarded if not dampened in a place like Hershey. Here, legacies of corporate service to community and management-labor cooperation, though tarnished, endure. On account of the Hershey Trust's customary control of the Hershey Company and financing of local and regional development, Hershey's model industrial community remains more or less intact and afloat—for the time being.

Hershey stakeholders do not imagine this untimely arrangement will continue forever, despite the perpetual nature of the trust. Yet they are invested in sustaining it for as long as possible, to pass on the "the gift" of Hershey to a next generation. They are committed to the social reproduction of the community, in which community is understood holistically to encompass the three key components of the founder's model: public township, business corporation, and philanthropy.

Public talk about the private trust—the gossip that preceded scandal and the chatter that persists—is rooted in a dilemma of social reproduction. The dilemma has become only more acute in recent years under the pressure of generational dynamics (namely, the dying out of older Hersheyites with first- and secondhand knowledge of the founding of the model community) and large-scale political-economic forces (not least among them the effects of the Great Recession), as well as other pressures such as shifting local and national demographics and cultural norms.

The trust is figured at the center of this dilemma of reproduction because of its unique agency in the community: as a surrogate for the founder, it holds together the threads of the Hershey tapestry. Accordingly, it has the power to rend and unravel the fabric of local life and livelihoods. The trust is, in this regard, both protector and "disruptor" (to use a term popularized by Silicon Valley) of the Hershey ecosystem. If recent generations of trustees are guilty of anything in the judgment of longtime Hershey stakeholders (to say nothing of allegations of self-dealing), they are guilty of failing to appreciate and prudently wield this relatively awesome power.

"THE GOOSE THAT LAYS THE GOLDEN EGG"

To better grasp the public power of the private trust, I visit the nerve center of civic governance in Hershey—a recently constructed administrative building across the highway from Hersheypark. On the outside, the building resembles the town's public schools, which themselves resemble low-security

151

correctional or holding facilities. Inside, it is equipped with high-end technology for responding to emergency weather and crime situations.

Derry Township police are headquartered here. A courtesy tour of their offices highlights the riot gear on reserve in case of large-scale disorder at the amusement park; potential terrorism is a serious concern. I meet a few officers who are huddled around a computer, watching surveillance video of a drunk driver crashing into a highway barrier the previous night. They chuckle and shake their heads: he was not hurt and he did not hurt anyone else, they assure me, to my relief. Drunk driving, underage drinking and drug use, and domestic disputes top the list of police priorities in this largely safe and quiet rural-suburban township.

In an administrative office on the top floor, I meet township manager Jake. A sensitive and lively longtime public servant and former township chief of police, he eagerly speaks to the role of the Hershey Trust in local public governance. "You have to understand," Jake tells me as I take a seat across from his desk, "when it comes to property owners in the township, the Hershey Trust is the big daddy." With control of the Hershey Company, outright ownership of the Hershey Entertainment and Resorts Company, ownership of a majority of land in the township, and sponsorship of the locally based Penn State Hershey Medical Center, it is well understood that "the trust looks out for its [own] interests."

The trust is especially "concerned about image." Jake points to the badge that until recently he wore as a police officer, which features a graphic rendering of the street signage at the intersection of Cocoa Avenue and Chocolate Avenue in downtown Hershey. Its initial design was a Hershey's bar, he explains, but the trust rejected that. "If a police officer were to do something wrong and the news puts the patch up there and it shows a Hershey's bar, it reflects badly." Instead, the trust hired an artist and developed the alternative logo for the police department. Officers wear the new badge with pride, Jake says: "When Hershey does something, they do it right. They put a lot of thought into it. Nothing looks shabby. Nothing brings discredit to the name. When you're working with Hershey, you know you're going to get a good product."

Jake's desk is adorned with U.S. Marines paraphernalia, including a small plaque inscribed with a heart-wrenching poem he wrote in honor of a close friend killed in battle. A native of nearby Lancaster, Jake entered the armed forces after graduating high school in the mid-1960s; it was a vocational trajectory his father had followed and his grandfather before that. After serving honorably as a marine in Vietnam, he entered law enforcement. When he arrived in Hershey in the early 1970s, the police department had been formed only recently and claimed just four officers; previously, private security hired by the trust patrolled the town as a constable power. Jake participated in a tenfold expansion of the force over three decades, designed to accommodate the increasing number of tourists who visit Hersheypark—up to several million annually. In the process, he refashioned himself personally and professionally from a marine into a "community protector." In Hershey, Jake says, "you [a policeman] feel more like a protector than anywhere else you could go."

Much of Jake's work for the township involves services to the various Hershey entities. A primary responsibility of the police, for example, is to ensure the town remains safe for tourists, who will not visit if there is "a reputation for being a troubled community." At the park's concert venues, officers in uniform and undercover officers in plainclothes direct car traffic, pursue drug and alcohol violations, and make assault-related arrests; occasionally they partner with state police on horseback, who have maintained headquarters nearby since the 1920s. "People come here to prey on the affluence we have," Jake tells me when I ask about crime in the township. "Nine out of ten people arrested in town are outsiders." The township has been "accused of hiding things from the press to make the community better," but he insists this is untrue: "The newspaper publishes all the arrests we make. The township has nothing to hide."

Cooperating with the "Hershey entities" to improve residents' quality of life is a primary concern of township management. Jake gives me an example of cooperation: the chocolate company is planning to build a new production plant in the outskirts of town. The plant will replace the original downtown factory, "19 East," which is slated for demolition. Innovations in efficiency in the new factory mean people will lose their jobs, "and nobody wants to see that." However, Jake explains, township residents will benefit in revenue from building permits as well as a tax assessment on the new plant. The trust and company are putting up land for a downtown improvement project involving a new intersection, bridge, and pedestrian underpass; the township is awarding construction contracts. This exemplifies, in Jake's view, the township's positive relationship with the Hershey entities: "It's all very cooperative and for the betterment of the community."

I ask about the financial condition of the township. Management is putting together its 2012 budget this month. It gets more difficult each year, Jake points out, "because no one ever wants a tax increase." Evidently, the township has not increased certain real-estate taxes since 1987. Next year's projected budget maintains these levels. Eventually taxes must be raised, he explains, but not in the wake of the national economic recession: "In retrospect, had we been smart in the good times, we would have built up a bank. A gradual tax increase would've been the way to go instead of the hammer coming down and hitting them hard."

In lean years like these, when local government revenues are stretched thin, taxes on Hershey entities become contested. Jake tells me about a new lawsuit filed against the trust by the Derry Township School District, which operates the public schools in Hershey. The lawsuit comes on the heels of state budget cuts in education precipitated by the 2007–2008 economic crisis and the subsequent election of austerity-minded Pennsylvania governor Tom Corbett. The substance of the dispute concerns taxes on Hersheypark and, more broadly, the trust's obligations to the school district. The trust pays an "amusement tax" on Hersheypark plus a parking tax (visitors pay to park their cars before entering); these tax revenues are shared between Derry Township government and the Derry Township School District. The trust is additionally responsible for a portion of the school district's annual operating budget—a provision stipulated by Milton Hershey in his last will and testament. The district's lawsuit essentially claims the trust owes more than it is giving. Township government is a mediator between the private trust and the public school district, as Jake sees it. "I wish the school district would ask the trust for more money quietly and in private instead of filing a lawsuit. If you sue now, you might win, but in the long run you lose that cooperative relationship."

The general impulse among township residents to avoid litigating matters involving the trust makes sense in light of local social history and regional political economy. Few communities of comparable size and modest tax base enjoy long-term relationships of reciprocity with a substantial private trust fund; in residents' view, litigation risks undermining that relationship and making an adversary of the trust. Litigation launched during the campaign to "Derail the Sale" of the Hershey Company was exceptional in that it came in response to what Hershey stakeholders—not only township residents but also Hershey Company employees, Milton Hershey School alumni, and others—perceived as an existential threat to the community at large. Settling disputes with the trust "quietly and in private," as Jake puts it, is the norm. "I'm wary about asking too much from the trust," Jake adds. "I just think you don't want to kill the goose that lays the golden egg."

But township residents are not united in resistance to formal litigation, as the school district's lawsuit demonstrates; nor are they united in protecting the "image" of the trust and avoiding public criticism, as fallout from the golf course scandal makes clear. Indeed, the concerned citizens of Hershey are divided over the nature of responsibility entailed in the uncommon relationship between private trust and public community. Precisely what is owed to whom, and how that responsibility is dispensed, is not a cut-and-dried contractual matter; it is an ongoing concern that evolves as new personalities, politics, and legal understandings enter the conversation. Local public opinion on the subject is decidedly mixed, but one trend is clear: Mr. Hershey's "gift" is no longer received and reciprocated in relative silence. People increasingly have a lot to say.

CRITIQUING TRUST

These are a handful of pertinent questions posed by my interlocutors in Hershey over the course of a year. Their animating concern is the nature of responsibility among the trust and its various stakeholders:

⊚ Is the Hershey Trust "corrupt"? Has it been "captured" by powerful players in state and national politics and industry?

- Is Pennsylvania acting as a prudent guardian of the trust's beneficiaries? Are those beneficiaries truly benefiting from their experience with the school?

- Should enrollment at the school grow? Is the school's mission outmoded? If so, might it be "salvaged"?

- What are the ethics of the trust's investments in local entertainment and resorts? Has the trust's investments made the town of Hershey more beautiful or more ugly to live in? Is the trust indebted to the township and its residents, or vice versa (or both)?

- What of the Hershey Company's relationship to the town? Should the company's headquarters remain local?

- Should the trust maintain formal control of the company? Ought state and federal government be more or less involved in oversight and regulation of the trust?

- And what—if anything—would Milton Hershey make of Hershey today?

Arguments about the status and future directions of the trust are motivated by different priorities and outlooks among stakeholders. Many put a premium on expanding enrollment at the school to serve more needy children—the raison d'être of the school trust fund in their assessment. Others emphasize a need for the trust to invest more in the local public community or at least to become more responsive to local public interests. Yet others prioritize intervention by state actors or activist trustees in order to bring about structural changes in the trust's governance that may redefine its mission in the twenty-first century. None of these stakeholder concerns necessarily excludes the others; they emanate from different perspectives on the larger question of responsibility involving the trust.

Hersheyites' concern with responsibility arises from an effort to sort out the obligation between the trust and its "external" publics: those groups of stakeholders who are affected by trust-led activities but who generally enjoy no legal or institutional standing to make direct claims on the trust.

Their concern with responsibility has both ethical and practical dimensions, which is to say, it has to do with abstract notions of fairness, equity, justice, and so on, as well as pragmatic issues such as collecting taxes, managing businesses, holding down jobs, and creating new ones.

There is also a social-cultural dimension to responsibility involving the trust, in that the identity of the Hershey community as a whole is forged in and through relationship to the trust; one might say relationship to the trust facilitates a sense of kinship ("fictive" as it may be) among Hershey-ites. This dimension is perhaps the most difficult to account for—identity is a social phenomenon notoriously tricky to identify—yet it is powerfully salient in conversations.

"We all have a responsibility to give back and to perpetuate this man's dream," explains Jeffrey, a recently retired Hershey Company executive and long-standing town resident. Jeffrey began his career with the company in the Midwest, then he relocated to corporate headquarters in Hershey, where he worked in sales and concluded his career in marketing in his mid-fifties. He lives with his wife in a handsome house downtown. Over glasses of Coca-Cola around the dining room table, I ask him about his understanding of the relationship between trust and community. "What has always intrigued me about this community is the man Milton Hershey and his perseverance to succeed," he begins:

It's interesting to take a look at the man himself and ask, What was his goal? What was his mission? What was his vision? And to try to roll the clock back to the turn of the century. What did we actually have here in Dauphin County? Farmlands, basically. And coal country. Now here comes a man that had a dream—a specific dream—to be successful at manufacturing candy. In order to succeed he realized he had to create an environment that would attract qualified people and also productive people to work in the factories. It was an incredible vision back at the turn of the century. He literally was an entrepreneurial type of person. And then you consider that with the massive wealth he garnered, he came across the idea of actually establishing a trust and he bequeathed all the money to the trust, in order to help those that are less fortunate.

Well beyond the tax burden he bears as a resident of Derry Township and the pension he enjoys from the Hershey Company, Jeffrey's feeling of responsibility toward Hershey implicates his own sense of honor and virtue. "It was an honor to work for the Hershey Company, where the majority of its profits ended up going back to help kids that needed help," he tells me earnestly. "At the end of the day you weren't a 100 percent capitalist pig. You were actually adding value back to society." Jeffrey and his corporate colleagues were prudent and judicious in the investment of money and marketing of products—"because the last thing we wanted to do was taint the imagery or compromise the fiduciary viability of the trust." Employees of the company "all had a firm understanding of our fiduciary responsibility to make sure that we succeeded. We wanted to make sure it wasn't on our watch that we compromised it."

He is skeptical, however, about the idealization of the founder: "Not a bad word is said about Mr. Hershey, but the truth is he wanted control of everything: every element, every store, every utility, everything. I've got to believe he was a son of a bitch!" Nonetheless, Jeffrey continues, "there is a paternal feeling of Hershey because of our benefactor—what he did and how he established it. . . . We're only here for a short period of time and we all, in our own little way, are stewards. We have to make sure that what transpires on our watch gets passed down to the next generation, whether it is keeping our houses tidy or whatever. It comes back to that model community and also to a certain amount of community pride, because this is a very unique society in relation to all the other crap that's going on. This one's working. It's a result, I think, of a lot of collective efforts from many different avenues coming in and coming out."

Despite his officially "retired" status, Jeffrey is well known for being active in the politics of the community. He is involved with the Democratic Party in Derry Township and volunteers financial services to the township school district, from which his daughter and son graduated. In 2002 he was heavily involved in the campaign to "Derail the Sale" of the company.

More recently, he has been involved in the public school district lawsuit filed against an arm of the trust implicating Milton Hershey's intentions for funding the township's public school system. Though thrown out of county probate court in relatively short order, the lawsuit affirms an ongoing division between, on the one hand, Hershey stakeholders such as Jeffrey who are prepared to make juridical claims on the trust and, on the other, those who look upon the trust and its local investments as a "gift" that should not be litigated or otherwise politicized.

A public critic of the trust in writing and in person since his retirement from the chocolate company, he recently published a letter to the editor of a local newspaper about the trust's governance, emphasizing that the original board of directors was made up of local families. Milton Hershey "trusted and had faith in those that lived directly in Derry Township to oversee the trust and do what was necessary and right to perpetuate his vision," he writes in the letter. The original board of directors did not take any compensation for their services: "It used to be an honor to serve the trust, but look at how things have changed. Compensation for trustees is rising in relation to returns, which have gone down." This compensation structure is simply "bad business," Jeffrey observes. The fact that trustees paid multiple times the value of a golf course on the verge of bankruptcy evidences their "naïveté of business." Moreover, he writes in his letter, "like a bad business" the trust has failed in its obligation of "social responsibility" to the Hershey community. The trust makes claims on the public township—pressuring the township to sell property to the trust cheaply and to keep competitors to the Entertainment and Resorts Company out of town, despite the tax benefits and jobs competitors could bring. The township in turn ought to make more claims on the trust, he argues, for example, through more contributions to the township's tax base.

"The Hershey Trust is a nest of politicians and lawyers, comparable in their ambition to the Barnes Foundation," Jeffrey tells me as he refreshes our glasses of Coca-Cola. He refers me to the documentary film *The Art of the Steal* (Argott 2009) about the ultimately successful effort by officers of the Barnes Foundation to depart from the legal will of founder Albert C. Barnes and to relocate the foundation's vast modernist and post-impressionist art collection from suburban Lower Merion, Pennsylvania, to Center City Philadelphia. As the film chronicles, Barnes, a chemist and an entrepreneur, was a fierce critic of Philadelphia elites during his lifetime and strongly resisted locating his art in Philadelphia. In the early 2000s, apparently because of inadequate funding for housing the collection, foundation officials asked courts to authorize relocation of the collection to Center City. *The Art of the Steal* features figures on all sides of the argument over whether to break Barnes's will, including members of the Lower Merion community, officials of Lincoln University (which had managed the collection), current Barnes trustees, journalists, and art historians. The strong editorial view of the film is that trustbusters—savvy politicians and businesspersons mostly—were, in the words of one player in the documentary, "destroying a man's will."[3]

In Jeffrey's judgment, the present-day challenge to Hershey's "unique society" is not dissimilar to what it was a decade ago, when the trust's board of directors was contemplating selling the company: "There could have been a catastrophic closure of multiple business entities in central Pennsylvania—because a lot of industries have built and invested around Hershey's business plan. It was an economic threat in 2002, and thank God the courts agreed with us." The threat today is less immediately economic than ethical: "You've got trustees taking advantage of their position for personal and political ends. Once you establish precedence for this type of attitude, it eventually compromises the purity and simplicity of the deed." "Of course," he adds, "this is how things work everywhere—not just in central Pennsylvania. Trustees have become almost drunk with glee or power and hubris—arrogance—everything we have seen over the last three years with the financial markets."

Jeffrey's critical views, developed from experience working in the company and residing in the town, are echoed as well as complicated by those with experience as students and employees of the Milton Hershey School: Hersheyites such as Bernard, a longtime alumnus and recently retired school employee. When I visit with Bernard in his home office, he points me to a brass statue on his desk. A replica in miniature of one that stands in the center of a water fountain at the entrance to Hersheypark, the statue depicts the founder dressed handsomely in a three-piece suit, hat in hand. For all the collectors of Hershey memorabilia I have encountered over the past year, I have not met the owner of a Milton Hershey statue until today. "Mr. Hershey is watching all of this," Bernard says with a wink as we sit down to talk trust.

In Bernard's view, the trust's current board of directors has "gotten political." He traces the origins of that politicization to the late 1980s and early 1990s—the last time in recent history when the "integrity" of the trust was intact. During that period, he explains, each of the leaders of Hershey's principal entities—the CEO of the chocolate company, the CEO of the entertainment company, the principal of the school, and the chairman of the trust—were, remarkably, alumni of the Milton Hershey School. Each was, in this sense, kindred to the trustor and to each other; they were "brothers." Each sat on the trust board and acted as one of the school's managers. There was little financial compensation for sitting on the board at that time: "It was an honor to be on that board and a privilege," Bernard says, echoing a common sentiment.

The organizational arrangement in the late 1980s to early 1990s "was getting back to where Mr. Hershey left off" when he died; however, for multiple reasons it did not last. For one, trustees were aging, and they retired from the board. Further, the school received a low grade by a regional accrediting agency (D'Antonio 2007: 250), which precipitated an overhaul of its curriculum and everyday practice—the notorious "Twenty-First Century Initiative" (see Chapter 3). As Bernard and many other alumni see it, these changes ultimately led to the attempted sale of the company in 2002 and the controversies involving the trust that followed.

Bernard graduated from the school in the early 1960s and returned there in a senior management capacity on the heels of "Derail the Sale." The "old days" are not as idealistic as they can sound, he tells me when I inquire into his student experience. In his era, an entrenched "bullying system" defined home life. "Growing up in the farm homes was really tough. Kids didn't have much of a built-in moral base." There was a tacit understanding that younger students would be bullied—"almost enslaved"—by older and larger students. "Sometimes it was physical; sometimes it was just doing errands and favors." Houseparents were generally complicit in this scheme, he recounts. Through the early 1960s, most male houseparents were hired by the school initially as dairymen; the majority did not have experience rearing children. They assigned management of the home to the eldest students. In the early 1960s, Bernard recounts, "the back of the bullying system was broken" when school managers—Hershey trustees—introduced a "middle division" of student homes. The middle division, which separated students into three rather than two age groups, is largely regarded as one of the most beneficial changes in the institution since its founding in 1909. It is, perhaps, the school's most innovative gesture.

These days, Milton Hershey School remains overall "institutional" and "custodial," Bernard observes. From a management perspective, it is run "much like a correctional facility." There are few opportunities to experiment with new approaches to care. "That's sad because the scale of the resources you have to invest. . . . You want to know you're doing the very best thing for students." Historically, the school has never been very creative or open to innovation, he explains. Creating the middle division was significant, but most of the other social changes at the school—changes around gender and race, specifically—were "imposed from outside," that is, in response to evolving national social norms and legal imperatives. The challenge of the school today, as Bernard sees it, is to innovate and improve "while staying within the mission, within the founder's intent."

Perhaps because he has experience as both a student and senior administrator, Bernard is one of the few Hersheyites I encounter who articulates a critique of the trust in terms of an oversight, or failure of foresight, on the part of the founder. "Mr. Hershey couldn't see ahead a couple generations to the people controlling the endowment today who don't actually care that much about his mission and vision," he tells me. "This is his fatal flaw of governance." Milton Hershey assumed that "private citizens who become members of the trust would treat the school in the same way that he and his colleagues would do"; he failed to establish "checks and balances." For Bernard, the intensifying secrecy among current board members is more disconcerting than their high level of compensation. "It is one of the most closed and secretive groups now." Such secrecy potentially shrouds attempts to steer the trust's fortunes away from the founder's intent and toward the interests of individual trustees. Simply replacing trustees with other personalities will not fix the "fatal flaw." A vital restructuring of the trust's governing protocols, Bernard suggests, is necessary to maintain the integrity of the founder's vision.

Bernard stops short of naming who or what might bring about a vital restructuring of trust governance or what shape that restructuring might take; but others, such as members of the nonprofit organization Protect the Hershey's Children, Inc., have made concrete proposals and acted both in courts of law and the court of public opinion. An occasionally controversial organization among Hersheyites—partly because of aggressive rhetorical tactics— Protect the Hershey's Children offers the most developed, formalized critique of the trust. "Our ranks include Milton Hershey School alumni, child care professionals, and others who share our desire to protect the Hershey's children," announces the organization's website (protecthersheychildren.org). The website also states that in Pennsylvania alone, "30,000 children are in foster care, costing the taxpayers millions. Managed prudently, the Hershey Trust can provide for thousands more of those children in desperate need."

Since 2002, Protect the Hershey's Children, Inc. (PHC for short) has been engaged in long-term, increasingly wide-scale criticism of trust activities. The organization began publishing a series of substantial essays about the school, the titles of which speak to the passion and frustration of its membership: "Factory for Miracles," "An Orphan's Trust Pie," "Anyone There, Anyone Care?" and "Gaming the System," among others. It has since set out and publicized seven reform goals:

- Ending MHS Board conflicts of interest
- Barring leadership self-enrichment
- Stopping misdirection of assets
- Removing partisan politics from all decisions
- Ending poor child welfare policies
- Hiring and promotion of MHS leaders on the basis of merit
- Creating an MHS Board whose core consists of child welfare professionals

PHC has authored several letters to the U.S. Internal Revenue Service, making a case for reviewing the trust's tax-exempt status. This appeal to federal authorities recalls the notorious case of an American trust run afoul of its philanthropic mission, the so-called Enron of charities: Hawaii's Bishop Estate. A significant, long-standing institution in modern Hawaii and one of the nation's wealthiest charities, Bishop Estate was established by Princess Bernice Pauahi Bishop in 1884 as a school for children with Native Hawaiian ancestry. Beginning in the 1990s, trustees were alleged to have "invested personal funds in business opportunities involving the trust, used trust funds to lobby extensively for changes in laws affecting their personal interests, involved the trust in state and federal political campaigns," all the while legitimating their actions in a legal brief that claimed the "traditional and customary prerogatives" of the dynasty of Princess Bishop (King and Roth 2007). It was not until students themselves began to complain about conditions at the school that public scrutiny was directed at trustees. The IRS eventually threatened to revoke tax-exempt status, and rapid reforms followed in 1999.

A book about Bishop Estate, *Broken Trust* (King and Roth 2006), chronicles the relationship between trustees and stakeholders in terms that many PHC participants use when talking about Hershey; indeed, PHC participants I meet cite the book when discussing reform efforts. Trustees of Bishop Estate had "always been political," writes Hawaii-based journalist David Shapiro in the introduction, "but the earlier generations of trustees were a different breed of political cat." Trustees sitting on the board in the late 1990s "knew little of the collegiality of a boardroom or the fiduciary duties owed by trustees. They were about gaining power by lining up voting majorities and divvying up personal fiefdoms. . . . Most important was the different way these trustees viewed themselves—not as servants of the princess, but as feudal lords, accountable to nobody" (2006: 4). The most important effect of the campaign to reform the estate, Shapiro writes, "was to energize the community spirit and elevate public expectations, ending the pervasive and demoralizing perception that official corruption was an inescapable fact of life in Hawai'i—the price of living in paradise" (8). PHC is effectively positioning itself like the campaign to reform Bishop Estate.

I meet with a chief advocate for PHC—a school alumnus trained as a lawyer who has been pushing hard for reforms for more than a decade. He is known among Hershey stakeholders as an outspoken and more than occasionally angry critic. "I've been questioning the school since day one," he tells me. "That's part of everyone's job, always." As a student in the 1970s and 1980s, he led an effort to allow students to go home on Thanksgiving vacation, which never had been permitted. He also participated in efforts to stop students from being kicked out for minor infractions: "I was a jailhouse lawyer" during his seven years at the school. "I always identified with child care needs because that's my history."

There has been progress at the Milton Hershey School, in his view. The academic programs today are much better than during his time as a student. The staff, teachers, and houseparents are generally well qualified. The buildings are essential resources. But, as he explains, issues involving governance and management have gotten worse: "Forty years ago, the trust had $300 million and there were 1,600 kids served. Today it's $8 billion, and there are only 200 students added. If you believe in luxury golf, grandiose buildings, and hundreds of millions of dollars in local construction contracts, then it's been a wild success—but the fact is, the Hershey Trust's mission is completely underutilized."

The advocate is careful to make sure I take note of national statistics: 540,000 children are in foster care today; 1.4 million children homeless; 6 million living in extreme poverty (half the level of federally defined poverty); 600,000 children's fathers incarcerated.[4] Single-parent households, poverty, substance abuse, emotional illness of the parent, medical condition of the parent or child—such are the "antecedents" for admitting children into at-risk child care facilities. Residential child care facilities across the United States are "a hodgepodge," the advocate observes. Even within states, there are different schemes for addressing at-risk children.

The model of child care at Milton Hershey School is successful "as a model," he explains. The physical model is in place—homes spread out across a beautiful natural environment—as well as the model of parenting by two married houseparents. However, he argues, managers of the school lack "sophistication and training" related to at-risk child care issues. The school admits students who are "easy to handle." That excludes children who stand to benefit most—in particular, minority applicants who are "weeded out" of the admissions process. Managers only know "brick and mortar solutions" to the problems they confront, including the serious problem of retention: they keep building. The school spent $800 million in infrastructure within the last decade—a "construction pigout" that, in his analysis, did little more than subsidize the personal fortunes of contractors in and around Derry Township.

A primary issue of concern for PHC is what happens to students when they graduate. The advocate is particularly alarmed by reports of suicide among alumni.[5] I ask if he anticipates reforms coming from Harrisburg. The state government is "the source of all corruption," he responds. Pennsylvania state governors historically have wanted goals outside the deed of trust—the state university medical center, for example—and they have found ways to accommodate "alternative illegal interpretations." Governors have had their inaugural celebrations at Founder's Hall—the large marble rotunda built on the school campus "supposedly as a monument to Mr. Hershey." The most recent governor to be elected avoided a celebration there only because of recent public attention directed toward the school and trust, he speculates.

As PHC members see it, wide public attention is finally turning to the trust because of a series of exposés written in the *Philadelphia Inquirer* (Fernandez 2011) and their own efforts. They are convinced that law and democratic systems eventually will bring about the reforms necessary to restore the school to what the donor originally intended: a home for as many desperately in need children as possible. And so, they insist, "This story will have a happy ending."

A "HAPPY ENDING"

Hersheyites like to point out that the chocolate company eventually may be sold despite their best collective efforts; the factory might be relocated outside of the township, as have many production lines already; the local entertainment and resorts industry eventually could collapse (it almost did, they recall, a few decades ago); the façade of the town could crumble; the remaining nuclear reactor at Three Mile Island could melt and make ruin of an entire region—not to mention the ever-present threat of tornadoes, hurricanes, floods . . . but the trust will go on forever. Nothing about the future of Hershey is promised but the trust.

In general, no one questions the fact of the trust's perpetuity. Everyone takes for granted that the trust will, thanks to the rule of law, perpetuate. The more pressing concern is, Who can be trusted with the trust? Will future trustees (who are appointed by present trustees) accommodate longstanding public stakeholders? Will they carry on the trust's customary relationship with the chocolate company and local community? If not—if the next generation board breaks with precedent—will they do so with the best interests of beneficiaries in mind? Will they innovate new, better ways to serve Milton Hershey students, or will they devise different ways of serving themselves?

As anthropologists George Marcus and Peter Dobkin Hall observe in *Lives in Trust* (1992), responsibility for managing a trust fund, in particular a family fund, tends to shift over time as a trust grows and matures. Initially, funds are managed by intimates of the trustor: family and close associates. Gradually, the responsibility for management is outsourced to more professional fiduciaries: wealth managers, lawyers, and the like. For beneficiaries, this managerial drift may be experienced as "dynastic dissolution": the sense that a great lineage is fading away, even though the trustor's wealth may be compounding at a healthy clip. Beneficiaries may choose to self-identify more strongly with the dynastic lineage as one way to counteract the feeling of dissolution, but few elect to get more involved in the technical intricacies of wealth management, which seemingly grows more complex by the day.

Among those who identify most strongly with the legacies and lineage of Milton and Catherine Hershey, the idea of outsourcing the trust's management to purely professional administrators is not ideal. Bureaucratic experts—characterized by "emotional detachment" and "forgetfulness of self," exercising duties and obligations "without regard to person" in "accordance with calculable rules . . . [to the exclusion of] love, hatred, and every purely personal, especially irrational and incalculable, feeling" (Weber 1954: 350–51)—may not keep the customs and values of the founding family in mind, even as they execute the letter of the Milton Hershey School deed of trust. And yet Hersheyites recognize that in the absence of disinterested experts, "self-interestedness" and incompetence all too often reign.

Is Hershey's distinctive dynastic arrangement in a state of dissolution? Is the Hershey lineage, "fictive" as it may be (because not rooted in biogenetic descent), fading away? Alumni of Milton Hershey School say the current generation of students lacks "the pride that comes from being a Milt"; they worry about a lost sense of heritage. Yet alumni themselves are filled with pride across generations, and presumably the newest, youngest cohorts among them will eventually feel similarly. Hershey Company employees point to the recruitment of outsider leadership as a sign of changing times; they worry that the chocolate company is becoming "a company like any other," one that "used to care about the community" but does no longer. Yet seemingly against the odds, the company remains headquartered in Hershey with a new factory under construction to replace the old one, and the Chocolate Workers Local 464 continues to be an effective advocate for labor's interests. Hershey residents, for their part, bemoan the sprawl of the "Hershey Entertainment Industrial Complex" and, in certain cases, the diverse newcomers moving into their neighborhoods; some wonder if the small town in which they grew up or chose to settle has been ceded to tourists and strangers. Yet Hershey today is no more or less a tourist town than it ever was (it is an attraction by design), and community members continue to find ways of welcoming newcomers despite lesser impulses to keep them out.

Hershey's quasi-dynasty appears to be thriving. Still, Hersheyites brood over the future of the local ecosystem. Will long-standing relations of reciprocity among township, company, and charity survive? "It all comes down to that trust board," one longtime resident puts it to me, echoing a common refrain.

The fate of Hershey does not rest solely in the hands of a trust fund's governance, to be sure. But decisions made by trustees will help determine, locally, the shape of things to come. Hersheyites are rightfully concerned with having a voice (which is not to say a vote) in decision-making processes. They understand that Hershey's trust was never a democratic institution in the sense of being governed by the people—it was always private property—

yet it exists solely to benefit the public interest. Recent scrutiny directed toward the trust is intended to clarify that interest; it is likely to endure if not accelerate in the years ahead. Incoming generations of trustees can expect that, whatever path Hershey's entrepreneurship and philanthropy take, ordinary citizens advocating for the public interest will be there to pave the way forward or, as necessary, block it. And that may suffice, for now, as a happy ending to the perpetual Hershey story.

⇒ CONCLUSION ⇐

I LEFT HERSHEY IN AUTUMN 2011 when the scandal over the trust was still new and its implications uncertain. Around this time, adjacent concerns related to Hershey attracted local and national public attention: the Milton Hershey School's refusal to admit a student diagnosed with HIV,[1] as well as the labor exploitation of foreign college students working in a regional facility that packages Hershey products.[2] The state government's probe into the trust proceeded amid these fresh headlines. Hersheyites could be forgiven for thinking the bad news would only get worse.

Pennsylvania's investigation into the Hershey Trust officially concluded in 2013 under the direction of a new attorney general, Kathleen Kane—the first Democrat and the first woman to be elected to this office in Pennsylvania. Among other findings, Attorney General Kane found that the golf course purchase was reasonable given fair-market values and the school's intended long-term use of the property; that evidence of self-dealing by trustees was insufficient; that allegations of illicit political contributions were unfounded because the contributions were made not by the trust itself but by its subsidiary, the Hershey Entertainment and Resorts Company; and that increases in compensation for board members were reasonable in comparison to peer institutions. No evidence of breaches in fiduciary duty was established (Pennsylvania Office of Attorney General 2013b).

Kane announced a new agreement with the trust that supplanted the one established after the attempted sale of the company in 2002. The agreement set out renewed guidelines for, among other things, conflicts of interest, board compensation and expenses, legal counsel, real estate, admissions and academic standards, student safety, and the reporting of relevant information to the attorney general's office. It reflected some key concerns of various critiques of the trust—calling on trustees to "use their best efforts to identify for election to their Boards [candidates] whose education, training and experience reflect the full range of the Boards' responsibilities," including "at-risk/dependent children" and "residential childhood education" (Pennsylvania Office of Attorney General 2013b: 2). But it stopped short of substantive reforms. "My office will continue to diligently monitor the activities of the Hershey School Trust to make sure that the use of Trust assets is entirely consistent with Milton and Catherine Hershey's donative intent," Kane remarked in a statement. "Their landmark perpetual generosity demands nothing less" (Pennsylvania Office of Attorney General 2013a).

In the hours and days following Kane's announcement, public responses appeared in the comments section of *Pennlive.com*, a regionally popular online news outfit run by the Harrisburg *Patriot News* (Malawskey 2013): "Just a big fat kiss on the cheek!" writes one commenter. "A slap in the face to taxpayers to say the Hershey Trust has been above board," comments another. "A watered-down agreement by influential people and politicians. A sad day for the legacy of Mr. Hershey's School," comments another. Yet another post consists simply of a dictionary entry for the word *conspiracy*— implying a secret plot between attorney general and trustees. Such are a handful of local interpretations of the state government's exercise of its *parens patriae* power over charities.

Disappointed the agreement did not go far enough and skeptical of the state's ability to enforce it, Protect the Hershey's Children, Inc. continued pursuing other means of holding trustees to account. The organization publicized cases of students allegedly expelled from Milton Hershey School because of their mental illness; it also began drawing public attention to the dearth of physically disabled students on campus. The evidence marshaled by PHC helped spur a Justice Department probe, beginning spring 2016 and ongoing as of this writing, into the school's compliance with the Americans with Disabilities Act.

In the wake of the attorney general's investigation, Hershey townspeople and company employees observed the demolition of the chocolate factory at 19 East Chocolate Avenue. Remaining portions of the facility were refurbished into offices for the company's growing international departments: Global Shared Services, Global Marketing, and Global Knowledge and Insights (Malawskey 2015). Concurrently, a few minutes' drive from 19 East, the golf course at the center of the scandal over the trust closed for business—bringing the number of golf courses in Hershey down to three. The trust announced that additional Milton Hershey School housing would be built on the property, reportedly to accommodate between three hundred and four hundred students.[3]

Hersheyites did not have to wait long for more newspaper headlines about their homegrown trust. In early 2016, news broke that the Pennsylvania attorney general was investigating violations of the terms of the 2013 agreement. This most recent investigation was precipitated by internal trust documents leaked to the press and attorney general's office that exposed infighting among trustees and raised numerous new concerns about misconduct and possible insider trading of Hershey Company stock.

Evidently, factions of trustees had been feuding since the 2013 agreement, and the chairman of the trust had been subjected to internal scrutiny for using his position to secure a summer finance internship for his college-aged son. A law firm hired by the trust to investigate the chairman's activities concluded he had engaged in no wrongdoing. Apparently in retaliation, the chairman accused two trustees of trading Hershey Company stock on insider knowledge. Internal legal bills mounted—$4 million alone for the report that exonerated the chairman—and four board members resigned, presumably in frustration at the toxic boardroom atmosphere.

When the attorney general's office got wind of the internal legal investigations and allegations of insider trading, it threatened the trust with legal action and set out to forge a deal that would supersede the one from 2013. The new agreement reestablished term limits that trustees previously had ignored; specified additional limits on the number of trustees who could participate in other Hershey corporate boards; set somewhat less generous caps on trustee compensation; spelled out a "conflict of interest policy" focused on perks, travel, and hotel reimbursements; reaffirmed the goal of a thirteen-member board made up of professionals with expertise relevant to the mission of the school; and determined a path for five longtime trustees to retire in the next several years (Pennsylvania Office of Attorney General 2016).

Attorney General Kane publicly announced the terms of the new deal in July 2016, but—as news reports and political pundits hastened to point out—she was prevented from officially signing off on it. Kane's license to practice law had been suspended stemming from accusations that she had leaked sealed grand jury documents to a reporter to embarrass enemies in Harrisburg and then lied about it under oath. One week after announcing the new agreement with the trust, she was formally charged with perjury and an assortment of obstruction-of-justice charges. Less than a month later, Kane was convicted in court on all counts and resigned her post.

The irony that the trust's primary watchdog was now a convicted felon was not lost on those Hersheyites who consistently have questioned the integrity of state oversight.

TREASURING THE TRUST

In summer 2016, the Hershey Company also made headlines. Yet again it became the subject of a high-value takeover bid, and yet again Wall Street turned its attention to the idiosyncratic relationship connecting the chocolate company, trust, community, and state government. This time the bid came from U.S. multinational Mondelez, makers of Oreo Cookies among other confections, and the number on the table reached $23 billion.

Analysts touted the deal as a potential blockbuster: Mondelez, once a branch of Kraft, is the second-largest confectionery in the world but has minimal U.S. presence. Hershey's, on the other hand, is one of America's largest candy companies but has struggled to expand outside North America. But the trust remained an X factor. Mindful of Wrigley's failed bid for the company in 2002, Mondelez tried enticing the board of trustees with assurances that the newly combined company would be called Hershey, that it would be headquartered in Hershey, and that local jobs and production would remain in place. Those efforts were in vain.

The trust rejected the offer without public comment, and Mondelez formally dropped its bid shortly thereafter. Analysts immediately began speculating that Mondelez itself was now a prime takeover target for some other, larger conglomerate—perhaps Kraft Heinz, Pepsi, or General Mills. For its part, Hershey's experienced a substantial dip in stock value; yet soon enough, Wall Street was again hailing it as an attractive bet for long-term investors (Hoy 2016).

On the heels of the failed deal, the announced retirement of Hershey CEO John Bilbrey precipitated speculation about his replacement and whether this was finally the moment for a newly constituted trust board to reevaluate its long-standing control of the company. The replacement turned out to be the first female CEO in Hershey's history, Michele Buck, an eleven-year veteran of the company who lives with her family in the community. That decision was publicly applauded for being progressive (a woman in the top leadership position) and, at the same time, conservative (an established insider committed to preserving the company culture). It gave little hope to those who would like to see a takeover.

As in 2002, the trust's refusal in 2016 to sell the Hershey Company exasperated financial and philanthropic observers who saw it as a dereliction of fiduciary duty to Milton Hershey students and a poor business decision for the Hershey Company. Among those observers, legal scholar Robert Sitkoff suggested in an interview with the *New York Times* that accepting Mondelez's bid was the fiscally and morally responsible decision to make; failure to do so was further evidence of the Pennsylvania commonwealth's indefensible interference in the private affairs of a charitable trust and business corporation (Segal 2016). Sitkoff pointed to the state law enacted after the canceled Wrigley's sale that required trustees to seek approval of any transaction involving control of the Hershey Company: "Imagine if the legislature of New Jersey passed a bill that said Princeton had to invest more than half of its endowment in one local company? That's what the Pennsylvania Legislature did in 2002. It's outrageous. The Trust is supposed to be rescuing needy kids" (Segal 2016).

Opinion on the Mondelez bid was not uniform, however. Corporate law scholar Steven Davidoff Solomon, writing in his capacity as *New York*

Times "Deal Professor," suggested that the Hershey Trust is putting "politics and relationships" over economics, and raised the possibility that this is legitimate and welcome. "While Hershey's stock price performance in the last three years has not been great, over the decades it has delivered outsize growth and profits while benefitting the local community and preserving an important way of life," Solomon writes. "While I wouldn't want many companies to be in Hershey's predicament [i.e., beholden to the controlling interest of a charitable trust] perhaps it is a jewel to be treasured, one that should be exempt from the laws of economics and today's hyper market efficiency. And perhaps it should stay that way" (Solomon 2016).

Reflecting on my year in Hershey, I am not persuaded by critics who insist trustees are duty-bound to sell the company and that neither the local community nor the state legislature has a right to interfere. Such critics tend to favor an abstract ideal of fiduciary responsibility over the sociolegal precedents and customary institutional arrangements unique to Hershey. Those who would urge trustees to sell the company tend not to account for the potential merits of an industrial foundation arrangement (along the lines Hansmann and Thomsen have argued [2012]; see Chapter 1). Likewise, they tend to overlook the fact that trustees are also managers of the school; trustees' duty to beneficiaries is not only fiduciary but also educational and moral. Indeed, board members may claim prudent reasons for protecting and nurturing the school's customary relations with the chocolate company and surrounding community. After all—as the county probate court found in 2002 in response to "Derail the Sale"—the trust's controlling interest in the company ensures an element of predictability in the economy of the larger community of which the school is a part. Board members may determine that this predictability has high value in a context of education and childrearing, especially among children whose backgrounds are characterized by displacement and precariousness.

Arguments in support of the trust's decision not to sell the company are independent of arguments in favor of reforms in Milton Hershey School management. Observers have encouraged top-to-bottom reforms that would bring the school in line with "best practices" in residential child care and at-risk youth education (I think here of criticisms by Robert Fernandez of the *Philadelphia Inquirer*, Pablo Eisenberg of the Center for Public and Nonprofit Leadership at Georgetown University, and Protect the Hershey's Children, Inc., among others). But such reforms are not incumbent upon the trust's surrendering control of the company. The Hershey Trust does not need to increase its $12 billion endowment to implement best practices or even to serve a greater number of students.

Some Hersheyites speculate that "Mr. Hershey" might have sold the company himself had he lived past 1945. He considered selling it earlier, they note; the start of the Depression evidently put a stop to negotiations. They muse that Milton Hershey was, above all, a money-minded businessman who ultimately could not resist an opportunity to optimize returns. Such speculation is not without merit. Ultimately, however, the decision to retain certain institutional customs and dispose of others is the prerogative not of Milton Hershey but of our contemporaries: sitting and incoming trustees, political office holders, legal and business professionals, and, most significantly, ordinary citizens acting together voluntarily in the public interest.

Arguably, the trust's control of the chocolate company warrants both preservation and cultivation. Trustees present and future should consider embracing this arrangement and experimenting with the possibilities of a uniquely American "industrial foundation." Preserving and cultivating the trust's controlling interest in the company means embracing the social—and financial—virtues of not-for-profit ownership of a business corporation, while remaining alert to the risks (e.g., a potential collapse in the North American chocolate market). It means striving for equity between on the one hand, the rights and interests of shareholders in the Hershey Company and, on the other, the rights and interests of shareholders in the Hershey "ecosystem"—all while prioritizing the rights and interests of the trust's beneficiaries.

In our Second Gilded Age, citizens in the United States and across borders are rightfully concerned with alternative models of corporate power that respect historically embedded social and economic ties, that offer greater predictability, and that grow both more slowly and more steadily than conventionally structured business corporations. Hershey's, under control of the Milton Hershey School Trust, is one such model: a "slow capitalist" enterprise. We should celebrate its difference and innovate upon it.

By the time this book is published, it is quite possible that the Hershey Company may already be sold—acquired, merged, spun off, maybe even liquidated. It is not hard to imagine a future scenario in which the brand name Hershey's is detached from anything chocolate or candy related and applied to some other global good or service (a chain of gated communities? a line of athletic-leisure wear? an online business school, Hershey U.?). But if Hershey's no longer exists, or exists in brand name only, it is not because the chocolate company was fated to be sold. Fate had nothing to do with it. Selling the company was a choice. Like all choices, it could have turned out otherwise—such is the "moral" of the Hershey story.

THE FUTURE OF THE ENTREPRENEUR-PHILANTHROPIST

During my time in Hershey, Pennsylvania and since, I have been challenged to consider the cultural power of the entrepreneur-philanthropist in our Second Gilded Age. From one perspective, the dominance of this figure in public life is cause for alarm. It is a sign that citizenship is receding; that ordinary citizens, who recognize that the state puts the welfare of corporations and special interests over the welfare of families and communities, are ceding their political agency to unelected, unaccountable, hyper-affluent private individuals, in the hope that they will advocate for the common good. In this light, we should be skeptical of the collective exuberance that greets each new announcement of a mega-philanthropic donation by a recently minted tech or finance billionaire. We should ask what it means for the legacy of democracy.

From another perspective, the dominance of this figure may be a sign that social norms around self-made wealth are evolving and progressing. It is becoming far less socially acceptable to make a fortune in business and hoard it for oneself and one's heirs. Successful entrepreneurs are expected to redistribute their personal wealth to benefit others. Today, the prestigious, noble, sexy, "cool" way to distinguish oneself from one's nouveau riche peers is to donate one's money strategically to people and causes who need it most. This emergent norm around self-made wealth may not directly benefit democracy, but it does not obviously harm it, either. In this light, we should salute the figure of the entrepreneur-philanthropist as a welcome cultural alternative to the miserly tycoon.

Other perspectives abound; only so much can be said without taking account of specific individuals. Bill Gates, founder of the Microsoft Corporation and the planet's wealthiest person, is a paragon of the twenty-first-century entrepreneur-philanthropist. Few would deny that the foundation Gates and his wife launched in 2000 is a force for good in the world. With an endowment reaching $40 billion, the Bill and Melinda Gates Foundation contributes to global health and global development, as well as libraries and education in the United States. It critically supplements, and in some respects surpasses, the investment capacity of nation-states. But celebrations of the Gates Foundation's virtuous efforts across the globe are accompanied by critical questions about the accountability of its three American trustees (Bill Gates, Melinda Gates, and Warren Buffet, who has pledged most of his fortune to the Gates Foundation). "The Gates Foundation's biggest challenge," observes legal scholar and philanthropist Joel Fleishman, "may be responding appropriately to the increased scrutiny it can expect as the steward of such a massive sum. The public attention drawn to a foundation governed by only three trustees who will oversee its annual spending of around $3.5 billion has already sparked public concern over its scale and the lack of broader accountability, as well as curiosity about how and how well the Gates Foundation will manage to spend such large amounts of money wisely and effectively" (2009: 47).

Concerns about the democratic accountability of private philanthropy are likely to grow more urgent as fortunes made in the early twenty-first century are converted into charitable dollars, particularly in the United States. Politics scholar David Callahan observes that American "big philanthropy" is becoming a power center equal to U.S. government, shaping politics and policy agendas: "We face a future in which private donors—who are accountable to no one—may often wield more influence than elected public officials, who (in theory, anyway) are accountable to all of us." This significant power shift is difficult to record and analyze because, as Callahan points out, "nonprofit laws allow rivers of money to sluice through society in opaque ways"; likewise, philanthropists and charitable organizations tend to operate "subtly. . . . Their fingerprints can be hard to see" (2017: 8). Hershey's trust is no exception in this regard, as the foregoing chapters attest.

In terms of its organizational structure, the Hershey Trust is not emblematic of the new philanthropy; it shares more in common with nineteenth-century charities than with modern, "third sector" foundations, as I have noted. However, the public scrutiny directed toward the trust is motivated by the same concerns about accountability that underlie public scrutiny of charitable organizations across the country and globe. The criticism that the Hershey Trust acts virtually like a sovereign in Hershey, Pennsylvania, is not unlike the criticism leveraged at the Gates Foundation in the developing world. The former may be regarded as an antecedent to the latter.

The situation in Hershey suggests that philanthropic organizations can deepen their commitment to accountability by attending to external stakeholders: people and organizations who are neither agents nor subjects of philanthropy but who are, for better or worse, caught up in its activities. As my analysis shows, the Hershey Trust's activities extend well beyond the formally circumscribed arrangement among trustor, trustee, and beneficiary and impact multiple publics, including Hershey community residents, Hershey Company employees, and Milton Hershey School alumni; though not recognized as official parties to the deed of trust, these external stakeholders clearly have an interest in decisions made by the trust and entitled to a voice. A similar observation can be made about philanthropic activity broadly construed. Donors and administrators can be more accountable by anticipating and responding to the interests and concerns of external stakeholders.

An opportunity also exists to broaden the public conversation about private philanthropy beyond the subject of donors and recipients. It is important to account for why and how donors give, what it is like to be on the receiving end of the gift, and what difference the donor-recipient relationship makes (its "impact," quantitatively and qualitatively construed). But aside from that relationship, there is much to learn about philanthropy from adjacent fields: communities in which charitable organizations are based and operate, industries and corporations that are impacted negatively or positively by philanthropic activity, informal social arrangements and cultural practices that arise out of formalized giving, and so on. There is also much more to uncover about the unintended consequences of philanthropy and the power of anti-philanthropic counterforces.[4] Philanthropists will likely be more effective, and democratic processes more robust, if we learn from external stakeholders about how philanthropy creates collateral impact (which is not to say collateral damage).

The foregoing chapters represent one attempt to look beyond the donor-recipient relationship toward other social arrangements produced and sustained by philanthropy. They also serve as a reminder that, in the United States, the association between charitable giving and consumer capitalism is long-standing and integral to modern American culture. Hershey's trust—a private charitable organization that owns a public business corporation—exemplifies the link, forged in in the United States in the early twentieth century, between the business of doing good and the business of selling and buying goods. That link endures in the twenty-first century, in which a growing market exists for brands and consumer goods that are associated with "doing good." Indeed, the Hershey Company may be regarded as an antecedent to emergent types of philanthropy-oriented business corporations. These include "social enterprises," in which a company implements a business model designed to achieve a socially beneficial goal; "double bottom line" or "benefit" corporations, which measure business success in terms of both profits and social impact; as well as companies and brands closely associated with the corporate social responsibility movement. The long-term social and economic effects of these novel corporate forms, and their consequences for democratic practice, are only beginning to come into view.[5] How these corporations will complement or clash with individual philanthropists and private foundations is an open-ended question.

Hershey's legacy of entrepreneurship and philanthropy, idiosyncratic as it may be, is a forerunner to the philanthropic-inspired capitalism and capitalist-inspired philanthropy that is increasingly familiar today. In this regard, the story of Hershey—the man, the town, the company, the charity—is as relevant as ever. The story provides a powerful myth for our times—not only in the United States, but anywhere consumerism prevails. It gives voice to the ordinary dreams and wishes of everyone who participates in consumer capitalist culture: the dream of becoming personally successful, and the wish that the most affluent among us will serve the common good. Hershey's is not the only popular story that speaks to the desires of modern consumer-citizens, but it is among the most persuasive and endearing. For this reason, it seems destined for a long shelf-life in our collective imagination.

NOTES

INTRODUCTION

1. The 2010 U.S. Census includes the following data about Hershey, Pennsylvania: population, 14,257; 81.5 percent white not Hispanic or Latino, 6.6 percent Asian, 6.2 percent African American, 3.2 percent Hispanic or Latino; foreign-born persons, 11.5 percent; educational attainment of bachelor's degree or higher (age 25+), 52.3 percent; median value of owner-occupied housing units, $243,800; per-capita money income in past 12 months, $35,605; persons below poverty level, 13.9 percent. For other census data related to Hershey and for a comparison with Pennsylvania state and national data, see U.S. Census Bureau 2010.

2. Michael D'Antonio's *Hershey: Milton S. Hershey's Extraordinary Life of Wealth, Empire, and Utopian Dreams* (2007) is the biography of record. For other histories of Hershey, see Castner 1983, Halbleib 2005, McMahon 2009, Shippen and Wallace 1959, Snavely 1935 and 1950, Sutcliffe 2003, and Whiteneck 2006.

3. *Black's Law Dictionary* defines fiduciary duty: "When one party must act for another. They are entrusted with the care of property or funds" (Garner 2014).

4. *Pleasantville* (Ross 1998) is a film about a brother and sister who are transported into a 1950s-era American family sitcom.

5. On traditions and "roots" of consumer capitalism around the globe, see Boon 1999, in particular, chap. 13, pp. 256–62.

6. On recent decades of cultural anthropology in and about the United States, see Greenhouse 2011. See also Cattelino 2010. On doing ethnographic fieldwork "at home," see Passaro 1997.

7. I do not claim to represent the ecosystem comprehensively or definitively. Mine is a partial and idiosyncratic account, based on my own interests and impulses as an ethnographer and, inevitably, limited by blind spots and biases; yet, I strive to depict general features of Hershey that any fieldworker would likewise observe. The approach I take is broadly interpretive, aimed at what social scientists call "thick description"

(following Geertz 1973 and 1983). The point is not only to describe "what goes on" in Hershey but also to account for its cultural significance.

CHAPTER 1

1. On scandal and gossip as informal mechanisms of social control among communities, see Rosen 2006. See also Fine et al. 2005; Scheper-Hughes 2002; White 2000.

2. In accordance with research ethics protocol, I have assigned pseudonyms to my interlocutors and modified some details of their identities.

3. For a history of Pennsylvania electoral politics, see Madonna 2008. Derry Township, in which the census-designated place of Hershey is incorporated and which was first incorporated in the eighteenth century, has voted Republican in most elections—local, state, and national—since the mid-nineteenth century; however, there are exceptions: in recent years, an independent was elected to Derry Township's board of supervisors.

4. *Black's Law Dictionary* defines "trust" as "an equitable or beneficial right or title to land or other property, held for the beneficiary by another person, in whom resides the legal title or ownership, recognized and enforced by courts of chancery" (Garner 2014). Modern American trust law is derived from common law in general and English law in particular, which allowed devoting property to a particular charitable purpose through the device of a charitable trust, beginning in the sixteenth century (Madoff 2010: 92). Though characteristic of common law systems, legal trusts are not unique to common law systems: consider, for example, the Islamic *waqf* (Arjomand 1998).

5. The status of the Hershey Trust was critical to the creation of the category of "supporting organizations" (509(a)(3) organizations) (DiRusso 2006: 213). The legislation allowed a supporting organization to retain control of for-profit enterprises. Such organizations derive their "freedom from income tax by reason of [their] relationship with other charities who enjoy broad public support" (209). Like charitable organizations, supporting organizations are understood to be providing some kind of public benefit such as poor relief, religious advancement, educational or scientific advancement, construction or maintenance of public works, and so on.

6. The Carlsberg Foundation apparently emerged from a personal conflict between the founder of the Carlsberg brewery—J. C. Jacobsen—and his son, Carl (Carlsberg Group n.d.). The family business was passed on to the foundation instead of the natural heir.

7. Jeffrey is referring to Flint, Michigan, the former General Motors factory town that sank into a deep economic depression in the 1980s after the company closed production facilities and which, in 2011, declared a state of financial emergency for the second time in a decade. Michael Moore's documentary *Roger and Me* (1989) is a vital document of Flint's struggles that doubles as an attempt to revitalize the community. See also Dandaneau 1996. Cf. Dudley 1994 on the closing of the Chrysler car plant in Kenosha, Wisconsin.

8. See Brody 2004; Klick and Sitkoff 2008; Komoroski 2003; Schramm 2006; Sidel 2003.

9. For a classic formulation of agency costs, see Berle and Means 1991 [1932].

10. Despite my multiple efforts to arrange a conversation, Mr. Reese would not commit to speaking with me. Evidently he was avoiding journalists in part because of the legal implications of press exposure; probably, as an ethnographer, I was associated with a sort of journalism. See Lederman 2004 on the "suggestive boundary problems" among anthropology, journalism, and other academic and professional disciplines.

CHAPTER 2

1. One might say Hershey's charisma resides, following Geertz (following Shils), in his symbolic relation to the active center of a social order. Charisma is "a sign, not of popular appeal or inventive craziness"—a routine misreading, Geertz suggests—"but of being near the heart of things." The center has "nothing to do with geometry and little with geography" (quote from Shils); the center is, rather, a "concentrated loci of serious acts . . . an arena in which the vents that most vitally affect its members' lives take place." It is involvement with the center that "confers charisma" (Geertz 1983: 122).

2. "M.S. was terribly knock-kneed" (Paul Wallace Research Collection, Box 1, Folder 33, p. 10). "He was of the old school" (Box 1, Folder 42, p. 1). "Mr. Hershey would do a favor" (Box 1, Folder 46, p. 1). "He talked in a high-pitched, eager, nervous voice" (Box 1, Folder 53, pp. 3, 2). "He did eat an enormous amount of candy" (Box 2, Folder 51, pp. 3, 9). "Mr. Hershey was a very fair-minded man" (Box 3, Folder 36, Item 33). "He told me his religion was the Golden Rule," recalls his personal nurse (Box 4, Folder 6).

3. Rowntree's—another English Quaker confectionery and a rival of Cadbury—modeled its company town at New Earswick on Cadbury's Bournville.

4. The Bournville Trust continues to operate; the Cadbury Company was acquired by Kraft in 2010 (after briefly being considered for purchase by Hershey Company; see Chapter 4).

5. Famously, the Cadbury factory inspired Roald Dahl's children's novel *Charlie and the Chocolate Factory* (1964). Dahl spent his adolescence at an English public school near the Cadbury Company (Shultz 1998). See also Mangan 2014.

6. On Hershey, Cuba, see Pérez 2012: 221–230 and Winpenny 1995.

7. P. A. Staples (1883–1956) was first hired by Hershey in 1921 to manage Hershey's Cuban holdings. Though little known in the community (because he lived and worked abroad), he became deeply trusted. A year before his death in 1945, and to the surprise of many in the company, Hershey appointed Staples as his successor. See Hershey Community Archives n.d.

8. For a cultural anthropological approach to Disney amusement parks, see Fjellman 1992.

9.This coincided with national environmental legislation such as the National Environmental Policy Act, the Clean Air Act, the Federal Water Pollution Control Act, and the Endangered Species Act.

10. The Three Mile Island incident had serious economic effects on Middletown, Pennsylvania—Hershey's neighbor—from which Middletown has had a difficult time recovering. For a history of the nuclear emergency at Three Mile Island, see Walker 2006.

11. In 2000, Hersheypark received the International Association of Amusement Parks and Attractions' Applause Award. "The award's aim is to recognise an amusement park or theme park whose management, operations, and creative accomplishments have inspired the industry through leadership, foresight, originality, and sound business development" (Liseberg Amusement Park 2014).

12. This is a national charity that raises funding for children's hospitals.

13. On "tough love" as a conservative Christian expression of compassion, see Burack 2014.

CHAPTER 3

1. The Murrie lineage is integral to Hershey's competition with the Mars corporation, as the Hershey Community Archives reports: "Shortly before the war, Forrest Mars, the son of Frank Mars, owner of the Mars Candy Company, was interested in marketing a new chocolate product. Forrest anticipated a chocolate shortage developing during the pending war. Forrest Mars teamed up with Bill Murrie's son Bruce to ensure a supply of scarce chocolate for their new product: M&Ms (short for Mars and Murrie) during the war years. After wartime quotas ended in 1948, Forrest Mars maneuvered Bruce out of the partnership and went on to become Hershey's largest competitor" (Hershey Community Archives n.d.). See also Brenner 1999.

2. On the chemistry of varieties of chocolate production, see Beckett 2008.

3. For a social-historical account of chocolate, beginning with cocoa's association with "food of the gods," see Coe and Coe 2013.

4. As Bruce and Crawford recount, John Harvey Kellogg—born into a family of Seventh-Day Adventists, trained as a physician, and eventually becoming one of the best-known figures in late nineteenth-century medicine—championed what he called "biologic living" (1995: 15), which stressed the health of the digestive tract. He devised the corn flake to combat "autointoxication," "the process by which materials left in the intestines due to constipation putrefied and caused disease" (17). Kellogg's Corn Flakes originated as a turn-of-the-twentieth-century health food, in other words.

5. This type of tour entails "an amusement ride system for conveying passengers past a display and including a support track having inclining and declining portions" (Broggie et al. 1971).

6. See a lovely description of these rooms in McPhee 1972.

7. The manager is referring to the lead character in the play *Death of a Salesman* (Miller 1949).

8. On the history and politics of the global cocoa bean market, see Off 2014.

9. As recently as 2007, Hershey collaborated with M&M Mars and other large chocolate producers to try to persuade the Food and Drug Administration to eliminate its stipulation that chocolate products sold in the United States must contain 100 percent cocoa butter in order to be labeled "chocolate" (Bridges 2007). The removal of the stipulation would have allowed candy companies to synthesize cocoa butter–like materials and include the ingredient in products labeled "chocolate." Removing the stipulation was projected to be profitable for the companies, since cocoa butter is the most expensive ingredient in milk chocolate. These efforts were thwarted after a coalition of boutique chocolatiers and chocolate enthusiasts successfully petitioned the FDA to maintain the stipulation (and M&M Mars withdrew from its collaboration with Hershey—publicly endorsing the standing stipulation and embarrassing Hershey executives, former company officials tell me).

10. *Theobroma cacao*; for a popular natural historical account of the tree and its cultivation around the world, see Young 2007.

11. On brand "jamming," see Klein 1999.

12. On the heels of the "Raise the Bar" campaign, Hershey announced it will "source 100 percent certified cocoa for its global chocolate product lines by 2020 and accelerate its programs to help eliminate child labor in the cocoa regions of West Africa" (Hershey Company 2012).

13. Ethnographic accounts suggest that CSR practices of business corporations around the globe are structured similarly to one another. See, for example, Benson 2008 on the CSR efforts of Philip Morris in the United States; Rogers 2012 on gas companies in Russia; Shever 2010 on Shell Oil in Argentina; and Welker 2009 on the Newmont Mining Corporation in Indonesia. Everywhere the discourse of CSR travels, it invites a connection between doing well (in terms of increasing shareholder value) and doing good for consumers, producers, and communities situated along a company's "value chain."

CHAPTER 4

1. The "quasi-pathological" character of optimism in American religions of healthy-mindedness is taken to an extreme in Christian Science, observes William James (1994: 96). Born of the Second Great Awakening (circa 1800–1830), Christian Science is "the most radical branch of mind-cure in its dealings with evil," which includes diseases (121). For its adherents, "evil is simply a lie, and any one who mentions it is a liar. The optimistic ideal of duty forbids [adherents] to pay it the compliment even of explicit attention" (121).

2. The Spartan is the totem of the school's sports league, whose colors are brown and gold—the colors of chocolate and caramel.

3. Dock was the author of *School Management* (1750), a colonial American treatise on pedagogy.

4. The term was introduced into professional psychiatric literature in the late 1980s (Lange et al. 2010).

5. As Warlde reports (2005, cited in Dillon 2009), it is difficult to calculate the number of social orphans globally and to distinguish them from numbers of "true orphans"; however, UNICEF has estimated there are a hundred million street children worldwide, a plurality of which live in Latin America.

6. See Chapter 2 for a discussion of *cy pres* in the case of the state university medical center.

7. Mothers dying at childbirth and one or both parents dying of illness were common causes of orphanhood in the nineteenth century, when many U.S. orphanages were established; social issues related to "unwanted children" became more salient in the twentieth century (Friedman 2009: 56).

8. Despite my best efforts, the educator who acted as president and CEO of the Milton Hershey School during its reform years would not agree to meet with me.

CHAPTER 5

1. The music of Bruce Springsteen is perhaps the most popular example.

2. This is evidenced by right-wing publicity around 2008 presidential candidate Barack Obama's comment about "bitter clingers." Obama's remarks were astute: "You go into these small towns in Pennsylvania and, like a lot of small towns in the Midwest, the jobs have been gone now for 25 years and nothing's replaced them. . . . And they fell through the Clinton Administration, and the Bush Administration, and each successive administration has said that somehow these communities are gonna regenerate and they have not. And it's not surprising then they get bitter, they cling to guns or religion or antipathy to people who aren't like them or anti-immigrant sentiment or anti-trade sentiment as a way to explain their frustrations" (quoted in Fowler 2008).

3. Since the production of the 2009 documentary, the Barnes Collection has opened in downtown Philadelphia. A visit to the collection reveals the extent to which the foundation has gone to preserve the intentions of Albert Barnes in mounting his collection: the rooms of the museum replicate the rooms of Barnes's home, and artworks are hung identically to the way Barnes hung them in Lower Merion. In the literature about the museum, however, Barnes's intentions are generalized: "The mission of the Barnes Foundation, which dates back to its founding in 1922, is 'the promotion of the advancement of education and the appreciation of the fine arts'" (Barnes Foundation n.d.). The more controversial details about Barnes's wish to locate the museum outside Philadelphia are, perhaps unsurprisingly, omitted.

4. For recent national data on foster care and foster populations, see Child Welfare Information Gateway 2013.

5. The most publicized case of suicide by an MHS alumnus was by a man who crashed his propeller plane into a Texas IRS building in 2010 (Brick 2010).

CONCLUSION

1. A lawsuit was filed by the AIDS law project of Pennsylvania with the U.S. Justice Department and won on the grounds that the school violated the Americans with Disabilities Act (U.S. Department of Justice 2012).

2.See Preston 2011a; 2011b.

3.Two significant books related to Hershey were published around this time. *Chocolate Trust*, by *Philadelphia Inquirer* journalist Bob Fernandez and based on his extensive reporting, is framed as an exposé of trustee negligence and corruption in the decades following Milton Hershey's death, with a special focus on recent decades (2015). It is a comprehensive journalistic account of the trust's operations and controversies. *Semisweet*, by alumnus and former Milton Hershey School president Johnny O'Brien, is a moving biographical account of student life in the "old days" and the author's homecoming as top administrator in the wake of the 2002 reconstitution of the board (2014). In evocative prose, it reveals the psychological dimensions of everyday life at Milton Hershey School in the mid-twentieth century—a mind-set that continues to shape and constrain the current administration's policies and practices.

4. Anthropologists' accounts of the unintended consequences of international development aid and humanitarian interventions are suggestive in this regard; see, e.g., Ferguson 1994 on the former and Bornstein and Redfield 2010 and Fassin 2012 on the latter.

5. For a succinct overview of "social enterprise" corporations and an analysis of the case of Participant Media, see Ortner 2017. I am indebted to Sherry Ortner for sharing a working draft of her essay.

REFERENCES

Ahlstrom, Sydney E. 2004. *Religious History of the American People*. Yale University Press.

Appadurai, Arjun. 1990. "Disjuncture and Difference in the Global Cultural Economy." *Theory, Culture & Society* 7: 295–310.

Argott, Don, director. 2009. *The Art of the Steal*. Film. 9.14 Pictures.

Arjomand, Said A. 1998. "Philanthropy, the Law, and Public Policy in the Islamic World Before the Modern Era." In *Philanthropy in the World's Traditions*, edited by Warren F. Ilchman, Stanley N. Katz, and Edward L. Queen. Indiana University Press. 109–32.

Associated Press. 2011. "Hershey Charity Scandal: Robert Reese, Ex-Hershey Official, Claims Wrongdoing." *San Diego Union Tribune*. February 10. http://www.sandiegouniontribune.com/sdut-ex-hershey-official-claims-charity-wrongdoing-2011feb10-story.html. Accessed April 10, 2017.

Barnes Foundation. n.d. "About the Barnes." http://www.barnesfoundation.org/about. Accessed October 18, 2014.

Barthel, Diane. 1989. "Modernism and Marketing: The Chocolate Box Revisited." *Theory, Culture & Society* 6(3): 429–38.

Bauman, Zygmunt. 2001. *Community: Seeking Safety in an Insecure World*. Polity.

Beckett, Stephen T. 2008. *The Science of Chocolate*. Royal Society of Chemistry.

Bellah, Robert, Richard Madsen, William M. Sullivan, Ann Swidler, and Steven M. Tipton. 1996 [1985]. *Habits of the Heart: Individualism Commitment American Life*. University of California Press.

Benson, Peter. 2008. "Good Clean Tobacco: Philip Morris, Biocapitalism, and the Social Course of Stigma in North Carolina." *American Ethnologist* 35(3): 357–79.

Berle, Adolf A., and Gardiner C. Means. 1991 [1932]. *The Modern Corporation and Private Property*. Transaction.

Bertrand, William. 2011. "Oversight of Public and Private Initiatives to Eliminate the Worst Forms of Child Labor in the Cocoa Sector in Côte d'Ivoire and Ghana."

Payson Center for International Development and Technology Transfer at Tulane University.

Bornstein, Erica and Peter Redfield, eds. 2010. *Forces of Compassion: Humanitarianism Between Ethics and Politics*. SAR Press.

Bridges, Andrew. 2007. "Battle Brewing Over the Definition of Chocolate." *New York Times*. August 9.

Boon, James A. 1999. *Verging on Extra-Vagance: Anthropology, History, Religion, Literature, Arts . . . Showbiz*. Princeton University Press.

Brenner, Joël Glenn. 1999. *The Chocolate Wars: Inside the Secret Worlds of Mars and Hershey*. HarperCollins.

Brettell, Caroline B., ed. 1993. *When They Read What We Write: The Politics of Ethnography*. Bergin & Garvey.

Brick, Michael. 2010. "Man Crashes Plane into Texas I.R.S. Office." *New York Times*, February 18.

Brody, Evelyn. 2004. "Whose Public? Parochialism and Paternalism in State Charity Law Enforcement." *Indiana Law Journal* 79.

Broggie, Roger E., and Bert W. Burndage. 1971. "Amusement Ride System." U.S. Patent 3,554,130.

Brown, Prudence. 1969. "Chocolate Town's Toothache." *Newsday*, August 19.

Bruce, Scott, and Bill Crawford. 1995. *Cerealizing America: The Unsweetened Story of American Breakfast Cereal*. Faber & Faber.

Burack, Cynthia. 2014. *Tough Love: Sexuality, Compassion, and the Christian Right*. State University of New York Press.

Cadbury, Deborah. 2011. *Chocolate Wars: The 150-Year Rivalry Between the World's Greatest Chocolate Makers*. PublicAffairs.

Callahan, David. 2017. *The Givers: Wealth, Power, and Philanthropy in a New Gilded Age*. Knopf.

Carlsberg Group. n.d. "The Carlsberg Foundation." https://carlsberggroup.com/who-we-are/the-carlsberg-foundation/Accessed April 10, 2017.

Castner, Charles Schuyler. 1983. *One of a Kind: Milton Snavely Hershey, 1857–1945*. Derry Township, PA, Literary Guild.

Cattelino, Jessica R. 2010. "Anthropologies of the United States." *Annual Review of Anthropology* 39: 275–92.

Child Welfare Information Gateway. 2013. *Foster Care Statistics 2012*. U.S. Department of Health and Human Services, Children's Bureau.

Coe, Sophie D., and Michael D. Coe. 2013. *The True History of Chocolate*. Thames & Hudson.

Crawford, Margaret. 1995. *Building the Workingman's Paradise: The Design of American Company Towns*. Verso.

Cuniberti, Betty. 1979. "Hershey: The Fans Dissolve—Bears a Team of Transients." *Washington Post*, April 8.

Dahl, Roald. 2007 [1964]. *Charlie and the Chocolate Factory*. Penguin UK.

Dandaneau, Steven P. 1996. *A Town Abandoned: Flint, Michigan Confronts Deindustrialization*. State University of New York Press.

D'Antonio, Michael. 2007. *Hershey: Milton S. Hershey's Extraordinary Life of Wealth, Empire, and Utopian Dreams*. Simon & Schuster.

DeNavas-Walt, Carmen, and Bernadette D. Proctor. 2014. "Income and Poverty in the United States: 2013." U.S. Census Bureau. www.census.gov/content/dam/Census/library/publications/2014/demo/p60-249.pdf. Accessed October 17, 2014.

Dewey, John. 2012 [1927]. *The Public and Its Problems: An Essay in Political Inquiry*. Pennsylvania State University Press.

Dillon, Sara. 2009. "The Missing Link: A Social Orphan Protocol to the United Nations Convention on the Rights of the Child." Suffolk University Legal Studies Research Paper Series Research Paper 09-02. http://ssrn.com/abstract=1136879. Accessed October 17, 2014.

DiRusso, Alyssa A. 2006. "Supporting the Supporting Organization: The Potential and Exploitation of 509(A)(3) Charities." *Indiana Law Review* 39(2).

Doan, Seth. 2011. "Hard Times Hit Hershey, Pa." Television broadcast. *CBS News*, March 5.

Dock, Christopher. 1750. *School Management*. Philadelphia County, Pennsylvania.

Dudley, Kathryn Marie. 1994. *The End of the Line: Lost Jobs, New Lives in Postindustrial America*. University of Chicago Press.

Durkheim, Emile. 1995 [1912]. *The Elementary Forms of Religious Life: The Totemic System in Australia*, edited by Karen E. Fields. Free Press.

Fassin, Didier. 2012. *Humanitarian Reason: A Moral History of the Present*. University of California Press.

Ferguson, James. 1994. The Anti-Politics Machine: "Development," Depoliticization, and Bureaucratic Power in Lesotho. University of Minnesota Press.

Ferguson, Priscilla Parkhurst. 2008. "The Big Business of Haut Chocolat." *Contexts* 7(2): 65–67.

Fernandez, Bob. 2011. "A Look at the Hershey Trust." Series of articles from March 2010 to November 2011. *Philadelphia Inquirer*. http://www.philly.com/philly/business/Inq_HT_Hershey_Trust.html. Accessed October 18, 2014.

———. 2015. *The Chocolate Trust: Deception, Indenture, and Secrets at the $12 Billion Milton Hershey School*. Camino.

Fine, G. A., V. Campion-Vincent, and C. Heath, eds. 2005. *Rumor Mills: The Social Impact of Rumor and Legend*. Aldine.

Fjellman, Stephen M. 1992. *Vinyl Leaves: Walt Disney World and America*. Westview.

Fleishman, Joel L. 2009. *The Foundation: A Great American Secret*. PublicAffairs.

Fowler, Mayhill. 2008. "Obama: No Surprise That Hard-Pressed Pennsylvanians Turn Bitter." *Huffington Post*, November 17. www.huffingtonpost.com/mayhill-fowler/obama-no-surprise-that-ha_b_96188.html. Accessed April 10, 2017.

Friedman, Lawrence. 2009. *Dead Hands: A Social History of Wills, Trusts, and Inheritance Law.* Stanford University Press.

Garner, Bryan A, ed. 2014. "Trust." *Black's Law Dictionary.* thelawdictionary.org/trust. Accessed October 18, 2014.

———. "Fiduciary Duty." *Black's Law Dictionary.* thelawdictionary.org/fiduciary-duty. Accessed May 15, 2017.

Geertz, Clifford. 1973. *The Interpretation of Cultures: Selected Essays.* Basic.

———. 1983. *Local Knowledge: Further Essays in Interpretive Anthropology.* Basic.

———. 2001. *Available Light: Anthropological Reflections on Philosophical Topics.* Princeton University Press.

Green America. 2011. "Hershey Ads Turned Inside Out: Winners Announced in 'Brand Jamming' Contest Critiquing Company's Child Labor Abuses." Press release (April 28). www.greenamerica.org/about/newsroom/releases/2011-04-28.cfm. Accessed October 18, 2014.

Green, Hardy. 2011. *The Company Town: The Industrial Edens and Satanic Mills That Shaped the American Economy.* Basic.

Greenhouse, Carol J. 2011. *The Paradox of Relevance: Ethnography and Citizenship in the United States.* University of Pennsylvania Press.

Halbleib, John F. 2005. *Hershey: Ideal Community for Orphans.* AuthorHouse.

Hansmann, Henry, and Steen Thomsen. 2012. "Virtual Ownership and Managerial Distance: The Governance of Industrial Foundations." Working paper, conference on Corporate Governance After the Crisis, Oxford, UK, January 13–14, 2002. http://tcgf.org/ceo/2012/documents/unrestricted/Hansmann%20Thomsen.pdf. Accessed April 10, 2017.

Harvey, David. 1989. *The Condition of Postmodernity.* Blackwell.

———. 2005. *A Brief History of Neoliberalism.* Oxford University Press.

Helyar, John. 2002. "Sweet Surrender." *Fortune*, October 14.

"Hershey Brand Jam Video Contest." 2011. Onlinevideocontests.com. https://www.onlinevideocontests.com/contest/2437. Accessed February 12, 2017.

Hershey Community Archives. n.d. "Murrie, William F. R.; 1873–1950." Hershey, PA. www.hersheyarchives.org/essay/details.aspx?EssayId=28. Accessed April 9, 2017.

———. n.d. "Staples, Percy Alexander; 1883–1956." Hershey, PA. www.hersheyarchives.org/essay/details.aspx?EssayId=35. Accessed April 9, 2017.

Hershey Company. 2010. "Our Story: Discover Hershey's History of Happiness." www.thehersheylegacy.com. Accessed October 18, 2014.

———. 2012. "Hershey to Source 100% Certified Cocoa by 2020." Press release (October 3). https://www.thehersheycompany.com/content/dam/corporate-us/documents/legal/source-100-certified-cocoa-2020.pdf. Accessed October 18, 2014.

"Hershey May Go on the Block." 2002. *Washington Post*, July 26.

"Hershey No Longer One-Industry Town." 1985. *Morning Call* (Allentown, PA), October 20.

Hirsch, Paul M. 1986. "From Ambushes to Golden Parachutes: Corporate takeovers as an instance of cultural framing and institutional integration." *American Journal of Sociology* 91(4): 800–837.

Ho, Karen. 2009. *Liquidated: An Ethnography of Wall Street*. Duke University Press.

Hoy, Laura. 2016. "Add a Little Sugar to Your Portfolio with Hershey's Stock [HSY]." Nasdaq.com (October 7). http://www.nasdaq.com/article/add-a-little-sugar-to-your-portfolio-with-hersheys-stock-hsy-cm690489. Accessed February 12, 2017.

James, William. 1994 [1902]. *The Varieties of Religious Experience: A Study in Human Nature*. Random House.

Jargon, Julie. 2007. "Hershey CEO Richard Lenny to Step Down." *Wall Street Journal*, October 2.

Joseph, Richard. 1967. "Hershey, Pa.: The Town Built on a Sweet Tooth." *Chicago Tribune*, September 17.

Keck, Margaret, and Kathryn Sikkink. 1998. *Activists Beyond Borders: Advocacy Networks in International Politics*. Cornell University Press.

King, Samuel P., and Randall W. Roth. 2006. *Broken Trust: Greed, Mismanagement, and Political Manipulation at America's Largest Charitable Trust*. University of Hawaii Press.

———. 2007. "Erosion of Trust." *American Bar Association Journal* 93: 48–67.

Klein, Naomi. 1999. *No Logo: Taking On the Brand Bullies*. Picador.

Klick, Jonathan, and Robert H. Sitkoff. 2008. "Agency Costs, Charitable Trusts, and Corporate Control: Evidence from Hershey's Kiss-Off." *Columbia Law Review* 108(4): 749–838.

Klott, Gary. 1984. "A New Class of Stock Is Proposed by Hershey." *New York Times*, August 28.

Klotz, Richard. 1973. *The Rise and Demise of the Hershey Junior College: An Historical-Descriptive Study of the Hershey Junior College, Hershey, Pennsylvania, 1938–1965*. Stiegel Print.

Komoroski, Jennifer L. 2003. "The Hershey Trust's Quest to Diversify: Redefining the State Attorney General's Role When Charitable Trusts Wish to Diversify." *William and Mary Law Review* 45(4): 1769–1802.

Lamme, Margot O., and Lisa M. Parcell. 2013. "Promoting Hershey: The Chocolate Bar, the Chocolate Town, the Chocolate King." *Journalism History* 38(4): 198–208.

Lang, C. Max. 2010. *The Impossible Dream: The Founding of the Milton S. Hershey Medical Center of the Pennsylvania State University*. AuthorHouse.

Lange, Klaus W., et al. 2010. "The History of Attention Deficit Hyperactivity Disorder." *ADHD: Attention Deficit and Hyperactivity Disorders* 2(4): 241–55.

Leach, William. 1993. *Land of Desire: Merchants, Power, and the Rise of a New American Culture*. Pantheon.

Lederman, Rena. 2004. "Towards an Anthropology of Disciplinarity." *Critical Matrix* 15: 60–74.

Liseberg Amusement Park. 2014. "The Applause Award." liseberg.com/en/home/En-tertainment/TheApplauseAward/. Accessed October 18, 2014.

Madoff, Ray D. 2010. *Immortality and the Law: The Rising Power of the American Dead.* Yale University Press.

Madonna, Terry G. 2008. *Pivotal Pennsylvania: Presidential Politics from FDR to the Twenty-First Century.* Pennsylvania Historical Association.

Malawskey, Nick. 2010. "Hershey Trust Probe Confirmed." *Harrisburg Patriot News,* October 7.

———. 2013. "Pennsylvania Attorney General: No Penalties, but Reforms for Hershey Trust." Pennlive.com (May 8). www.pennlive.com/midstate/index.ssf/2013/05/penn-sylvanias_attorney_general.html. Accessed October 18, 2014.

———. 2015. "Old Is New Again at Former Hershey Factory." Pennlive.com (August 6). http://www.pennlive.com/midstate/index.ssf/2015/08/hershey_factory_19_east_chocol.html. Accessed February 12, 2017.

Mangan, Lucy. 2014. *Inside Charlie's Chocolate Factory: The Complete Story of Willy Wonka, the Golden Ticket, and Roald Dahl's Most Famous Creation.* Penguin.

Marcus, George E., and Peter Dobkin Hall. 1992. *Lives in Trust: The Fortunes of Dynastic Families in Late Twentieth-Century America.* Westview.

McKean, Erin, ed. 2005. "Weird." *New Oxford American Dictionary,* 2nd ed. Oxford University Press.

McMahon, James D. 2009. *Milton Hershey School.* Arcadia.

———. 2010. "2010 Coretta Scott King Women for Diversity Award Winner: Catherine Elizabeth 'Kitty' Hershey (Posthumously)." *Women Connect Magazine,* Spring: 10–12.

McPhee, John. 1972. "The Conching Rooms." *New Yorker.* www.newyorker.com/maga-zine/1972/05/13/the-conching-rooms. Accessed April 10, 2017.

de la Merced, Michael J.. 2010. "Hershey Won't Challenge Kraft for Cadbury." *New York Times,* January 22.

Merry, Sally Engle. 1984. "Rethinking Gossip and Scandal." In *Toward a General Theory of Social Control,* vol. 2, edited by Donald Black. Academic.

Miller, Arthur. 1998 [1949]. *Death of a Salesman: Certain Private Conversations in Two Acts and a Requiem.* Penguin.

Milton Hershey School Alumni Association. n.d. "Dearden House." www.mhsalum.org/dearden-alumni-campus/facilities-overview/dearden-house/. Accessed October 18, 2014.

Mintz, Sidney W. 1986. *Sweetness and Power: The Place of Sugar in Modern History.* Penguin.

Moore, Michael, director. 1989. *Roger and Me.* Film. Warner Bros.

Morris, Jack. 1970. "Hershey's Troubles: Big Chocolate Maker, Beset by Profit Slide, Gets More Aggressive." *Wall Street Journal,* February 18.

Moskin, Julia. 2008. "Dark May Be King, but Milk Chocolate Makes a Move." *New York Times,* February 13.

REFERENCES

"M. S. Hershey Dead; Chocolate King, 88." 1945. *New York Times*, October 14.

Murrie, Richard Wallace. 1939. "The Story Behind a Hershey Bar: The History of the Foundation and Subsequent Growth of the Hershey Chocolate Corporation, and the Simultaneous Development of the Model Industrial Community of Hershey, Pennsylvania." Senior thesis, Department of History, Princeton University.

O'Brien, John A. 2014. *Bittersweet: An Orphan's Journey Through the School the Hersheys Built*. Rowman & Littlefield.

Off, Carol. 2014. *Bitter Chocolate: Anatomy of an Industry*. New Press.

Ortner, Sherry. 2017. "Social Impact or Social Justice? Film and Politics in the Neoliberal Landscape." Unpublished lecture.

Passaro, Joanna. 1997. "'You Can't Take the Subway to the Field!': 'Village' Epistemologies in the Global Village." In *Anthropological Locations: Boundaries and Grounds of a Field Science*, edited by Akhil Gupta and James Ferguson. University of California Press.

Paul Wallace Research Collection. 1974. Hershey Community Archives. Hershey, PA.

Pennsylvania Office of Attorney General. 2013. "AG Kane Announces Reform Agreement with Milton Hershey Trust and Milton Hershey School." Press release (May 8). www.attorneygeneral.gov/Media_and_Resources/Press_Releases/Press_Release/?pid=990. Accessed October 18, 2014.

———. 2013. "Hershey Trust Agreement." May 8. www.scribd.com/document/140233918/Hershey-Trust-Agreement-May-8-2013. Accessed April 9, 2017.

———. 2016. "2016 Hershey Agreement." July 29. www.attorneygeneral.gov/uploadedFiles/MainSite/Content/Related_Content/PressReleases/2016%20Hershey%20agreement.pdf. Accessed April 9, 2017.

Pennsylvania v. Board of Directors of City Trusts, 353 U.S. 230 (1957).

Pérez, Louis A., Jr. 2012. *On Becoming Cuban: Identity, Nationality, and Culture*. University of North Carolina Press.

Preston, Julia. 2011a. "Foreign Students in Work Visa Program Stage Walkout at Plant." *New York Times*, August 17.

———. 2011b. "Pleas Unheeded as Students' U.S. Jobs Soured." *New York Times*, October 16.

Re Milton Hershey School Trust, 807 A.2d 324 (Pa. Commw. Ct. 2002).

Rogers, Douglas. 2012. "The Materiality of the Corporation: Oil, Gas, and Corporate Social Technologies in the Remaking of a Russian Region." *American Ethnologist* 39(2): 284–96.

Rogers, John. 1967. "A New Concept in Medical Teaching: Can We Bring Back the Family Doctor?" *Boston Globe*, December 10.

Rosen, Lawrence. 2006. *Law as Culture*. Princeton University Press.

Ross, Gary, director. 1998. *Pleasantville*. Film. New Line Cinema.

Rusk, Howard A. 1965. "The Hershey School and Its Philosophy of Dignity in Working with the Hands." *New York Times*, June 13.

Safford, Sean. 2009. *Why the Garden Club Couldn't Save Youngstown: The Transformation of the Rust Belt*. Harvard University Press.

Samadi, Nina. 2011. "Amusement Parks in the U.S." *IBISWorld Industry Report 71311*. IBISWorld.

Scheper-Hughes, Nancy. 2002. "Min(d)ing the Body: On the Trail of Organ Stealing Rumors." In *Exotic No More*, edited by Jeremy MacClancy. University of Chicago Press.

Schramm, Carl J. 2006. "Law Outside the Market: The Social Utility of the Private Foundation." *Harvard Journal of Law and Public Policy* 30: 355–415.

Schultz, William Todd. 1998. "Finding Fate's Father: Some Life History Influences on Roald Dahl's Charlie and the Chocolate Factory." *Biography*: 463–481.

Segal, David. 2016. "Backstabbing and Threats of a 'Suicide Parachute' at Hershey." *New York Times*, July 30.

Sherzer, Jack. 2002. "Chocolate Thunder: 500 Rally Against Sale." *Harrisburg Patriot News*, August 3.

Shever, Elana. 2010. Engendering the Company: Corporate Personhood and the "Face" of an Oil Company in Metropolitan Buenos Aires. *PoLAR: Political and Legal Anthropology Review* 33(1): 26–46.

Shippen, Katherine Binney, and Paul Wallace. 1959. *Milton S. Hershey*. Random House.

Sidel, Mark. 2003. "Struggle for Hershey: Community Accountability and the Law in Modern American Philanthropy." *University of Pittsburgh Law Review* 65: 1–61.

Snavely, Joseph Richard. 1935. *Milton S. Hershey: Builder*. Private printing.

———. 1950. *The Hershey Story*. Private printing.

Solomon, Steven Davidoff. 2016. "Another Hershey Deal May Come Unwrapped. Maybe It Should." *New York Times*, July 5.

Spielberg, Steven director. 1982. *E.T. The Extra Terrestrial*. Film. Universal Pictures.

Sutcliffe, Jane. 2003. *Milton Hershey*. Lerner.

Tarabay, Jamie. 2010. "Original Hershey Chocolate Factory Set To Close." Radio broadcast. *National Public Radio*, October 6.

U.S. Census Bureau. 2010. "QuickFacts." www.census.gov/quickfacts. Accessed April 9, 2017.

———. 2010. "QuickFacts: Hershey CDP, Pennsylvania." https://www.census.gov/quickfacts/table/PST045216/4234144,00. Accessed April 9, 2017.

U.S. Department of Justice. 2012. "Justice Department Settles with Pennsylvania School for $715,000 over Exclusion of Child with HIV." Press release (September 12). Office of Public Affairs.

Veblen, Thorstein. 2007 [1919]. *The Theory of the Leisure Class*. Oxford University Press.

Vidal v. Girard's Executors, 43 US 127 (1844).

Villalonga, Belén, and Raphael Amit. 2009. "How Are U.S. Family Firms Controlled?" *Review of Financial Studies* 22(8): 3,047–91.

Walker, Samuel J. 2006. *Three Mile Island: A Nuclear Crisis in Historical Perspective*. University of California Press.

Wallace, Anthony F. C. 1988. *St. Clair: A Nineteenth-Century Coal Town's Experience with a Disaster-Prone Industry*. Cornell University Press.

Wardle, Lynn D. 2004. "Parentlessness: Adoption Problems, Paradigms, Policies, and Parameters." *Whittier J. Child. & Fam. Advoc.* 4: 323.

Weber, Max. 1954. *On Law in Economy and Society.* Edward Shils, trans. Simon and Schuster.

———. 2001 [1905]. *The Protestant Ethic and the Spirit of Capitalism.* Routledge.

Weiner, Matthew, director. 2013. "In Care Of." Television episode. In *Mad Men.* Written by Carly Wray and Matthew Weiner. AMC, June 23.

Welker, Marina A. 2009. "'Corporate Security Begins in the Community': Mining, the Corporate Social Responsibility Industry, and Environmental Advocacy in Indonesia." *Cultural Anthropology* 24(1): 142–79.

Welker, Marina A., and David Wood. 2011. "Shareholder Activism and Alienation." *Current Anthropology* 52(3): 57–69.

West, David J., and J. P. Bilbrey. 2011. "Hershey's." Conference presentation, Consumer Analyst Group of New York, February 23.

White, Louise. 2000. *Speaking with Vampires: Rumor and History in Colonial Africa.* University of California Press.

Whiteneck, Pamela C. 2006. *Images of America: Hersheypark.* Arcadia.

Winpenny, Thomas R. 1995. "Milton S. Hershey Ventures into Cuban Sugar." *Pennsylvania History* 62(4): 491–502.

Winter, Greg. 2001. "Hershey Breaks Tradition in Naming New Chief Executive." *New York Times,* March 13.

Wooden, John, and Jay Carty. 2009. *Coach Wooden's Pyramid of Success.* Revell.

Yonay, Ehud. 1972. "It's Not *All* Sweetness in Hershey, Pa." *Newsday,* May 11.

Young, Allen M. 2007. *The Chocolate Tree: A Natural History of Cocoa.* University Press of Florida.

Zunz, Olivier. 2011. *Philanthropy in America: A History.* Princeton University Press.

INDEX

of chocolate in, 80–85; as marketing for Hershey company, 145; memorialization of Milton Hershey, 9–10; as model community, 43, 143, 151, 158; municipal government of, 151–155; Pennsylvania Dutch culture and, 41, 44–46, 60, 123, 143; politics of, 17–18; proposed sale of Hershey company and, 13, 32; relationship to Hershey Trust, 71, 151–152, 154–155, 157, 159, 179; religious institutions in, 60–69; transition away from company town, 49–50, 56–59, 86, 168

Hershey Company, 1, 7, 77–78, 105; attempted takeover of, 173–175; branding and, 1, 7, 60, 80–81, 97, 144–145, 147, 177; CEOs of, 17, 93, 161, 174; concept of "service" and, 146–147; corporate social responsibility (CSR) and, 96–102, 187n12; cultural changes at, 91–96, 168; "Derail the Sale" campaign and, 28–32; downsizing at, 84–86, 89; dual-class stock mechanisms and, 103–104, 106; early days of, 144–146; global strategy of, 105; Hersheypark and, 51; during Hershey's "golden age", 45; labor-management relations within, 77–78, 84–91; manufacture of chocolate by, 80–85, 89–91, 94–96, 187n9; marketing efforts of, 91–92, 94–95, 144–146; Mennonite principles and, 145–146; Milton Hershey School and, 5, 97, 100–101; optimization and, 81; products produced by, 2–3, 78–80, 90, 94–95; profitability of, 35; proposed sale of, 13, 16, 28, 30, 93, 174; Reese's company and, 37; relationship to Hershey Trust, 6, 13, 22, 91–92, 103–107, 173–177; shareholder value maximization and, 102–107; stock value of, 106, 147–148, 174; unions at, 84–89, 91

Hershey Entertainment and Resorts Company, 19, 50–52, 138, 170

Hershey Junior College, 43, 49–50, 53–54

Hershey Medical Center. *See* Penn State Milton S. Hershey Medical Center

Hersheypark, 8, 25, 44, 47, 50–52, 153–154, 186n11

Hershey School. *See* Milton Hershey School

Hershey Trust. *See* Milton Hershey School Trust

"Hillary Girls," 23–29

Ho, Karen, 102

industrial foundations, 6, 22–23, 35, 175–176

inequality, 4, 70–71

Italian population of Hershey, 45–47, 49, 60, 63, 69, 71; Catholicism and, 63, 65, 68–69

Kane, Kathleen, 170–171, 173

Kellogg, John Harvey, 186n4

Klick, Jonathan, 34–35

labor unions, 149; at Hershey Company, 84–85, 89, 91

Lamme, Margot O., 145

Leach, William, 8–9, 146

"Little Italy," 46

Madoff, Ray, 20, 53

Marcus, George, 10, 167

Mars Company, 7, 35, 91–93, 105, 186n1, 187n9

Mennonites, 123, 145–146; Milton Hershey as, 2, 41, 109, 123, 145–146

Merry, Sally Engle, 16

Milton Hershey School, 2–3, 7, 162; admission qualifications, 54, 115, 117–118; alumni relations and, 137–142, 168; behavioral issues at, 121–123, 125–127, 131–132; books about, 189n3; bullying in, 161–162; changes in student body, 131–135; changes to during 1990's, 137–138; corporal punishment and, 121, 126, 140; corporate social responsibility

ACKNOWLEDGMENTS

I AM INDEBTED to the citizens of south-central Pennsylvania who shared time with me during my fieldwork and since: residents of Hershey; employees of the Hershey Company; students, alumni, houseparents, and administrators of the Milton Hershey School; and those associated with Penn State Hershey Medical Center, Hershey Entertainment and Resorts Company, and Derry Township School District and administrative offices.

I owe a special thanks to Tammy Hamilton of the Hershey Community Archives, James McMahon of the Milton Hershey School Department of History, and Carole Hite Welsh of the Derry Township Historical Society for archival assistance; Michael Hussey of Widener Law School and David Maxey, Esq., for introductions to trust law; Terry Madonna of Franklin and Marshall College for insights into state electoral politics; and the offices of Stephen R. Reed in Harrisburg and Edward G. Rendell in Philadelphia for lively conversations about the state of Pennsylvania and the state of the union.

At Princeton University, I have been privileged to work with the extraordinary Drs. James Boon and Carol Greenhouse. Without Jim and Carol's keen attention, erudition, compassion, and humor, I would never have taken the risk of walking the high wire of ethnographic research—much less in my "hometown," a short 125 miles west of campus.

I am indebted to Princeton's Department of Anthropology faculty members and administrators who supported me in my research and writing: João Biehl, John Borneman, Isabelle Clarke-Decès, Elizabeth Davis, Gabriela Drinovan, Abdellah Hammoudi, Rena Lederman, Alan Mann, Carolyn Rouse, Lawrence Rosen, Mo Lin Yee, and Carol Zanca. I also thank Didier Fassin of the Institute for Advanced Study for the opportunity to audit penetrating courses on the anthropology of morals and public anthropology and to sit in on Thursday lunch seminars in the School of Social Sciences; and Peter Singer of the University Center for Human Values for the opportunity to think otherwise about ethics as an assistant instructor in "Introduction to Practical Ethics" (fall 2014).

Among other friends and colleagues at Princeton and beyond, I would like to thank Celeste Alexander, Adam Becker, Theo Brasoveanu, Brookes Brown, David Callahan, Hewsen Chen, Priscilla Cohen, Leo Coleman, Christoph Cox, Talia Dan-Cohen, Rohit De, Mark Dixon, Mollie Dixon, Cristina Domnisoru, Jesse Dylan, Frederick Errington, Leah Feldman, Aurelien Fraisse, Leslie Geddes, Jonathan Geller, Deborah Gewertz, Kristina Gonzalez, Gwen Gordon, Eva Harman, Jeff Himple, Christina Hultholm, Graham Jones, Stanley Katz, Jens Klenner, Raphael Krut-Landau, Pablo Landa, George Laufenberg, Sura Levine, Alphonso Lingis, Peter Locke, Ricky Martin, Nikos Michailidis, Sarah Milov, Amy Moran-Thomas, Paul Muldoon, Anh-Thu Ngo, Claire Nicholas, Sherry Ortner, Andrew Parker, Heath Pearson, Daniel Polk, Bridget Purcell, Erin Raffety, Sebastian Ramirez, Mark Robinson, Joel Rozen, Allison Schnable, Saul Schwartz, Marissa Smith, Joseph Tsiamoglou, Matt Tyrnauer, Matthew Weiner, and Sam Williams. I am also deeply indebted to old friends from Hershey and Hampshire College (my undergraduate alma mater) who encouraged me in this project: Caroline Black., E. J. Cyran, Amanda Dennis, Chris Dickson, Dave Grant, Eric Imhof, Colin Milne, Allison Rung, Laura Seiverling, Michael Sherrard, Brian Shotzbarger, George Simms, Rob Swanger, Seth Wessler, Boyd Williamson, Michael Winslow, and Padraic Wood.

My research and writing at Princeton was made possible by a fellowship from Princeton University; pre- and post-fieldwork research grants from the Princeton Institute for International and Regional Studies; conference and travel grants from the Office of the Dean of the Graduate School; and the Fellowship of Woodrow Wilson Scholars (2011–2013). I also wish to thank the UCLA Department of Anthropology for the opportunity to serve as a visiting lecturer. Unbeknownst to them, the exceptional students who partook in "The Business and Culture of Documentary Film" (summer 2016) were helping me think through the final stages of my Hershey manuscript.

Peter Agree of University of Pennsylvania Press has given me a world-class introduction to publishing. I am indebted to him, Noreen O'Connor-Abel, the anonymous readers who offered supremely constructive feedback, and the whole Penn Press team.

My greatest debts are to my courageous and beautiful partner, David Hsu, and to my family: George and Janette, Ted, Irene and Jim (1934–2008), Kathryn and Deni, and Bill and Zoey.

This book is dedicated to my parents.